The Practice Educator's Handbook

The **Practice** Educator's Handbook

SARAH WILLIAMS and LYNNE RUTTER

4th Edition

Series Editors
Keith Brown
and **Steve Keen**

Learning Matters
An imprint of SAGE Publications Ltd
1 Oliver's Yard
55 City Road
London EC1Y 1SP

SAGE Publications Inc.
2455 Teller Road
Thousand Oaks, California 91320

SAGE Publications India Pvt Ltd
B 1/I 1 Mohan Cooperative Industrial Area
Mathura Road
New Delhi 110 044

SAGE Publications Asia-Pacific Pte Ltd
3 Church Street
#10-04 Samsung Hub
Singapore 049483

Editor: Kate Keers
Development editor: Sarah Turpie
Senior project editor: Chris Marke
Project management: Deer Park Productions
Marketing manager: Camille Richmond
Cover design: Wendy Scott
Typeset by: C&M Digitals (P) Ltd, Chennai, India
Printed in the UK

Library of Congress Control Number: 2018965493

British Library Cataloguing in Publication Data

A catalogue record for this book is available from the
British Library

ISBN 978-1-5264-2390-0
ISBN 978-1-5264-2391-7 (pbk)

At SAGE we take sustainability seriously. Most of our products are printed in the UK using responsibly
sourced papers and boards. When we print overseas we ensure sustainable papers are used as measured
by the PREPS grading system. We undertake an annual audit to monitor our sustainability.

Contents

Foreword from the Series Editor

Practice education has never had a more important role in the development and delivery of quality social work practice. This new edition of The Practice Educator's Handbook has been updated and has new practice material on building supervisory relationships with learners and the importance of good quality supervision to support learning and practice.

Practice education and the skills that practice educators bring are increasingly seen as vital not just for social work students undertaking a social work programme but for the whole profession as it seeks to be steeped in learning and development drawing upon research and best practice. Practice educators have seen their role develop to include the support of newly-qualified social workers in their first year of practice. This role is rightly being expanded to include supporting the continuous professional development of all social workers as the profession increasingly recognises the value of lifelong learning.

This new edition has been written to support practice educators and all social work professionals involved with the facilitation of learning within the profession.

As with the previous three editions, the aim is that this text will encourage you and the social work profession as a whole to reach even higher standards. This has never been as important as the current time. Social work services face ever increasing pressures and this high-quality practice education is critical in order for the profession to develop and to serve its clients well.

All texts in the series have been written by people with a passion for excellence in social work. This book is no different. Other books in this series may also be of value to you as a practice educator as they are written to inform, inspire and develop social work practice.

Professor Keith Brown
National Centre for Post-Qualifying Social Work and Professional Practice, Bournemouth University

Introduction

Structure of the book

In the opening chapter we set the scene by providing an opportunity to find out more about how professional development can be supported through learning that takes place in work-based settings. The book then follows the domains set out in the Practice Educator Professional Standards for Social Work (PEPS) (CSW, 2012a) with five key parts.

- Part One, Domain A: Organise opportunities for the demonstration of assessed competence in practice.

- Part Two, Domain B: Enable learning and professional development in practice.

- Part Three, Domain C: Manage the assessment of learners in practice.

- Part Four, Applying learning from Domains A–C to address challenging practice situations.

- Part Five, Domain D: Effective continuing performance as a practice educator.

As each part of the book covers a large area of practice, we have split each of these main parts into a number of manageable chapters. You can read a part from start to finish or you can dip into a chapter depending on your specific interest or the amount of time you have available.

The terms 'work-based learning' and 'practice learning' are both used to describe the learning that takes place within a work setting. Generally speaking, however, there are no agreed definitions for either of these terms and they are frequently used interchangeably (Nixon and Murr, 2006). Therefore, throughout this book we will refer to all learning that is located in the workplace as 'work-based learning'.

Who is this book aimed at?

This book has been written for busy social workers involved in supporting, enabling and assessing learners in the workplace. It is aimed primarily at people with responsibility for either qualifying social worker students or newly-qualified social workers (NQSWs) during their first year of professional practice, but it will also be of interest to those with responsibility for other professional learners such as students from other professions, people undertaking post-qualifying awards and those undertaking other forms of continuous professional development.

The book has been written specifically to support those undertaking practice educator awards which meet the staged requirements of the Practice Educator Professional Standards (CSW, 2012a) and will be particularly useful for social workers who are new to a practice education role. It will also be of interest to more experienced practice educators seeking support to reflect critically on their practice and further develop their professional capability.

This fourth edition has been fully updated to include developments in social work education since 2015, with the inclusion of a new chapter in Part Four which explores aspects of formal supervision within the practice educator role.

How will the book support your practice?

We aim to present an easy-to-read book that will challenge you to take a critical, evidence-informed approach to your thinking and to your practice. Although the book will give you some useful ideas to use within your work with learners, it will not provide you with a 'bag of tricks' that can be pulled out and applied in an unthinking manner. It blends practical information and advice with material aimed at developing an understanding of key concepts and research that will encourage you to think about how and why adults learn in a professional context and how their practice can be assessed fairly and accurately. Throughout the book we have included examples drawn from our own practice and life experiences together with ideas about practice provided by others who have been involved in work-based learning situations. These examples and ideas aim to illustrate how we, as individuals, may have approached a particular situation. These examples represent our individual views on practice and are intended to provide a starting point for you to critically think through your own approaches and not to provide templates for you to apply in practice.

This book should therefore be seen as a handbook to guide your thinking rather than as a textbook concentrating on delivering content. It attempts to offer sufficient theory and discussion to help you gain new understanding in enabling the learning of others but does not give a comprehensive coverage of the literature in this complex area (that has been provided by a number of other excellent books). It uses activities and reflection points to encourage you to think about the application of the ideas we present to your own areas of practice. Research summaries are also included throughout. A summary is provided at the end of Chapter 1 and for each of the following five parts of the book to provide a quick outline of the main ideas presented. Suggestions for further reading are also provided to enable you to explore issues raised in greater depth and extend your knowledge further.

This book will obviously support the development of practice education knowledge and skills but will also support your wider professional development. The integration of practice education within qualified social workers' professional roles can be seen as a natural extension in many respects. Skills and abilities required for the enabling of others through a learning and development process are obviously aligned with those used for social work with people who use social services (e.g. use of discretion, anti-discriminatory practice) and with those used when working alongside other professionals (e.g. communication, diplomacy). It is apparent that much prior experience will be relevant to this subject area and a great deal of material that is covered in this book and in associated programmes will be transferable to other areas of practice, such as supervision and management, as well as to direct work with service users and carers.

Chapter 1
Practice educators and work-based learning

Introduction

Have you ever spent time considering what makes you special? Not you as a person (although we are sure you are), but you as a professional. What knowledge, skills and attributes have enabled you to undertake the task of supporting and safeguarding some of the most vulnerable people in society? Have you asked yourself how you reached the stage in your professional development you are at today? How you gained your knowledge, built your skills and developed your attributes? And – rather importantly since this is a book for practice educators – how you can now use your learning more effectively to undertake the vital role of supporting the development of others?

In this opening chapter we will introduce some ideas that encourage you to think more deeply about these fundamental questions. We will also aim to convince you (if that still needs to be done!) that increasing your capability as a practice educator is not just an important contribution to your profession, but is also a key part of your own development as an experienced professional. We will start by looking at theories that explain how people make the journey from novice to expert. Then move on to think more specifically about the attributes that professionals need to function more effectively in the workplace. We will look at all of these issues against the backdrop of developments in the wider social work profession. The themes we introduce will be further developed in later chapters, where we will also consider how the ideas discussed can be applied to practice situations. Towards the end of this chapter we will look at the contributions practice educators can make to the wider professional learning process in the workplace and think about how values will inform the approach that you take when you are supporting the learning of others.

Why is work-based learning and assessment such an important part of professional education?

Gaining experience in the workplace is widely considered to be an essential component of professional education (SWRB, 2010). It provides an opportunity for learners to find out about the realities of practice, extend classroom-acquired skills and knowledge, improve performance and be assessed actually doing the job that they are being prepared for. However, involvement in work-based learning can be a frustrating, confusing and confidence-sapping experience. Learning experiences are often ad hoc and hard to control; learners can be exposed to sharply contrasting approaches and be given conflicting advice while having to navigate the minefield of a complex and unfamiliar organisation. These challenges arise primarily because social work is such a messy and uncertain profession

(Knott and Scragg, 2016), but also because work environments, unlike classrooms, have not been specifically designed to support learning. Working environments are difficult to predict and control and the needs of learners are often, not unexpectedly, put in second place to those of the organisation.

Because work-based environments are such unpredictable and complex places to learn, the quality and nature of the outcomes achieved can also be unpredictable. In the next section we will begin to think about how people actually learn from 'messy' experiences in the workplace and what the implications of this will be for you as a practice educator.

How do professionals learn in the workplace?

When we ask people attending our courses to describe how learning happens at work, most start by talking about formal events or activities such as in-house training, supervision, shadowing or being taught about new processes by more experienced workers. Although these types of activities are important, research suggests that formal learning is by no means the only, or even the most significant, way that people learn in the workplace (Eraut et al., 1998; Wenger, 2000; Ford et al., 2005; Nixon and Murr, 2006). While we are at work, whether we are consciously aware of it or not, learning is continuous – with everything we see, hear or do having the potential to shape the way that we think and practice in the future (Wenger, 2000).

ACTIVITY **1.1**

Reflect back on something you have learnt at work that has made a difference to the way that you approach your professional role. Do you think that informal learning played any part in how you gained this new knowledge or skill? Try to think quite deeply about this question – not just considering how you gained new information or ideas but also how you decided whether or not you agreed with what you had learnt and how you gained confidence in applying that learning in practice.

Comment

It is worth remembering that even in learning situations that we think of as formal there are aspects of informal learning – for instance, coffee breaks during seminars where a learner has the opportunity to talk about the material presented by the facilitator with their colleagues. The informal 'chat' is an important part of the learning process as it helps them review what was heard, consider how that new information changes existing ideas and form and test 'theories' that incorporate the new knowledge. Similarly, in a work-based setting, informal learning will often enhance and reinforce more formal learning experiences. For example, students can learn a great deal from shadowing experienced workers and reflecting formally on their observations. But learning does not necessarily end there – later in the day or even the week a casual conversation with a fellow student, colleague or service user may give a new insight into the work that was observed. Of course, it is not always a conversation that triggers informal learning – further practice experiences, personal experiences, hearing something on the news, watching a film or a television programme or reading a book with a storyline or character that makes a learner think more about a situation they have encountered at work can also be influential.

In work-based settings learning almost always tends to occur through a blend of formal and informal experiences, some of which may not even be explicitly recognised as part of the developmental process (Eraut, 1994). Therefore, when planning, enabling and assessing the learning of others, it is important to consider the whole workplace learning context and not just the parts of that context which are under your direct control.

CASE STUDY *1.1*

Delia is a final-year student in a Children and Family team. She has been in the placement for a month and her practice educator, Georgia, believes that she is now ready to take more responsibility for her own cases. Before Delia starts to work independently, Georgia reminds her about the organisation's Lone Working Policy, which was first introduced during induction. Georgia illustrates how the policy should be used to guide practice by talking about how she applies it when she herself visits service users. She is confident that Delia understands that she should always let someone know when she arrives to visit a service user and when she expects to leave.

However, after two weeks Georgia discovers that Delia has not always followed the policy, occasionally moving from one visit to the next without checking in with the nominated person in the office. When she asked Delia why she had been doing this, Delia told her that she was doing exactly what she knew other people in the office regularly did when they were making low-risk visits. She said that it was often really difficult to get through to the office on the phone and she was worried about arriving late.

Georgia realised during the supervision conversation that there was a contradiction between the Lone Working Policy and what Delia saw happening in practice. In practice learning situations it is not unusual for learning to be primarily driven by what is perceived to be the norm rather than formal 'teaching'. This is because people, in group situations, are heavily influenced by social norms and are therefore likely to conform to the behaviour of groups to which they aspire to belong (Turner, 1991). Being aware of social norms in the workplace and the pressures that they may place on learners will help you to be clearer in your supervision sessions about what is expected from the learner.

One of the biggest potential drawbacks of any learning system that relies so heavily on the next generation of professionals learning from the last is that while this can be an excellent way of passing on desirable behaviours and valued skills, it is equally good at maintaining those behaviours and practices that need to be changed. Although, in the case study above, Delia was clear about why she was not following the policy, we are not always so aware of how our views and behaviours are being influenced. As a practice educator, you can help the learners you support to gain an insight into their own learning processes by explicitly discussing with them when and how they have gained new skills and/or ideas. This has two key functions: first to increase their awareness of maximising opportunities for learning in the workplace and second to encourage a more critical approach to the influences on their thoughts and practice.

REFLECTION POINT

One of the things that can be confusing for learners in the workplace is the mismatch between what they are told and what they see. As experienced workers we often take shortcuts that should not be taken by someone with less experience. These shortcuts can become the social norm or the accepted way to practise in established teams. Can you think of any examples of this kind of behaviour in your own team? How do you think this would impact on a learner joining the team?

So, while we can see that it is reasonable to argue that learning in the workplace is an essential part of an individual's preparation for professional practice, we need to be aware that the provision of appropriate professional learning within the workplace is not always a straightforward process. This is particularly true when, like now, there is a drive for major changes in the way that a profession is required to function. In the next section we will move on to explore why this point is especially pertinent in the current climate and look at how the government is promoting an agenda for reform in the social work profession.

Placing work-based learning in the wider social work context – the agenda for reform

Over the last thirty years, the social work profession in England has frequently come under the spotlight and been found seriously wanting (e.g. Laming, 2009). A succession of serious case reviews have identified inconsistencies and service failings against a backdrop of increased caseloads, funding constraints, staff shortages and rapid turnover in many agencies. Since 2009, government and public concerns about the competence, effectiveness and sustainability of the profession have led to a rapid succession of reforms and regulatory initiatives (SWTF, 2009b; SWRB, 2010; CSW, 2012a; DoH, 2015; DfE, 2018). These have aimed to address the perceived shortfalls in initial education and continuing professional development as well as weaknesses in supervision and leadership at both strategic and operational levels. Most recently, the Children and Social Work Act 2017 has led to the establishment of a new specialist professional regulatory body for social work – Social Work England – due to become operational during 2019. This new body will take over regulatory responsibility for social work from the Health and Care Professions Council (HCPC) with key responsibilities for registering social workers, setting standards for education and training and determining fitness to practise. At the time of writing this edition the future direction of travel to be taken by Social Work England is uncertain as consultations on all aspects of social work regulation and education are underway.

REFLECTION POINT

What do you think we have learnt from the reforms of the last ten years? What changes do you think Social Work England should now make to ensure that the profession is fit for purpose?

How have the changes introduced in the last decade helped practice educators ensure professional learners are fit to practise?

Reforms introduced during the last decade in England have included two developments of particular significance to practice educators. The Social Work Task Force review (2009b) highlighted that the standards used for the assessment of social workers were unclear, inconsistent and unfit for purpose. Following an extensive consultation, the Social Work Reform Board developed the first (of two) standards aimed at addressing this issue – the Professional Capabilities Framework (PCF). The intention was to provide a nationally agreed, generic framework that set out expectations for social workers at every stage of their career. This was particularly significant for practice educators because, although there had been previous sets of standards (e.g. National Occupational Standards), the PCF was the first to provide a developmental framework against which students at each stage of their education and working in any context could be judged. Following an extensive consultation, the PCF was reviewed and refreshed in 2018 by the British Association of Social Workers (BASW) in conjunction with Research in Practice. At the time of writing it is used by all qualifying social work programmes in England to guide learning and benchmark the assessment of students in practice placements.

In February 2014, the Department of Education (f) published a review that looked specifically at the education of children's social workers which concluded that in addition to the generic PCF there was a need to specify 'what newly qualified social workers should know and be able to do at the end of their first year in professional practice' (Narey, 2014). The Knowledge and Skills Statement for Child and Family Social Workers was published to meet this need (DoH, 2014), with a similar framework for social workers working in adult services following in 2015 (DfE, 2018). The PCF and Knowledge and Skills Statements are currently used in parallel, with the PCF setting generic standards for all social workers and the KSSs building on the PCF to provide occupationally relevant standards for those working in specific roles. A guidance statement produced by BASW (2018) as part of the 2018 refresh of the PCF maps the KSS to the PCF and helps practice educators understand how the standards can be used both separately and together to provide a benchmark for practice expectations.

Although the introduction of both the PCF and the Knowledge and Skills statements represent important developments in social work education, it was the introduction of the PCF that led to a step change in terms of driving forward change. This is because the PCF (BASW, 2018):

- sets a clear expectation that social workers will continue to develop their skills and knowledge throughout their career and not just up to the point of qualification;

- acknowledges the complexity of practice by encouraging a shift in focus from the assessment of discrete competences towards a holistic appraisal of overall professional performance;

- emphasises the central importance of reflective practice.

To understand why these features of the PCF (BASW, 2018) are quite so significant and how they are supporting a change in the way that learning in the workplace is enabled and assessed, we will now move on to explore the differences between social work competence and capability.

From competence to capability – promoting a new way of thinking about practice

Historically, the assessment of competence in a range of specified areas, primarily at the point of qualification, was used to determine if social workers were fit for practice (Williams and Rutter, 2010). However, more recently, it was recognised that a different approach was needed (SWRB, 2010, 2012). There was a growing recognition that competences were a bit like the ingredients used to make a cake – important elements of practice, but not enough when judged in isolation to ensure a successful professional outcome. Although having the right ingredients is a good starting point, anyone who has made a cake will know that there is more to baking than putting good quality ingredients into a bowl and hoping for the best! Like social work, a cake is more than the sum of its parts. The way the ingredients are brought together, the length of time that the batter is mixed, the temperature of the eggs and count-less other factors will determine how the cake turns out. Subtle differences in techniques together with the knowledge and flexibility to react to the unexpected – such as missing ingredients or an unreliable oven thermostat – will make a huge difference to the finished product. Similarly, while it is important that social workers develop all the right competences (or ingredients), it is the way that those competences are brought together that ensures they can deal with uncertainty and practice effectively in more challenging and complex settings.

Since it is, at least in part, the ability of some social workers to deal with complexity, respond flexibly and use professional judgement confidently that has drawn past criticism (e.g. Munro, 2011) we can see why the refocus from the assessment of competence to the promotion and evaluation of a more holistic and critical approach to practice may be needed. This process of holistic and continuing learning is often described as the development of professional capability (Barnett and Coate, 2005).

So, what exactly is professional capability?

Although most of us could recognise a capable practitioner, understanding why exactly they are capable or knowing how to support a novice social worker to take the necessary steps in their journey towards capability is much harder. This is because there is no set formula for 'capability'. You can't say to a learner 'if you always do it like this you will be fine'. The whole point is that capability is the capacity to use the knowledge, skills and attributes you have (or can gain) flexibly and responsively. It is about being able to use professional judgement to practise slightly differently in each situation that you meet in order to do the best job that you can at the time. The PCF (BASW, 2018) provides useful guidance, but although it gives an indication of the elements that practitioners should be bringing together when they perform capably, it is less clear about what the bringing together actually means – except of course in terms of the need to produce a desired outcome (which we can only know has been achieved with the benefit of hindsight!).

RESEARCH SUMMARY *1.1*

Barnett and Coate (2005) undertook research with learners to understand how the learning process can prepare them more effectively for future professional roles. Although they accept that the nature of professionalism and the professional role is contentious, they suggest that it is possible to identify a number of key features that learners need to develop in order to be effective in their career. These include adaptability, reflexivity, flexibility, creativity, critical analysis and evaluation, problem-solving, team working, critical thinking, self-reliance, critical self-awareness, open-mindedness and recognition of multiple perspectives, being able to deal with uncertainty and change, motivation to learn and develop, and the ability to learn how to learn.

Barnett and Coate proposed that learners who actively incorporate these skills in their practice will be effective career-long practitioners who can work independently, deal with complexity and embrace change because they will:

- *understand the need to keep knowledge and skills up to date and identify gaps in existing capability;*

- *have the skills and motivation needed to update knowledge and skills independently;*

- *evaluate new learning and place it in the context of what is already known;*

- *understand how to adapt and transfer learning from one situation to another, ensuring that they can function effectively when faced with new situations;*

- *reflect critically on their own practice and the practice of others and use this for the purposes of learning and development;*

- *be able to articulate and critically evaluate their knowledge to make decision-making more systematic;*

- *be able to use critical thinking skills to solve problems and take responsibility for decision-making;*

- *be able to work effectively with others, recognising and valuing complementary skills and knowledge;*

- *have professional humility and be open to listening to the views of others;*

- *have a critical understanding of, and adherence to, an appropriate professional value base.*

Based on Barnett and Coate (2005)

Exploring the model that Barnett and Coate based on their research, which has underpinned some of the thinking behind the PCF (CSW, 2012c), is a useful starting point for thinking more about how we can support the development of capability through work-based learning (Barnett and Coate, 2005). The model consists of three interlinking circles each representing an aspect of professional capability – knowing, acting and being. Reflective practice is absolutely central to the model and applying the approaches that are suggested here will help you to support the development of reflective practice in the learners with whom you are working.

More about knowing

Most people would agree that a social worker needs to have a sound working knowledge of current legislation and an understanding of the theory and research that underpins and informs their practice (Thompson, 2005). Barnett and Coate (2005) agree that a relevant knowledge base is an important foundation for practice, but suggest that it is not just having the knowledge that is the most important aspect of being a capable professional. After all, having knowledge does not mean that you know how to evaluate or apply it, and knowledge without these transferable skills is at best worthless and can at worst be dangerous. Barnett and Coate (2005) therefore suggest that professional education should focus not only on gaining knowledge but also on developing skills in knowledge acquisition, analysis and evaluation and an understanding of how to critically apply knowledge to practice situations.

This makes sense for three reasons.

- Knowledge goes out of date very quickly so social workers need to keep their knowledge base under review and update it regularly.

- Information is readily accessible so it is no longer as important to hold knowledge in our heads. This means that we can access the 'best' information available to us at any given time.

- There is rarely one right answer or one way to solve a problem – social workers need to think critically about the knowledge they access, understand that there will often be multiple sources of information that may be contradictory or conflicting, and be open-minded about evidence that goes against their existing beliefs.

Ideas for practice – developing a learner's capacity for knowing

There are direct implications that arise from Barnett and Coate's research for you as a practice educator. To provide effective support for a learner, you need to model the use of research skills, critical analysis and critical evaluation in your own practice – something many people attending our courses say they lack confidence in doing. Take advantage of any opportunities that arise to explore and extend your skills in this area – how about suggesting that as a team you add a slot to meetings where you take a critical look at a journal article together?

In your work with learners it will, of course, be important to provide opportunities for them to gain new knowledge, but in order to promote 'knowing' you must also think about how you can maximise opportunities for learners to explore, analyse and apply their knowledge in a variety of contexts. You will find more ideas about how this can be achieved in the following case study and in later chapters of the book.

CASE STUDY **1.2**

Germaine is a drug and alcohol worker based in a community project and is an experienced practice educator. He is currently working with James, a final-year social work student. In a supervision session Germaine suggests that James reads about various approaches that could be used with the young people in the project and recommends some relevant recent research papers. He asks James to select two contrasting approaches and bring notes to the next supervision session about what he understands to be the strengths and weaknesses of the two approaches. In the supervision session Germaine helps James to deepen his critical understanding of the approaches by encouraging him to analyse and evaluate them in depth, making the learning more relevant by thinking about how they could be used with specific service users.

More about acting

This domain focuses on the way that professionals 'act' in practice situations and on the underlying skills and attributes that guide and define their actions. I'm sure we would all agree that social workers need to develop a range of practice skills that enable them to work with service users, carers and other professionals. However, Barnett and Coate (2005) suggest that it is not just the development of specific skills per se that demonstrates capability but the ability to avoid standardised practice through a commitment to continually updating and developing skills, critically evaluating actions and adapting practice to achieve best possible outcomes in each individual practice context.

Ideas for practice – acting

When designing learning activities for students and other learners you will be helping them to develop within the acting domain if you incorporate activities that encourage them to reflect on, critically analyse and evaluate the skills they use in their practice and provide opportunities to explore alternative approaches wherever possible. This will help to reinforce an understanding that there is usually more than one approach to working in a complex situation and that there is almost always no single 'right approach' or 'right way' to do something. Activities that help learners to identify and analyse the subtle differences between apparently similar service users and situations can be particularly useful (case studies can be a good way of doing this). As with support for the development of 'knowing', you can play a key role through modelling a critical approach to practice and by ensuring that learners are supported to reflect critically on the skills that they are using in their work with service users.

More about being

The 'being' domain is central to the Barnett and Coate (2005) model and is the area in which it varies most significantly from other, earlier models of professional development (Williams and Rutter, 2012). According to Barnett and Coate (2005), learning in this domain, which includes developing a sense of self-awareness, self-confidence, emotional resilience and a commitment to reflective practice, is fundamental to effective professional performance in a modern world. The integration of both personal and professional values into approaches to practice was considered by Barnett and Coate to be an essential aspect of the development of 'being'. (An exercise in the next section of this chapter will encourage you to begin to look at your own value base with regard to enabling others.)

Again, the model has clear applicability in work-based learning situations, underlining the importance of maximising opportunities for the development of professional reflexivity, professional self-awareness, the confidence to work independently and take responsibility for one's own practice and one's own professional development. The development of 'being' attributes is crucial to success in social work and other allied professions. It is therefore important that we consider ways in which we can support social work learners at all stages of their careers to develop within this domain. You will find ideas for how you can support learning in the 'being' domain throughout the rest of this book.

The Barnett and Coate model stresses the importance of developing an integrated capability across all three domains to produce professional capability. It follows that learning and teaching should be designed to ensure that integration takes place between all three domains and that educators help learners to make links between their experiences. With work-based experiential learning there is the potential for this to happen because in real-life situations learning cannot be separated into neat compartments. As we will see later, an essential component of work-based learning is reflection on 'whole practice experiences' and many theorists believe that it is through the act of critical reflection on experience that professional learning is achieved (Eraut, 1994; Moon, 1999; Fraser and Matthews, 2008; Beddoe, 2009).

The role of the practice educator in work-based learning

The main focus of the chapter so far has been fairly and squarely on the needs of the people who should be at the centre of any learning process – the learners. However, as we draw the chapter to a close I would like to shift our attention to those who are working in support of the learning process – the practice educators. The task you are facing when you agree to take on a practice educator role is not a small one. And the responsibilities that come as part of that role are serious and can at times become burdensome. However, for me, the role has brought more professional satisfaction than almost anything else I have been involved in at work. I have found that becoming, and continuing to be, a practice educator has been a significant driver for my own continuing development – as I have frequently realised, there is nothing that makes you question your own practice more than having to explain it to someone else!

As a practice educator you need to have confidence in your own professional capability before you can support the development of capability in others – and that may mean that you need to build aspects of your own practice alongside the learning you are undertaking for this new role. Because undertaking the practice educator role will make you think about professional capability you may well find yourself 'ahead of the game' in your workplace – understanding more than many of your colleagues about the importance of underpinning aspects of professionalism like emotional resilience and emotional intelligence. For this reason, practice educators are often able to contribute more to workplace learning than they can achieve simply through their work with individual learners. This may be through a formal contribution, such as taking a lead responsibility for an aspect of team development or providing mentor support to a colleague, but is more often through supporting the informal types of learning that we discussed earlier – being the person who quietly asks those curious questions which lead to a perspective shift or being the one who mentions an interesting new piece of research to other members of your team. In the remaining chapters of the book we will explore in some detail how you can use your practice education capability to fulfil the roles and responsibilities of a practice educator. You will quickly realise that this now involves more coordination and quality assurance than was traditionally the case – although you will be the 'conductor' of the learning experience there will be many 'players' involved in supporting and assessing a learner's progress – and it will be down to you to make sure that they understand how they can contribute effectively and fairly to the process. By doing this you may find that you are making another contribution to the overall development of your team as you help increase understanding among your colleagues of how to facilitate the learning of others.

REFLECTION POINT

As a social worker, your values are an important element of your practice and of your professional capability. Values will influence all your decisions and actions and will be just as important in your work with learners as they are in other areas of your professional practice. Thinking critically about your value base will help you to understand how your values will impact on your practice. Consider your values with respect to facilitating and assessing practice and think about how these values differ from your more familiar professional value base. Why do you think you hold these particular values? Can you link them to any specific experiences that you have had as a learner or as a practice educator? How do you think that your values will guide and influence your practice with learners?

These are the GSCC (2002) values for practice educators that have been incorporated into the PEPS (CSW, 2012a).

- Identify and question their own values and prejudices, the use of authority and power in the assessment relationship, and recognise and act upon the implications for their assessment practice.

- Update themselves on best practice in assessment and research on adult learning and apply this knowledge in promoting the rights and choices of learners and managing the assessment process.

- Respect and value the uniqueness and diversity of learners, recognise and build on strengths and take into account individual learning styles and preferred assessment methods.

- Accept and respect learners' circumstances and understand how they impact on the assessment process.

- Assess in a manner that does not stigmatise or disadvantage individuals and assures equality of opportunity. Show applied knowledge and understanding of the significance of poverty, racism, ill health and disability, gender, social class and sexual orientation in managing the assessment process.

- Recognise and work to prevent unjustifiable discrimination and disadvantage in all aspects of the assessment process and counter any unjustifiable discrimination in the ways that are appropriate to their situation and role.

- Take responsibility for the quality of their work and ensure that it is monitored and appraised; critically reflect on their own practice and identify development needs in order to improve their own performance, raise standards and contribute to the learning and development of others.

As can be seen, these values advocate certain approaches and processes for the task of enabling learning by ensuring practice is of a high professional standard and that it is ethical, non-discriminatory and fair.

ACTIVITY **1.2**

Write a few words on the skills, knowledge and personal qualities you are bringing to the role of practice educator.

Remember that skills and knowledge are often transferable from other areas of your life. For instance, you may never have had experience of supporting adults to learn in a formal setting but you may know that you are good at breaking tasks down into simple-to-understand steps and can explain them to people.

Think about how you will need to build on these skills, knowledge and attributes as you become more experienced within the role. What new knowledge will you need? What skills will you need to develop? Where will values fit in? Remember that it is not always possible to draw clear distinctions between knowledge, values and skills.

It may help you to draw a mind map (or other representation, table, list, pictures, etc.) of the things that you think you need to learn to help you become a more effective practice educator. Include your ideas about how this learning will be achieved (e.g. 'I need to know more about how adults learn. I will learn about this by reading, attending workshops and by reflecting on my experience of working with a learner').

Comment

This exercise will provide you with an analysis of your existing skills, knowledge and values and will encourage you to think about areas for further development. This could form the basis for a personal development action plan. You could consider asking your line manager and/or colleagues what they think are your strengths and development needs that may be relevant to the practice educator role, as this would give you another perspective on your capability.

Chapter summary

- Learning is taking place in every workplace all of the time – each time something new is encountered there is the potential to learn from it.

- If professional education and frameworks for continuing development are to be fit for purpose, they must ensure that they promote the development of skills and attributes that will enable professionals such as social workers to be effective in their role in this rapidly evolving and complex work climate.

- Effective work-based education should focus not only on learning and assessment for the demonstration of practice competence but also on bringing the competences together into a cohesive whole, which some describe as the development of professional capability.

- Success in the workplace is dependent not just on the development of a fixed set of competences but critically on the development of a range of transferable skills and appropriate professional attributes that interlink to form professional capability.

- As a social worker, your values will be important in guiding your approach to the task of supporting and assessing learning in practice.

FURTHER READING

Barnett, R and Coate, K (2005) *Engaging the curriculum in higher education.* Maidenhead: Open University Press.

BASW (2018) *Professional capabilities framework for social work in England* – guidance on using the 2018 refreshed PCF.

Part One

Domain A: Organise opportunities for the demonstration of assessed competence in practice

Meeting the requirements of the Practice Educator Professional Standards (CSW, 2012a)

The material in this part links to the following domain standards.

Domain A: Organise opportunities for the demonstration of assessed competence in practice

1. Take responsibility for creating a physical and learning environment conducive to the demonstration of assessed competence.

2. Devise an induction programme for social work students that takes into account a learner's needs and their previous experience.

3. Negotiate with all participants in the workplace, including service users and carers, the appropriate learning opportunities and the necessary resources to enable the demonstration of practice competence.

4. Work openly and cooperatively with learners, their line managers, workplace colleagues, other professionals, service users and carers in the planning of key activities at all stages of learning and assessment.

5. Coordinate the work of all contributors. Ensure they are fully briefed, understand their roles and provide them with feedback.

6. Complete an audit and provide feedback on practice learning opportunity in line with the Quality Assurance for Practice Learning framework.

7. Monitor, critically evaluate and report on the continuing suitability of the work environment, learning opportunities and resources. Take appropriate action to address any shortcomings and optimise learning *and* assessment.

8. Contribute to the learning and development of the agency as a training organisation. Help to review and improve its provision, policies and procedures and identify barriers for learners.

Introduction to Domain A

When I organised my son's eighth birthday party I had everything planned down to the last detail. I researched and selected party games, shopped around for interesting prizes and worried about which children to invite. I considered and then reconsidered all sorts of different food before finally settling on what I hoped would be the perfect menu – a menu that would have something for everyone, would not give too much of a sugar rush or lead to any nasty allergic reactions. In the run-up to the party I had 'to do' lists pinned all over my kitchen and every spare moment was filled with activities related to the organisation of those two short hours. On the big day it was worth it. Although I knew of course that things could still go wrong, the careful planning made me more confident and provided me with a range of plan Bs for times when the plan As didn't quite work out. So, for instance, when I discovered during a game of Pass the Parcel that I had mis-calculated the number of layers and did not quite have enough prizes to go around, I had a bag of spare goodies to hand and was able to placate the child who had missed his turn. Later, when another boy fell over and cut his knee in the garden, the first aid kit was waiting by the back door and I could stick a plaster on the cut with minimum fuss.

Although you may feel that my approach to my son's birthday says more about my personality than about organisation in general, I have included this example from my own experience to highlight the value of planning and preparing for significant events. Most people would agree that when outcomes really matter, good planning and preparation are important. We can all think about times when a lack of organisation has led to disappointing results in both our personal and professional lives. For me and for my son the outcome of that particular party was very important and I was fortunate because I could choose to prioritise my time to invest in planning and preparation. However, in work situations we do not always have the luxury of time or the autonomy to choose how to spend it. We have many competing priorities and very often planning for learning opportunities, quite understandably, comes low down on our list of things to do. But is this something that is acceptable within our professional role?

In Part One (Domain A) we will be primarily thinking about planning and organising learning experiences for social work students on practice placements. These students will be spending between 70 and 100 days in your workplace and the outcomes of the placement matter a great deal, both to the student and to everyone else involved. However, in our experience, less time is commonly given over to organising student placements than I spent planning my son's two-hour-long birthday party. When planning for placements is skimped, we have often found that things go wrong – students struggle or even fail to meet their objectives, service users can be disadvantaged and problems can arise within teams or even the wider organisation. Because the outcomes of social work placements really do matter and the consequences of poor planning and organisation have such far-reaching and serious consequences, workplace learning is not something that can be left to chance (Shardlow and Doel, 1996). It is therefore important that practice educators are able to spend time planning placements before they happen and have sufficient resources to ensure that the learning experience is effectively organised from beginning to end.

Part One will provide you with the opportunity to think critically about the way that learning should be planned and organised in the workplace. It will also enable you to explore a range of organisational strategies that you can use as a practice educator. Most of the examples that have been included relate to social work students but many of the principles underpinning the examples apply equally to other learners, such as newly-qualified social workers or people undertaking continuing professional development.

Part One builds on the key themes introduced in Chapter 1 and looks at how you can organise and manage learning to ensure both the demonstration of competence and the development of professional capability. We will show that the way that learning is managed can have a significant impact on learning outcomes and that some management strategies are more likely than others to support the development of capability.

Part One is divided into three: Chapters 2, 3 and 4. Chapter 2 provides an introduction to the issues covered within Part One and links back to Chapter 1. We look at some of the reasons why it is important to encourage learners to take some responsibility for planning and organising their own learning and stress the importance of taking a partnership approach. At the end of Chapter 2 we identify seven key elements of organisation that are particularly important for work-based learning. In Chapter 3 we move on to explore the first of these elements, effective planning and preparation, in more detail. Chapter 4 covers the remaining six elements.

Chapter 2
Managing learning: taking a partnership approach

In the previous chapter, we introduced the idea that poor planning can have serious consequences for learners and others involved in their learning in the workplace. We are going to open this chapter with a case study that illustrates what can happen when a practice educator fails to devise a plan B for the first day of a placement. We will see that the consequences of this oversight have the potential to be far reaching, with negative impacts on the learner, the service users and the member of staff who has to deal with the additional work created by an unexpected student when they are already overstretched.

CASE STUDY 2.1

Beate arrives on the first day of her placement as a student in a residential project for people with learning disabilities to find the door firmly locked with no obvious way to get in. She rings the doorbell but gets no answer. She tries a telephone number she has been given and after a long delay the phone is answered. The person on the other end of the phone sounds flustered and although she is friendly, clearly has no idea who Beate is or why she is there. After a short wait she lets Beate in and takes her into the office, explaining that she is an agency worker and that the manager is sick. The project is very short-staffed and she is working alone. She vaguely remembers from a team meeting that a student was due to start sometime soon but can't remember what plans, if any, had been made. She suggests that as there seems to be nothing else organised, Beate might like to spend the day getting to know the residents in an informal way – maybe watching some TV with them or giving them support to do their washing. She then tells her that she is very busy and needs to get on – gesturing towards the lounge and saying that some of the residents will be getting up soon.

ACTIVITY 2.1

Take a few minutes to think about this situation and then answer the following questions:

- *How do you think Beate would be feeling at this point?*

- *How do you think the experience of this first day could impact on her learning in the placement?*

(Continued)

ACTIVITY **2.1** *continued*

- *What about the residents – how could they react to meeting Beate in this way?*
- *How might the agency worker be feeling and what could she have done differently to have improved the management of Beate's first day?*

Comment

In answering these questions try to put yourself into Beate's shoes and imagine how you would be feeling. To extend the activity and take a more critical approach, you could give Beate two contrasting character traits (confident and anxious?) and see if you think this would make a difference to how she would react.

Although the situation described in the case study would be somewhat unsettling for any student, the actual impact of this experience and the student's ability to cope with this degree of independence on their first day is likely to vary widely. If Beate was a confident woman with experience of working in a similar residential setting, she would probably have taken the day in her stride. She would have felt positive about her ability to communicate and support people with the completion of everyday tasks. She would have known the questions to ask the agency worker in order to take advantage of the learning opportunities that the day was still able to offer. She may even have welcomed this chance to meet the people she would be working with in an informal way. However, a less self-assured student with no experience of working in this type of setting could have found the lack of support and structure extremely alarming.

Although I doubt that any self-respecting practice educator would plan such an unstructured start for a student, the unexpected does sometimes unfortunately happen. This case study will hopefully have made you think a little more about what it would be reasonable to expect someone to be able to cope with in a new learning situation and how much responsibility students should be taking for their own learning. In the next section we will move on to look at why this is something we should be reflecting on and why it is generally considered a good thing for professional learners to be in control of their own development.

Who should plan and organise work-based learning?

In Chapter 1 we introduced the idea that social work learners should be encouraged and supported to take responsibility for managing their own learning, as the ability to do so is fundamental to their development as effective professionals (Barnett and Coate, 2005). The Professional Capabilities Framework includes the ability to recognise and respond to one's own learning needs within the professionalism domain, with all social workers from the point of qualification onwards expected to be able to take responsibility for aspects of their own learning. Theories of adult learning also stress the central importance of learners taking some or all of the control for how and what they learn.

Historically, learning theories did not distinguish between childhood and adult learning, but in 1980 Malcolm Knowles began a long-running debate by claiming that adult learners have distinct characteristics and that learning outcomes are improved when educators have an understanding of their needs and motivations. Knowles's (1980) claims formed the basis of his theory of 'andragogy' (the study of adult learning) and although many of his ideas are contentious and are now considered oversimplifications (because many of the characteristics he identified can apply equally well to some children and are by no means universal in adults), they are still thought to be a helpful starting point for any discussion about adult learning (Walker et al., 2008).

RESEARCH SUMMARY **2.1**

Andragogy – a theory of adult learning

Knowles developed the following 'principles' to describe adult learners.

- Adult learners are autonomous and self-directed. *Adults have a different self-concept from children and most adults have reached a point of development where they see themselves as independent and capable of making their own decisions. If they come into a learning situation and have little or no autonomy, they may feel disempowered, and Knowles believed that this could reduce the quality of their learning.*

- Adult learners have a wealth of knowledge and experience. *Adults approach education with an existing bank of knowledge and experience gained from educational, life and work experiences and this is a resource and foundation for future learning. Knowles believed that adults learn most effectively when they are encouraged to build on and develop their existing knowledge and when they are respected as people who already have skills and knowledge.*

- Adult learners are goal-orientated. *Adults are most motivated to learn things that will help them achieve specific goals. Adults will therefore learn most effectively when the benefits of learning activities are specifically linked to the achievement of learning or life objectives.*

- Adult learners are relevancy-orientated. *Adults are most motivated to learn things they see an immediate use for, particularly learning which will help them 'solve a problem' that they have currently in their lives. Adults will therefore learn most effectively when clear links are made between what they are learning about in 'theory' and how they can use their new knowledge in practice.*

Based on Knowles (1980)

Implications for practice educators

There are some clear implications for practice educators in Knowles's (1980) ideas. If we accept his 'principles' as guidance on how to work with adult learners we can see that we will help adults to learn most effectively when we do the following:

- Encourage and support them to be active participants in their learning – for example, by setting some or all of their own learning objectives, by selecting and designing their own learning experiences and by taking some responsibility for monitoring and assessing their own progress and achievements.

- Form an 'adult to adult' partnership with them that fully takes into account, recognises and values their existing skills and knowledge, and uses this as a basis for further learning and development.

- Help them to understand how their learning experiences are linked to their learning needs and goals.

The first two principles are particularly relevant to managing and organising learning in the workplace and will have significant implications for the way that the relationship between the practice educator and learner is established and maintained. You will see how these principles are relevant at all stages of managing and organising learning experiences as Part One unfolds and you will be given opportunities to reflect on how you can incorporate them into your practice. We will also look at some of the ideas put forward by other writers such as Prosser and Trigwell (1999), Biggs (2003) and Beddoe (2009) and consider how they have helped us to understand that the relationship between a learner, an educator and the learning context are more complex than andragogy (Knowles, 1980) suggests.

ACTIVITY 2.2

Reflect on Knowles's principles for adult learning and consider how well they describe you as a learner. It may help you to answer the following questions.

- *Do you always learn most effectively when you are able to be in control of your own learning or can you think of times when you would prefer to be more directed by a 'teacher'?*

- *Do you think that it is important for a practice educator to find out about what a learner already knows? How does it feel to be a learner whose previous knowledge and skills are not taken into account by a teacher?*

Comment

This exercise will help you to begin to think about some of the reasons why Knowles's theory of andragogy (1980) is controversial. Most people find that the extent to which they want to manage their own learning varies from situation to situation and will be dependent on a number of complex interacting variables such as confidence levels, context, learning task, time pressures, etc.

Different learners, different contexts, different management approaches

Every adult learner and every learning situation is unique. We have already seen that encouraging adults to take an active responsibility for their own learning can enhance their learning outcomes (Knowles, 1980, 1990). In the next section of this chapter we will consider how the extent to which this is possible or even desirable will vary considerably from situation to situation.

REFLECTION POINT

Work-based learning is not the same as classroom learning because it occurs in complex situations that involve real service users whose welfare can be directly affected by the learner's actions. It is a situation where mistakes can have serious consequences and this can lead to high levels of uncertainty and anxiety in learners (Walker et al., 2008; Doel, 2010). This anxiety can quite reasonably reduce the learner's inclination to take risks and increase their need for security and direct guidance (Prosser and Trigwell, 1999). Practice educators will also have some strong motivations to 'keep control' of work-based learning as they normally carry some level of responsibility for their learner's workload and will feel responsible for the success or failure of the learning experience. As a consequence they may be tempted to 'play it safe' and keep as much control as possible of the management of the learning experience. In this way they can be assured that the learner will learn what they need to know and they can demonstrate that they have done their job thoroughly and efficiently. This means that practice educators and learners need to balance the considerable educational benefits of encouraging the learner to take responsibility for their own learning with the risks and stresses involved in doing so.

When deciding how to divide responsibility for managing learning with a learner, it is worth asking yourself what is behind your decision and how your approach to risk has influenced your and your learner's thinking.

A number of factors need to be taken into account when decisions are reached on how responsibility for organising and managing learning is distributed between the practice educator and the learner. These factors include:

- characteristics of the learner (confidence, motivation, expectations, ability, etc.);

- prior experiences of the learner (personal, work, educational);

- stage that the learner has reached in the learning process (novice, near-qualified, post-qualified, etc.);

- nature of the learning objectives (fixed, e.g. PCF (BASW, 2018), determined by learner, determined by employer, clear or ambiguous, etc.);

- nature of the assessment process (fixed, e.g. format provided by university, negotiable, fully understood by the learner, etc.);

- nature of work involved (e.g. level of complexity, level of inter-professional, inter-agency work involved, etc.);

- nature of the learning context (e.g. good or poor culture of learning for learning, support and resources available to the learner);

- level of responsibility the learner is taking for practice and the risks attached to the work they are undertaking;

- who is accountable for the learner's practice (learner, practice educator or other);

- what safeguards are in place to ensure quality of service to the learner and quality of the overall learning experience (e.g. supervision, monitoring and reviews);

- what resources the learner has the authority to access or mobilise – some things may have to be organised and managed by the practice educator or a manager with appropriate levels of authority.

CASE STUDY 2.2

Hope is a second-year student on a BA (Hons) social work course at Exbury University. She is a 22-year-old black woman who lives with her parents near the university. She has a good academic record and has told her practice educator in a pre-placement meeting that she is confident meeting new people, self-motivated and enjoys a challenge. Although this is her first placement she has had some experience of working as a volunteer in youth groups and does part-time work in a residential home for older people. She started her placement at The Grove, an independent drug and alcohol drop-in centre, two weeks ago.

Gavin, her 35-year-old white male practice educator, recently completed a practice educator programme and knew that he 'should' be encouraging Hope to take responsibility for her own learning. He therefore took what Hope had told him about her confidence levels into account and suggested that she took responsibility for organising and managing part of her induction programme. Hope enthusiastically agreed to do so and after a brief initial introduction to the project she was given a list of visits to make to other agencies that had close links to The Grove. Gavin gave her some leaflets about the projects and suggested that she should make contact with the organisations and arrange visits during the first month of her placement. Although she was told that the visits would be useful, she was not really given much guidance on what her objectives for the visits should be.

After three weeks in the placement Hope had failed to arrange any visits. She told her practice educator that she had tried but although she had left numerous messages for people, no one had returned her calls. This seemed unlikely as the practice educator was in regular telephone contact with several of the agencies and knew that they had a good record of returning calls. Hope still seemed confident and said she would keep trying to make contact. The practice educator sensed that she was becoming anxious about the situation and reflected that she probably needed more help than he initially thought with organising her induction.

ACTIVITY **2.3**

What do you think is really happening in this case study? What factors are involved in Hope's failure to organise induction visits? What would you have done differently if you had been Hope's practice educator:

- *in the first supervision where you talked about induction?*
- *at the end of the first week in the placement?*
- *after three weeks?*

Comment

This activity will encourage you to think about how you will begin to judge how and when it is appropriate to encourage a learner to take some responsibility for managing his or her learning. You can use the questions set out above to help with your analysis. An area to focus on is the way that Gavin judged Hope's ability to manage her own learning – could he have asked some different questions to find out more? Maybe he could have asked Hope to give him some examples of previous situations when she had used similar skills?

In some situations practice educators will need to take a lead role in the organisation of the learning process, while in others the learner themselves can take some or all of this responsibility. The balance of responsibilities for managing learning can change over time as the learner grows in confidence, becomes more familiar with the learning context and is clearer on how they can meet their objectives. In a learning experience, such as a student placement, the learner would normally be expected to move from a position of early dependence towards greater independence over the course of the placement. You can help learners to become more independent by providing appropriate safe opportunities in which they can take responsibility for their learning along with support and encouragement to do so.

However, it is sometimes not enough to provide opportunities, support and encouragement to learners, as some have never developed the underlying confidence, skills and attributes needed to take on this level of responsibility. Some learners, particularly those who are inexperienced or whose previous educational experiences have not required them to manage their own learning, may need help to develop their ability to manage time, prioritise tasks, problem-solve and research information as well as help to build self-confidence and motivation (Barnett and Coate, 2005). Support with the development of these underlying skills and attributes should not be seen as added extras or things which are outside the practice educator's remit. This is because these skills and attributes will not only improve their ability to manage their learning but are transferable to other areas of their professional practice and will enhance their more general professional capability, for example, in the PCF (BASW, 2018) domains of professionalism and knowledge.

Student social workers and newly-qualified social workers (NQSWs) commonly lack the confidence, skills, local knowledge and networks that they need to manage their own learning processes effectively and safely. They are also in situations which are likely to cause high levels of anxiety and it has been shown that in such circumstances people tend to want more direct guidance and support (Prosser and Trigwell, 1999). It is therefore common for students and other people who are new to learning situations to initially need considerable help organising and managing their learning. Throwing people in at the deep end is rarely a good strategy and our own experience of setting up student placements has shown us that where this approach is adopted, placements often do not get off to a good start.

Not all learners need high levels of initial support with the management of their learning and experienced social workers undertaking post-qualifying education or continuous professional development based in their own workplace will often be able to take some or even all of the responsibility for organising their own learning experience. It is, however, worth remembering that even experienced professionals sometimes lack confidence in a new learning role. It is therefore important not only to understand what the 'learner' is like in their more familiar professional role, but also to know about their previous experiences as a learner and about their level of self-confidence and competence with regard to the specific learning they are undertaking (Prosser and Trigwell, 1999). It is only by developing a good understanding of the learner and the learner's context that it is possible to establish how much support the learner will want and need with organising and managing their learning in the workplace.

Getting to know the learner and working with the learner to reach joint decisions about important issues such as how their learning will be managed will be achieved most effectively when there is a learning partnership between the learner and the practice educator. We will now look at how learning partnerships and other key objectives relating to effective work-based learning can be achieved by focusing on seven elements that provide an effective foundation for successful learning opportunities.

The seven elements of organising work-based learning

Work-based learning by definition is taking place in a situation where learning is not the number one priority. In social work environments the needs of the service users and their carers will often, quite rightly, take priority over the needs of learners. And so practice educators and learners will therefore be faced with a careful balancing act to ensure that:

- the needs of the learner are met;

- the learner can balance their learning with other aspects of their workload;

- all others within the work environment (service users, carers, colleagues, etc.) are considered, respected and not significantly disadvantaged as a result of the learning taking place.

While a perfect balance will always be difficult to achieve, paying attention to the following will improve the outcomes for all involved.

1. Effective planning and preparation

    Ensuring that the needs of the learner can be met, that the impact of the learning on others has been considered, that appropriate resources can be made available and that the learning experience can be accommodated within the organisation.

2. Setting clear expectations

    Ensuring that all involved in the learning experience understand their respective roles and are clear about what is expected from them.

3. Providing an effective learning environment

    Attending to all aspects of the learning environment and ensuring where possible that it is adapted to meet each learner's individual needs.

4. Ensuring effective communication

    Ensuring that good strategies and processes are in place to facilitate effective communication between all interested parties.

5. Providing appropriate support and monitoring progress

    Ensuring that all aspects of the learning experience are monitored and supervised adequately and that appropriate support is provided to the learner throughout the learning experience.

6. Undertaking regular reviews of progress

    Ensuring that progress is formally reviewed at agreed intervals and that there are strategies in place to deal with any problems that may arise.

7. Evaluating the learning experience

    Ensuring that the learning experience is evaluated and that information received is used to feed into the planning process for future work-based learning.

In the next two chapters we will look at each of the above in greater detail.

Chapter 3
Effective planning and preparation (Element 1)

Building sound foundations is a crucial part of providing an effective learning experience, with overall success dependent, at least partly, on the quality of the planning and preparation that takes place (Shardlow and Doel, 1996; Walker et al., 2008). Our experience of working with university-based social work programmes at both pre- and post-qualification levels supports this idea and has shown us that a significant number of the common problems associated with learning in the workplace can be attributed to failures in the planning and preparation stages.

Managing any form of work-based learning is a complex task (Grey, 2002) and, when learning experiences are organised at the last moment, there is often not enough time to ensure that adequate resources are in place to meet learners' needs. Last-minute placements for social work students are sometimes unavoidable, for instance when a planned placement falls through, but unless a great deal of extra care is taken, they can turn into poor experiences for both the learner and the organisation providing the placement. Even when learning takes place in a learner's own workplace, things can go wrong if time has not been taken to ensure that adequate planning and preparation are undertaken: for example, resources not available, no time for discussion of learning/personal reflection on learning/ feedback, lack of workload relief.

Planning and preparation should ideally start at the moment you first consider the possibility of providing support for learning in your workplace; this could be a request from a local university for a placement, a discussion with a colleague about providing mentoring support or involvement with a NQSW. It should continue through the early stages of the learning process. The tasks involved in planning and preparation can usefully be broken down into the following stages (although not all will be needed for all forms of learning):

- making the decision to provide a learning opportunity;
- consulting with and involving your agency in planning and preparation;
- consulting with and involving the learner in planning and preparation;
- planning and organising an induction programme.

Working through each of the relevant stages in a systematic way will help you to ensure that sound foundations are put in place for work-based learning experiences. It is unlikely that this will be a linear process because you will probably find that you need to revisit and revise some of your earlier plans in light of information gained throughout the planning and preparation process. For instance, you will need to consult your colleagues and managers about the possibility of supporting a learner at a very early stage when you may not know much about the learner or their course. At a later stage you will need to go back to them again with any new information gained from talking to the learner in more detail.

We will now consider each of these planning and preparation stages in further detail.

Making the decision to provide a learning opportunity

The first stage of the planning and preparation process involves working with your team to decide whether a placement or other learning opportunity can reasonably be provided in your workplace at this time. It is important to include everyone who will have a role in the placement, as the presence of a learner will have an impact on team dynamics and possibly on individual team members' workloads.

Whether you and your team are new to supporting work-based learning or have some previous experience, it is worth analysing your current position to ensure that you make an appropriate decision. This decision can be considered to be made up of two parts. First, is it appropriate for you/your organisation to support a learner at this time? Second, is it possible to meet this particular learner's needs? Saying 'yes' to a learner when you or your organisation are not in a position to fully support them and provide the opportunities they require is likely to end in, at best, a disappointing experience for all involved and, at worst, setting up the learner to fail.

CASE STUDY 3.1

Exbury University approached Rosebank Day Centre and asked them if they could take a second-year social work student on a 70-day placement. The manager, Sandra, who is the only qualified practice educator at the day centre, knows that she will be going on maternity leave for the last three weeks of the placement and is still unsure who will be covering for her in her absence. However, the team really enjoys having students on placement and the service users have been asking when the next student is coming. The university really values the placement as it has always been well organised and evaluated positively by students.

Sandra decides that she will say 'yes' to the student, having negotiated with a colleague, Nathan, who is also an experienced practice educator and the manager of a nearby residential project. They have agreed to share the placement and the practice educator responsibilities between the two projects. Nathan will take over the placement for the last few weeks and Sandra will contribute to the final report before she goes on maternity leave. The university is very pleased with this arrangement as it means that a valued placement can go ahead.

ACTIVITY 3.1

What do you think of Sandra's compromise? What plans will Sandra and Nathan need to make to ensure that the joint placement runs smoothly? Who else do you think they should have consulted?

Comment

The compromise reached by Sandra certainly seems reasonable, although it would still be important for her to think ahead and predict what could still go wrong. Although this would be no guarantee of success, it would help Sandra and Nathan to put plans in place to avoid foreseeable problems. The case study does not mention consulting with either the student or staff at the two projects. Would you have involved them, or do you think that their input was not needed at this stage?

In some situations, circumstances may dictate that there is no option but to say 'no' to the provision of a learning opportunity, but in others, even when circumstances are not ideal, it may be possible to make reasonable changes which ensure that the learner's needs can be met. To help you reach a decision, you should consider if the experiences you can offer within your workplace match the learner's needs (Doel et al., 1996). It may be helpful to consider the following questions.

Questions to ask about your organisation

- What impact will a learner have within the organisation – will we need to make any changes and do we have the necessary resources to meet an additional team member's needs?

- Could there be any negative consequences of the placement for service users and carers – can these be minimised or avoided?

- What learning opportunities can we provide? Can we link with any other agencies or organisations to extend the opportunities we can offer? Can any other workers within the organisation offer specialist opportunities? Do agency policies or procedures limit any opportunities that can be offered?

- What previous experience do we have of supporting learning in the workplace? What can we learn from that previous experience to help us in this situation?

- How will other people such as colleagues, service users and other professionals need to be involved and what is their attitude to involvement in supporting learning? What skills do they have? Do they have any development needs to support their involvement?

Questions about you as practice educator

- Do I have the time, knowledge, skills, motivation and resources to support the learner? Will there need to be any organisational changes to support me in my role as practice educator (workload relief, extra training or support, supervision for my role as practice educator)?

- How will the needs identified above be met – is it feasible and realistic to meet these needs within the resources and in the time available?

Questions about the learner and their course

- What will the learner need to gain from the learning opportunity and can we meet these needs?

- What do they already know? What can they already do? What previous experience have they had that is relevant to this workplace?

- Do they have specific learning needs, or any other additional needs, and can we meet these needs?

- What does the learner's course require from the learning opportunity (learning and assessment requirements, commitments required from the work-based practice educator, such as attendance at meetings, etc.)?

- What support will the course offer to me as the practice educator?

You can use the information gained by answering these questions to help you reach a decision about whether or not to offer a placement. Remember that very few learning situations are perfect and you will almost certainly need to make some compromises to make the placement work. Decide what is essential, what is desirable and where there are difficulties. Try looking creatively at whether or not problems can be solved.

REFLECTION POINT

Think about your own workplace. How are decisions about student placements made? Could this process be improved? Could there be more consultation? Do you think this would increase your team's commitment to and involvement with student placements?

Consulting with and involving your agency in planning and preparation

Once you have decided that you can provide a placement for a student or can support a learner such as an NQSW, you need to start work on planning the learning experience itself. It is important that you continue to involve key people from within your organisation such as line managers, colleagues, service users and carers, because all of these people will have contact with the learner and may become involved in the learning and/or assessment process. You may also need to involve people from outside agencies if the learner will be working with them on a regular basis.

It is worth thinking about why and how you want other people to be involved before you open any discussions. By thinking things through in advance you will be much clearer about your objectives and will be more likely to succeed in achieving them.

REFLECTION POINT

Think about what the benefits are for you and the learner of involving other team members and colleagues from other agencies in the learning and assessment process. There will be a number of benefits such as having others to share the workload and provide back-up support to the learner in your absence and also in terms of the way the learner is supported with their development. Learners will have the opportunity to work with a range of social workers and other professionals and this will expose them to different perspectives and approaches. This experience will help them to learn to be more flexible and adaptable in their practice (see Part Two for more information about this). You may also wish to involve other people in assessment of the learner's competence (see Part Three for some reasons why this is a good idea).

The involvement of people who receive services in social work education has been mandatory in England since 2003. This means that it is now standard practice for service users and carers to be asked to provide feedback on a learner's performance. Unfortunately, because of the widespread use of standardised feedback forms and the poor support provided to those whose opinion is being sought, this is often reduced to mere tokenism (Pearl et al., 2018; Walker et al., 2008). Thinking creatively and consulting widely at the planning and preparation stage of a placement can make this process more meaningful. Ensuring that people who receive services and their carers are involved not only in the provision of feedback but are given the opportunity and support to work in partnership with learners to help them understand how their practice can be improved (Askheim et al., 2017).

Managers will also need to be included in the planning process as they need to understand the implications for practice educators in terms of workload and flexibility, as this may mean that changes to work practices or support mechanisms are required. Thinking about what your needs are going to be and having an open discussion with your line manager about them at an early stage is really important because it may be difficult to make changes later. Don't assume that you will have workload relief or that your manager can provide you with support and guidance on your practice educator role unless you have checked this in advance.

You should also not assume that other people will feel positive about working with a learner or about contributing to a learning experience. Learners can bring extra work and disruption to a workplace; their presence can be challenging to staff because they bring new ideas and question established practice. Service users and carers may be concerned about working with a 'learner' rather than an experienced member of the team or may be anxious about meeting a new face. Experience with marginal and failing students in the past may have reinforced negative views and pressures of work may be forcing people to concentrate their energy on what they see as the core elements of their work. This will almost certainly not include involvement in learning.

However, despite the challenges that can come with supporting work-based learning many social workers do feel very positive about getting involved, recognising that a core part of their professional role is to support the development of others. Having learners in the workplace brings advantages – new ideas can be refreshing and energising and students can often undertake projects or 'added value' pieces of work that your team does not normally have the resources to complete. Service users and carers often enjoy working with learners because they feel that they get more time and attention as the learners have reduced caseloads. Some even positively enjoy helping the student to learn.

It is likely that your team, service users and carers will include people with both positive and negative views towards students and other learners. An important part of the planning process is to provide information and reassurance to everyone who will be involved and include them, where possible, in major decision-making. This will ensure that you take their views into account and that they understand what you are expecting from them if they agree to have an involvement in the learning process. Experience shows that it is difficult, if not impossible, to provide a good-quality learning experience within a workplace without the full cooperation of all involved, so investing time and energy in consulting and involving others is definitely worthwhile.

The following section will help you to think about who needs to be involved and how you can go about supporting and encouraging their involvement with all stages of the learner's experience in your workplace.

Consulting with and involving the learner in planning and preparation

In Chapter 2 we established the importance of the development of an effective learning partnership between the practice educator and the learner as a basis for a successful learning experience (Knowles, 1980). The foundations of this partnership need to be built during the planning and preparation stage.

In a social work placement the first point of contact (after there has been an agreement in principle about a placement) between student and practice educator will normally be a phone call or email to arrange an informal workplace visit. The purpose of this meeting is to spend a little time with the learner, beginning the process of getting to know them, finding out about their specific learning needs and exploring how these needs can be met in your workplace. It is best if the meeting takes place a few weeks before the start of the learning experience. This will provide sufficient time for both the learner and the practice educator to undertake any preparation that is agreed at the meeting. This type of meeting is particularly important when a learner is coming into a 'placement' from outside the team, but can also be valuable for people learning within their own work environment because their learning needs will often be different from their working needs.

As well as finding out about the learner, the meeting will also provide the opportunity for you to let them know about your expectations and give them information about you and your work environment. Although pre-placement meetings are usually fairly informal, planning will help to ensure that both you and the learner get the most out of the time you spend together. Drawing up an agenda will help give structure to the meeting and ensure that key issues are covered. Sharing this agenda with the learner before the meeting and encouraging them to add agenda items is a good idea as this gives you both a chance to prepare for the meeting and bring any relevant information on the day. Working in this way sends the learner a clear message that they will be expected to take an active role in their own learning and provides a good starting point for an effective learning partnership.

It might also be a good idea to suggest that the student does a small amount of reading about your service user group or the services that you provide before the meeting – maybe you could send a link to a website that would be helpful. This will again send a message regarding your expectations about the student taking some responsibility for their learning – all but the most confident students would welcome some signposting to relevant materials; however, don't expect them to do too much at this stage.

Work-based learning brochures

How are students and other new learners going to find out about your organisation and about you as a practice educator?

People do not generally remember or understand large amounts of information provided verbally in early meetings so it is worth considering how you will ensure important details are provided, understood and remembered (Mullins, 2005). Doel et al. (1996) encourage those responsible for managing learning in the workplace to provide clear, brief, jargon-free information for newcomers in the form of a brochure. They suggest that a brochure should contain information about the practice educator, the team in which the learning will take place and the agency as a whole, covering professional experience, specific knowledge, skills and experience of individuals within the team, previous experiences of supporting work-based learning, and information about the service users with whom the team works.

Doel et al. (1996) also suggest looking for creative and meaningful ways of conveying information to learners rather than the brochure being made up of questions and answers. This could include, for example, providing information in the form of descriptions of typical days, profiles of service users or examples of work undertaken by other learners. It may even be a good idea to ask current or past learners to contribute to the brochure because they will be able to provide the learners' perspective on what should be included.

Although this is a very good idea, it is worth considering that, as with any brochure, creation is not the end of the task. Information will need to be regularly updated and revised to ensure that an up-to-date picture of the organisation is presented at all times. Brochures, even in their simplest form, require an investment of time and effort. Involving other team members in the production of the brochure can spread the load as well as being a useful team-building exercise which will help people to feel involved in the provision of practice learning opportunities. To avoid spending time 're-creating the wheel', it is worth considering what resources you could draw on for inclusion in the brochure. These could include mission statements, leaflets about services, etc. It is also worth thinking about whether you can collaborate with other practice educators in your agency to pool general resources, possibly coming up with some sections of the brochure that can be used across the organisation with others specifically developed for each workplace. Working cooperatively in this way may also help build supportive relationships with other practice educators, which will be useful at every stage of supporting work-based learning.

ACTIVITY 3.2

One of the things that it is useful to include in a brochure for new learners is a profile of you as a practitioner and as a practice educator. This will help the learner find out about you, your particular areas of expertise, experience and interest.

Try writing a profile that you could give to a social work student or an NQSW joining your team. What will you include?

Comment

There is no right or wrong approach to writing a profile. You need to think carefully about what information will be useful to the learner and what will help them see you as someone who is able to support them in a positive and skilful way. As part of your deliberations you should consider where to place appropriate boundaries, as this will help you to think about what to include and what to leave out.

In my role as a practice educator I normally provide learners with a brief summary of information about myself and my work experience. I include material in the profile about how I learn and how I approach new ideas, as I think this is a useful way to introduce these topics. I give basic outline information about my personal life including that I am a mother of teenaged children, because I believe that this gives me a specific perspective on my work. Not everyone feels comfortable about sharing details of their private life and you will need to make your own decision about this. You need to think about power issues as part of sharing information with a student – do you expect them to share information with you that you wouldn't be prepared to share with them? If so, how will this affect your relationship?

Planning and organising an induction programme

The value of a good induction programme for any new person in a working environment is widely recognised and is a vital part of ensuring competence to practice (Mullins, 2005).

Most organisations that employ social workers will have in place some form of induction process for new employees. Some may also have a specific procedure for students on placements. Since September 2012 all newly-qualified social workers have been required to undertake an Assessed and Supported Year in Employment (ASYE) (CSW, 2012a) and as part of this have been provided with very specific packages of support and assessment. When you plan the induction of a student or a newly-qualified social worker the first obvious step is to investigate the policies, procedures and resources already available within your organisation. These will normally provide guidance and structure for the induction process but will usually need to be tailored to meet the needs of each individual. Further useful resources relating to induction and the ASYE are available from Skills for Care and the BASW websites.

Induction involves the introduction of a new person to the culture and environment of an organisation and should include an introduction to its policies, practices and members of staff (Mullins, 2005). In a social work agency an important part of this induction includes an introduction to the service users and carers who engage with the service, including activities that enable the new person to begin to understand their perspective, needs and wishes. A properly planned and designed induction programme will provide reassurance, aid motivation and improve performance. The induction period for a new worker generally extends over the first few months of employment. Clearly, when a learner is on a relatively short placement or other similar brief learning experience, the induction period will be shortened and it is important that the programme is designed to take this into account. Although it may be useful to get some ideas from a standardised induction process used within your organisation, each learner's induction should be developed individually, taking into account their specific needs for learning and support.

Where possible, learners should be encouraged to identify their own needs and take some control over the management of the induction process in line with adult learning principles (Knowles, 1980). However, it is important to remember that people in new situations often feel anxious and don't know what they don't know. This difficulty, even for confident learners, with identifying exactly what they should be learning about in an unfamiliar organisation means that some clear advice and guidance will be required from you in your role as practice educator. It has been shown that students normally welcome support from a knowledgeable practice educator at this stage of their learning experience (Parker, 2006).

It is always worth remembering that people find it very difficult to absorb large amounts of information in a short space of time, particularly in new situations. Even though we know that this is the case, we may still have to restrain ourselves in early supervision sessions because we feel that we need to make sure we have told the student everything they need to know. The design of the induction programme should allow for a staged approach to learning with an option for information to be revisited and reviewed (Mullins, 2005).

Induction plans

A written copy should be given to the student including times and locations of activities. People responsible for each element of the plan need to be clearly identified with their contact details. The plan should include:

- *detailed plans for the first day to include the layout of the building, initial introductions to your team, health and safety, parking, expenses, etc.;*

- *introductions to key people – maybe some pre-arranged meetings to discuss their role, etc.;*

- *shadowing opportunities – with you and with colleagues;*

- *visits to other agencies – not all at once at the beginning as the student needs to get to know your team before they can understand the wider context in which you work;*

- *essential training – e.g. computer systems, etc.;*

- *suggested reading – policies, procedures information about methods and approaches specific to your service, relevant research, etc.;*

- *reflection time – make sure you build this in to allow the student to think about and learn from their experiences;*

- *time with the practice educator.*

Based on Maclean and Lloyd (2013)

You may also wish to consider an induction checklist on which you can tick things off as they are covered. You should think about how you ensure students have access to information that they will need during their induction and throughout their placement. Many practice educators put together induction folders containing key policies and procedures, information about the team, meeting dates, etc. An induction folder can be used to complement a brochure such as the one described earlier, and can be personalised for each individual student.

ACTIVITY 3.3

What would you need to include in an induction programme for a social work student on their final placement in your workplace? How will you stage the programme so that you ensure you don't give too much information at once? Could the responsibility for delivering induction be shared? How would you encourage the student to take some responsibility for the management of the induction programme?

Comment

Remember to include information about your workplace, policies, procedures, the community you serve, service users, your team and other linked organisations, etc.

We started this chapter by stressing the important role of planning and preparation in work-based learning experiences and have explored ways of ensuring that learners can be enabled to have the best possible start. However, while we have been clear that the likelihood of a learner's success will be reduced by a lack of preparation and planning, there are many other factors that can affect the outcomes and overall effectiveness of learning experiences. In the next chapter we will move on to explore some further aspects of managing workplace learning and consider the practice educator's role in this process.

Chapter 4
Organising learning (Elements 2–7)

Element 2: Setting clear expectations

It is very important that everyone involved in a learning process has a shared understanding of what is expected from them (Knowles, 1990; Neary, 2000; Maclean and Lloyd, 2013). If there is any confusion or disagreement about expectations at the start of the learning experience it is likely that problems will develop. This could lead to difficulties with the achievement of learning objectives, reductions in the quality of service provision, problematic relationships with colleagues or a breakdown in the relationship between the learner and the practice educator.

CASE STUDY 4.1

David was a social work student undertaking his first placement in a small school for children with learning disabilities. Staff at the school provided support to the children at meal times and expected that David would do the same. This expectation had not been discussed at the pre-placement meeting or included in the learning contract. David did not see how helping with lunch met his learning needs and so decided to use lunchtime to catch up with his reflective recording. David's colleagues felt that he should be helping with lunch because chatting with children informally over a meal gave an insight into their perspectives and helped build and maintain relationships. When Janine, the practice educator, explained why she felt that it was important to get involved, David happily did so. He said he wished he had understood the value of this experience from the start of the placement as he felt that he had inadvertently put relationships with his colleagues and children at risk through his behaviour.

Before any learning experience begins there should be agreement about a number of issues, including:

- the learning objectives;
- the learner's individual learning needs;
- what learning opportunities will be provided;
- what resources will be required to support learning;
- what support will be provided to the learner (supervision/mentoring, etc.);

- assessment methods and criteria;

- practical arrangements such as working times, line management and sickness;

- any general expectations relating to the learner's behaviour in the placement;

- procedures to follow when things go wrong.

A generally accepted way of formalising agreements about learning is through a contract. The term 'contract' is one with which most adults are familiar – we have employment contracts, contracts regarding housing and even occasionally contracts regarding personal arrangements such as partnerships. Contracts are binding agreements for people to carry out specific behaviours, often within a specified timescale. Before signing any form of contract it is important that all of the key people fully understand the implications of the agreement and their role within it.

Learning contracts are documents drawn up by those involved in a learning experience (for students in work-based learning this is usually the practice educator, the on-site supervisor (if relevant), the learner and the tutor from the learner's college/university course). They specify what the learner will learn, how this will be achieved, what resources will be available and the criteria that will be used for measuring success (Neary, 2000). Encouraging the learner to be actively and meaningfully involved in the process is important (Knowles, 1990). But remember that contracts are often drawn up early in the learning process, at a time when learners may be feeling anxious and powerless. They may not want to admit weaknesses or expose a lack of understanding. It is therefore important that you in your role as practice educator work in close partnership with the learner ensuring that they are empowered to contribute meaningfully to the process and are confident enough to make their needs and wishes known.

Learning contracts are usually agreed at a meeting that takes place between key individuals before, or shortly after, the start of a learning experience and are a very important part of the overall learning process. The exact timing of the contract meeting is open to debate (Walker et al., 2008). Some people believe that the contract should be drawn up before the start of the learning experience while others do so within the first few weeks of the placement. Both approaches have advantages and disadvantages. Contracts are most effective when they are used as 'working documents' which are reviewed and if necessary revised at regular intervals, helping to keep learners and practice educators focused on the agreed learning objectives and assessment targets. If used in this way, the timing of the drawing up of the contract is probably not that critical, as changes can be made within the first few weeks as and when they are needed.

When a contract has been drawn up, Neary (2000) suggests reviewing it before finalising it by considering the following questions:

- Are the learning objectives clear, understandable and realistic? Do they describe what the learner proposes to learn?

- Are there any other objectives that should be considered?

- Do the learning opportunities seem reasonable, appropriate and efficient ways of achieving objectives?

- Are there other opportunities that could be utilised?

- Are the assessment criteria and means of validating them clear, relevant and convincing?

- Could other evidence be sought?

Many learning programmes will have their own specified way of assessing and collecting evidence for work-based learning. The contract will therefore usually include some material that is specified and non-negotiable, such as competences to be met and certain require-ments for assessment, together with material that can be individually negotiated to meet the needs of a learner and/or the agency. It is very important to familiarise yourself with any guidance and requirements provided by learning programmes, including pro formas deve-loped for learning contracts. Seek advice from the learner's tutor or placement coordinator if you have any doubts about what is required.

Although learning contracts are most commonly used for 'placements' and for the Assessed and Supported Year in Employment (ASYE) their value in other work-based learning situations, such as within mentoring, peer support or other forms of learning such as continuing professional development, should also be considered. Formalising agreements through contracts protects the interests of the learners and their workplaces and ensures that the needs and expectations of both are clearly communicated.

Element 3: Providing an effective learning environment

Think about your own experiences of work-based learning. What do you particularly remem-ber? What helped you to learn and what made learning difficult? Whenever we ask these questions on practice education courses we get a wide variety of answers but, if we had to select the ones that are most commonly given, they would concern the relationship with the practice educator. This anecdotal finding has been strongly supported by research find-ings based on social work and nursing practice learning (Lefevre, 2005; Parker, 2008; Smedley and Morey, 2010).

What you do and the way that you interact with the learner is probably the single most important thing that will influence the quality of a learner's experience. But when practice educators are asked to list what a learning environment is made up of, they often completely forget that they themselves are a central part of it.

People do not learn in a vacuum. They learn within a context made up of many variables that interact in a complex way and uniquely impact on each individual and their learning process (Marton et al., 1984). Getting the learning environment right and ensuring that it supports and encourages appropriate learning is an important aspect of the overall management of any work-based learning experience. Knowles first introduced the concept of a 'learning environment' in 1970. In his early work he explored the importance of physical needs (warmth, comfort, resources, etc.) and psychological needs (safety, appropriate level of challenge, respect, being treated as an adult, etc.), concluding that if these were not met, adults' learning could be seriously impaired. We can all remember a time when we have sat in an overheated or freezing room and found it almost impossible to do anything but wish for the session to end. Simple things like being too hot or too cold or not having a comfortable chair or a desk to write on can have a surprisingly big impact on learning. We also find it hard to learn when we don't feel safe or are anxious; we can get put off by challenges that we think are too hard or can be inclined not to try when we perceive tasks to be too easy. But the situation is not straightforward, as there is always interplay between the factors that make up the learning environment. For example, people who are strongly motivated learners are much less likely than others to be affected by factors such as the room's temperature.

Knowles (1990) also looked at the impact of social and cultural aspects of the environment and showed that these could also influence learning outcomes. He believed that if any of a learner's needs were not met, the quality of their learning could be reduced and that they may 'vote with their feet' and opt out.

The relationship with the practice educator, relationships with other people providing support to the learner and the general atmosphere within the workplace are all important parts of the learning environment (Ellison, 1994, cited in Lefevre, 2005). Lefevre (2005) found that students valued practice educators who were supportive, friendly, relaxed, open and respectful and were available and ready to share ideas. Although the majority of students would agree that having a practice educator with these attributes would support effective learning, there is not universal agreement among learners about other aspects of the learning environment. It is therefore unwise to make assumptions about an individual's needs based on a generalised impression of what a 'good' learning environment is.

Research has clearly shown that individual learners have very different needs and different ways of prioritising those needs (Biggs, 1999). Furthermore, it is the way that the learner perceives the environment that is significant to their learning and not any absolute measure of what is provided for them (Ramsden, 1992; Prosser and Trigwell, 1999). It is quite possible for different learners to perceive the same environment in substantially different ways, influenced by factors such as their previous learning experiences, expectations, motivation to learn, approach to learning and personal values (Prosser and Trigwell, 1999).

So, returning to the relationship with the practice educator, although most learners would say that having a 'good' relationship with their practice educator was important to their learning, Lefevre's research (2005) showed that each student interviewed used different words to describe what worked for them. What one student would perceive as cold and formal, another might interpret as professional and efficient.

CASE STUDY **4.2**

James and Julie have both just started placements in the same social work team. The team works in a cramped and noisy office with insufficient desks and computers to go around. James finds the noise, bustle and lack of personal space very stressful. He finds it hard to concentrate, hates not knowing if he will have a desk to work at and would rate the office as a very poor learning environment. Julie by contrast loves the 'buzz' in the office and feels that she learns a lot by hearing other people work and being able to talk things over with colleagues. She would rate the learning environment as good, even though she sometimes has to share a desk or phone.

Talking to the learner to find out what is important to them individually will help you to plan a learning environment within your organisational and resource constraints that comes as close as possible to meeting their individual needs. It will also help you to develop a relationship with the learner that is appropriate and meets their needs.

A very important aspect of the learning environment is the degree of inclusivity that it offers. Tisdell (1995) said that a learning environment should:

- acknowledge that all individuals bring multiple perspectives as a result of gender, class, age, sexuality, etc.;

- recognise that learners' identification with social groups is multiple and complex;

- reflect the experiences of learners and value these as a basis for learning and assessment;

- acknowledge the power disparity between teacher and learner.

Learners who feel marginalised and disempowered will not have their psychological, social or cultural needs met and this is likely to have a negative impact on their learning (Knowles, 1990; Prosser and Trigwell, 1999). Parker (2008) found a clear relationship between the inappropriate use of power and a breakdown in placements for social work students.

Learners arriving in placements are particularly likely to feel disempowered and marginalised and it is an important part of a practice educator's role to work in partnership with others to create an inclusive, supportive learning environment that meets each individual learner's needs. However, it is not just learners new to a workplace who may feel this way. Experienced workers can be 'destabilised' by new learning and, as a result, may feel disempowered. For example, social workers on a post-qualification 'critical thinking' course frequently comment that the processes involved in developing their critical thinking skills lead to an initial loss of professional confidence. Furthermore, because employers and colleagues are not always ready for the challenges that can result in increased criticality, learners report feelings of dissonance and, in some cases, even marginalisation. Practice educators can support individual learners with these sorts of experiences and can also work with others to ensure that team members and managers are open to new ideas and appropriate challenges.

Getting to know and forming a supportive relationship with individual learners is an important part of ensuring that the environment provided is inclusive and empowering (Smedley and Morey, 2010). Discussing and valuing previous experience, acknowledging and discussing difference without sentimentalising it, together with challenging stereotypes and checking assumptions, all have an important role to play (Doel et al., 1996). Some 'differences', such as physical disability or ethnic background, may be relatively visible while others, which may be of equal importance to learners, may be less obvious.

ACTIVITY 4.1

Here are some examples of different people. What specific preparations would you need to make to ensure that the learning environment was suitable for them? Would their circumstances mean that you would have to make any day-to-day changes within your work environment to ensure that their needs were met?

ACTIVITY **4.1** *continued*

- *Michaela is a 46-year-old Croatian woman who came to the UK two years ago and is retraining as a social worker. Her spoken and written English are good, but she has limited experience of living in this country.*

- *Jethro is a 23-year-old man with severe dyslexia. He uses a specialist computer program to help him write and needs support with reading complex material.*

- *Helena is a 33-year-old single mother with two children under the age of five. One of her children has a physical disability. The learning opportunity is within an adult team that provides services for adults with various disabilities.*

Comment

The changes you will need to make will depend partially on your own individual work environment. All three people described above could thrive in a workplace but would need some adjustments. You need to take into account relevant legislation, e.g. the Equality Act (2010). This Act makes it unlawful to discriminate against people with a disability in the workplace. It also places a responsibility on employers to make reasonable adjustments to meet the needs of people with disabilities. You should bear in mind that dyslexia and other similar disabilities are covered by the Equality Act (2010).

The learning environment not only has an influence on the likelihood of the success or failure of work-based learning, it will also have an impact on the quality of the learning that takes place. Returning to one of the key themes of this book – the development of professional capability – we can see that the learning environment provided can play an important role in determining whether learners simply demonstrate competence or are supported to develop their capability.

Thompson (2006) stressed the importance of creating a culture within workplaces that supports all individuals to learn and develop. The following list draws on some of Thompson's ideas. An effective learning environment will be one in which:

- people are open to considering different approaches;

- people have a desire to look at issues from a service user/carer perspective;

- mechanisms exist for seeking service user and carer feedback;

- there is a willingness to learn from experience and there is an environment that supports critical reflection;

- it is possible to learn through safe experimentation and explore new ways of working;

- there is an expectation that learning will be shared;

- there is enthusiasm for an evidence-based approach to practice;

- there is good communication across professional boundaries;

- opportunities exist for people to share ideas and express opinions.

The provision of an effective learning culture supports the development of professional capability because it encourages social workers at all stages of their development to be open to new learning and to take a more critical, evidence-based approach to their practice (Hafford Letchfield et al., 2008).

Although practice educators obviously play an important role in the provision of a culture for learning, work-based learning is most effectively supported when a learning culture exists across the whole organisation (Senge, 1990). A recent study by Beddoe (2009) suggests that there is considerable doubt that organisation-wide cultures can exist in large social work agencies. This is because learning is often directed in a top-down way by senior managers (who tell people what they need to learn rather than basing learning strategies on service user needs and what workers want to learn) and also because current managerialist and blame cultures have low levels of tolerance for learning from mistakes.

On a more optimistic note, however, Beddoe (2009) concluded that even when organisation-wide cultures did not effectively support learning at a team level, it was still possible to create an effective learning culture. As a practice educator with a specific interest and skills in work-based learning you can have a direct influence on how the team culture develops.

See Part Four for more information on how a culture for learning can be provided within the supervisory relationship.

Element 4: Ensuring effective communication

Few people would disagree that effective and open communication is critical to the success of work-based learning situations. Most of us can remember times when failures in communication have led to misunderstandings or breakdowns in information transfer. When this happens in situations where people are learning, the potential for serious consequences for all involved is very significant. Learners may not have their needs met, tasks may be completed incorrectly or not at all, and service users and carers may receive an incomplete or poor-quality service.

In this element we will explore some key aspects of communication within work-based learning situations.

Communication with the learner

The imbalance of power within the relationship will have an impact on communication between the practice educator and the learner (Shardlow and Doel, 1996; Parker, 2008). For a student, the practice educator occupies an authority role and has the power to assess their practice and ultimately will have a say in whether or not they qualify as a social worker. They may also have the power to provide or limit access to resources and learning experiences and can have an influence on the opinions of others in the team.

However 'good' the relationship is that develops between the learner and the practice educator, the learner will retain a degree of apprehension as a result of the power held by the practice educator. Communicating openly about mistakes, uncertainties and concerns can be difficult when the learner is aware that their overall performance is being judged. Learners may also be reluctant to criticise or question the practice of the agency or the practice educator because they may fear the consequences of such behaviour.

Awareness by both the learner and the practice educator of the impact of this power imbalance, together with open discussions about what this will mean in practice, can help to mitigate these negative effects on communication. It is a good idea for the practice educator to raise the issue of power right at the start of the relationship and to talk about how any concerns the student may have can be allayed.

Communication between the practice educator and the university/training provider

Good communication between those responsible for supporting learners in the workplace and the learner's education/training provider helps to ensure that learning experiences run smoothly and problems that arise are dealt with effectively. Both practice educators and programme providers will need to take some responsibility for establishing and maintaining effective working relationships. You will need to make sure that, where possible, you attend meetings for practice educators that are arranged by the university and carefully read all written material that is provided relating to the placement. Don't assume that just because you worked with the university in the previous year that systems and procedures will be the same. Before the placement starts read the placement handbook and ask for clarification about anything that you are uncertain of.

In a study which looked at communication between higher educational establishments and employers, Kemp (2000) showed that creating a collaborative relationship between universities and work-based learning providers was not just desirable but essential when learners were studying for qualifications that required:

- substantial practical skills and an in-depth knowledge base;
- integration through reflection and underpinning values;
- validation by professional and academic authorities.

Furthermore, Kemp (2000) showed that the formation of an effective collaborative relationship was not a simple or linear process. Her research indicated that two interdependent factors were significant in the development of such relationships: shared values and open communication. She found that collaborative working was successful when effective professional relationships developed between staff in universities and in placement agencies, as this enabled direct communication to take place between key individuals.

If a problem arises within the placement it will be much easier to deal with if you have already been in communication with a tutor or practice learning coordinator from the university.

Element 5: Providing appropriate support and monitoring progress

Monitoring the learning/assessment experience is an important part of ensuring quality in terms of learning outcomes, practice performance and the interface between the two. Although the assessment of learning and the achievement of learning objectives/ competences is an important part of the monitoring process, practice educators do not just monitor learning opportunities to measure whether learning is 'on track' (assessment). The monitoring role undertaken by practice educators is much wider and encompasses all aspects of learning and the learning environment. This will involve asking a series of questions.

- Is the learner's practice good enough for the role they are undertaking – does it meet agency standards; is the learner's work of a high enough quality to meet service users' needs (protecting service users and the agency)?
- Are the learner's support needs being met (protecting the learning process)?
- Is the learner able to meet their learning objectives (protecting the learner)?
- Is the quality of the learning experience good enough (developing the agency)?

Practice educators have a number of methods at their disposal that can be used to check the progress of the learner and the overall process of the learning experience, including:

- formal supervision (or practice tutorials);
- informal supervision (working alongside learners);
- evaluations of the learner's written records/assignments/reflective records, etc.;
- formal observation of practice;
- feedback from colleagues, managers, service users and carers and the learners themselves.

It is likely that a combination of the above methods would be used to monitor the success of a work-based learning opportunity as this will ensure that a variety of different perspectives are taken into account and that the interests of all involved in the learning environment are considered.

The practice educator will play a key role in monitoring the learning experience, working in partnership with the learner to draw together and analyse the information gained from the process. However, where possible, the practice educator should encourage learners to be partly responsible for monitoring their own progress. They can do this by supporting them in self-assessment and keeping track of progress towards objectives. This can be done formally in supervision where learners can be asked to report back on and evaluate progress since the last session. Most university qualifying programmes now build in processes that encourage students to monitor their own progress with the achievement of the Professional Capabilities Framework (PCF) (CSW, 2012c).

For a more in-depth exploration of some of these methods for monitoring learning experiences, see Part Three.

Element 6: Undertaking regular reviews

Regular reviews are an essential part of the quality-assurance process for work-based learning, providing both practice educators and learners with an opportunity to check progress with the achievement of objectives. Reviews draw on information gained through the monitoring processes described above and ensure that, when required, action is taken to keep learning experiences on track. Learning contracts should be used within the review process to check that intended learning outcomes are being met and that all involved are meeting their commitments.

Most learning programmes will have formal points of review where there will be the opportunity to review the contract, review objectives, monitor progress and devise an action plan for the remainder of the learning experience. Social work degree courses usually have formal review points in the middle and at the end of each practice learning opportunity (as a minimum). The dates of these reviews are usually included in the learning contract to ensure that all involved in the placement know when they will take place and can prepare appropriately. Reviews are usually undertaken at a meeting but may in some cases be paper exercises.

Where learners are not studying through a formal programme, it may be worth agreeing points at which reviews will be undertaken between the learner and the practice educator. This will ensure that progress is regularly reviewed and that plans are made to help learners with the achievement of their goals.

CASE STUDY 4.3

Jacob is half way through his placement in a Looked After Children team. He has settled in well and has developed a good working relationship with Diana, his practice educator. Diana is aware that they are approaching the mid-point of the placement and, to help Jacob prepare, they go through together the pro forma that will be used at the mid-way meeting. Diana encourages Jacob to take the lead, reflecting on and evaluating his progress to date. They refer to the records Jacob is completing for his portfolio together with supervision notes and feedback from service users and colleagues. Although there has been an ongoing dialogue about progress in supervision, Jacob finds this preparation session with Diana very reassuring as it enables him to get an overview of his progress. They both identify that there may be a problem evidencing the professional leadership domain of the PCF (CSW, 2012c) and agree to bring this up at the mid-way meeting.

A week later Diana and Jacob meet with the tutor from the university to review Jacob's progress to date. At the meeting Jacob raises the issue of lack of evidence for the professional leadership domain and he, Diana and the tutor explore ways in which evidence could be provided. Diana is able to offer a few suggestions and as part of the review a specific objective is set for Jacob to deliver a short training session within a team meeting.

Element 7: Evaluating the learning experience

Every learning experience that you facilitate as a practice educator will be unique. Each learner and course that you work with will provide you with potential for reflection on your experiences and consequential professional growth. In order to evaluate the placement, you will need to gather information from the learner, from colleagues, from service users and from carers. You can bring this information together with your own thoughts and feelings to evaluate the placement as a whole. You will be able to draw out points of learning for you, for the learner and for your organisation. It is a good idea to undertake some or all of this evaluation with the learner – continuing the learning partnership and bringing it to a logical conclusion. In Part Five we will develop this theme further and look at how you can learn from your experiences and continue to develop as a practice educator.

However, it is important not only that you continue to develop your skills as a practice educator but also that the organisation that you work in continues to develop and become a more effective environment for learning. Peter Senge introduced the concept of learning organisations in the early 1990s. A learning organisation is one that engages with systematic thinking, teamworking and work-based learning of all forms. A learning organisation will be an effective organisation because the learning of individuals is integrated into the whole. Learning organisations should avoid the same mistakes being repeated and provide an environment in which workers can respond flexibly to new challenges (Senge, 1990; Gould, 2000).

Within a learning organisation each worker has a responsibility for his or her own personal commitment to continuous development as well as a shared responsibility for supporting the development of others. Within such an environment it is clearly important to learn from experiences of supporting learning in the workplace. To do this, each learning experience should be evaluated and the results of this evaluation incorporated into planning future learning opportunities.

Shaw (2004) suggests that for evaluation to make a real contribution to the development of an organisation there must be:

- an evaluation culture which sustains honest enquiry;
- a commitment within the organisation to development (in other words, the results of the evaluation will be taken on board by the organisation, not just the practice educator);
- learning-based practice (the evaluation must lead to changes in practice when necessary).

In this respect an organisation must have structures that enable the dissemination of information across levels and be able to develop and redevelop meaning for itself to bring about change (Wenger, 2000; Nixon and Murr, 2006).

If you are working as a practice educator for a social work student you will not only need to be involved in evaluating your experience within your own organisation but will also be required to complete an evaluation for the university so that they can monitor the quality of the placements that their student has undertaken. The student will also complete an evaluation. Universities placing social work students will have their own systems for evaluating placements and you will need to contribute to these for each placement that you are involved in. There are currently plans to introduce a standardised national system for evaluating placements: the Quality Assurance for Practice Learning framework (QAPL).

ACTIVITY *4.2*

How will you go about evaluating learning opportunities that you support as a practice educator?

Are there mechanisms in place to ensure that your own learning and that of your learner can contribute to your organisation's learning and improve support and opportunities for future learners?

How will you ensure that what you learn from the evaluation will help inform others in your organisation?

Comment

There is a danger that evaluation can become a superficial process – a tick-box exercise. Think carefully about the evaluation and communication systems that are currently in use in your organisation and consider whether they really do help both you and your organisation to learn from your experiences.

Summary of Part One Domain A

- The effective management of learning experiences is of central importance and the process should ensure that:

  - the needs of the learner can be met;

  - the learner is able to balance their learning with the rest of their workload;

  - others within the work environment are not disadvantaged as a result of learning taking place.

- It is important to develop a learning partnership which encourages the learner to take an active role in the management of their own learning.

- The way that learning is coordinated will vary significantly depending on the nature of the learning that is taking place and the specific needs of each individual learner.

- Key elements in the effective organisation of work-based learning are:

  - effective planning and preparation;

  - setting clear expectations;

  - providing an effective learning environment;

  - ensuring effective communication;

  - providing appropriate support and monitoring progress;

  - undertaking regular reviews;

  - evaluating the learning experience.

FURTHER READING

Beverley, A and Worsley, A (2007) *Learning and teaching in social work practice.* Basingstoke: Palgrave Macmillan.

A very readable guide to learning and teaching in social work, covering the necessary learning theory as well as the key aspects of the learning partnership.

Edmonson, D (2014) *Social work practice learning.* London: Sage.

A really helpful look at placements written for students. The chapter on planning and beginning placements is particularly relevant.

Maclean, S and Lloyd, I (2013) *Developing quality practice learning in social work.* Rugeley: Kirwin Maclean Associates.

Section B is a very readable practical guide for practice educators.

Part Two

Domain B: Enable learning and professional development in practice

Meeting the requirements of the Practice Educator Professional Standards (CSW, 2012a)

The material in this part links to the following domain standards.

Domain B: Enable learning and professional development in practice

1. Teach the student using contemporary social work models, methods and theories relevant to the work, powers and duties, and policy and procedures of the agency, demonstrating the ability for critical reflection.

2. Establish the basis of an effective working relationship by identifying learners' expectations, the outcomes which they have to meet in order to demonstrate competence, and their readiness for assessment. Agree the available learning opportunities including multi-professional contexts, methods, resources, and timescales to enable them to succeed.

3. Discuss, identify, plan to address and review the particular needs and capabilities of learners, and the support available to them. Identify any matters which may impact on their ability to manage their own learning.

4. Discuss and take into account individuals' learning styles, learning needs, prior learning achievements, knowledge and skills. Devise and deliver an appropriate, cost-effective teaching programme, which promotes their ability to learn and succeed.

5. Make professional educational judgements about meeting learners' needs within the available resources, ensuring the required learning outcomes can be demonstrated in accordance with adult learning models.

6. Identify which aspects of the management of the learning and assessment programme learners are responsible for in order to achieve their objectives. Describe and agree the roles of the work-based assessor in mentoring, coaching, modelling, teaching and supervision.

7. Establish how the learning and assessment programme is to be reviewed. Encourage learners to express their views, identify and agree any changes and how disagreements on any aspects of it are resolved.

8. Advise learners how to develop their ability to manage their learning. Deal with any difficulties encountered by them.

9. Support the student in gathering evidence according to programme requirements.

Additional learning outcome for practice educators at Stage 2

1. Apply an appropriate range of supervisory models, roles and skills, which recognise the power dynamics between assessor and learner.

Introduction to Domain B

So far we have seen that your role as an educator is to enable the development of competence and capability, i.e. to develop people who will be effective career-long practitioners able to work independently, deal with complexity and embrace change. In addition, we have established the overall ideals of working in partnership with the learner and of promoting self-direction within the learning environment.

Part One has shown that getting to know a learner is a key part of developing the ideal partnership and, in order to optimise practice learning and assessment, learners' needs and expectations need to be met through a well-structured and organised learning experience. Part Two takes the next step and looks at how to provide suitable learning opportunities that also incorporate the ideals of partnership and self-direction, and which enable the type of learning and professional development that generates competence and capability.

The chapters in Part Two relate to four key aspects of enabling learning and professional development in practice.

Chapter 5. Understanding learners

Chapter 6. Developing learning objectives

Chapter 7. Considering learning theories

Chapter 8. Designing learning opportunities

Before we start, we need to understand that the goal of developing competent and capable practitioners (whether they are students, novices or experienced workers) influences each of these four aspects of enabling learning and professional development in practice. It does this by setting certain standards or underpinning requirements from the outset.

For understanding learners (Chapter 5), our goal demands that learning is about developing learners' critical thinking and practice, and this involves enabling the development of their own personal approach and understanding of practice. Understanding learners is therefore underpinned by a requirement to enable learners to take an active part in their learning and for them to adopt as independent an approach as possible within the boundaries of safe and acceptable social work practice.

However, it can be seen that one of the main dangers here is assuming someone is ready to be enabled in this way. If a learner is not used to taking an active role in their own learning or to thinking independently with the material or ideas with which they are provided, it can be a source of great anxiety. For example, a mature practitioner who has known only a more traditional style of education will probably need a great deal of support before they are able to learn more independently. However, another mature student may be quite confident and fairly self-directive from the start because they have previously undertaken a distance learning course.

Understanding learners, therefore, requires you to be able to adopt a critical and flexible style that seeks out and allows for individual difference when enabling learning. This is where you can embed your learner-centred approach further by truly understanding learners and being able to work from where they are rather than where you assume them to be or would prefer them to be.

For developing learning objectives (Chapter 6), our overall goal of developing competent and capable practitioners demands a holistic view of practice learning and social work tasks. As we have seen, social work practice involves more than just a thorough understanding of explicit regulatory competences. In a learning context, placing too much emphasis on competencebased learning and assessment has a number of inherent dangers, because focusing on definable skills and outputs alone can limit and reduce what practice is about (Doel et al., 2002). There is also a need to be aware of the more implicit processes that guide and inform our decisions and actions, such as the use of intuition, deliberation, judgement-making, critical analysis and evaluation, and incorporate them into learning schemes where possible.

When considering learning theories (Chapter 7), our overall goal of developing competent and capable practitioners takes account of the notion that there is no one overall definition of 'learning'. Learning is a very complex and situated phenomenon; different people learn in different ways and the same person will learn differently in different situations. It follows that there is no single 'right' theory or method to enable it. This is a perfectly acceptable and even liberating position to be in. It means a range of theories can be considered critically and used to devise the most appropriate activities which allow learners to develop their personal understanding and approach.

Finally, designing learning opportunities (Chapter 8) will need to enable learners' capabilities for working independently, dealing with complexity and embracing change. A structured learning opportunity is a planned and structured piece of work that prepares, enables and consolidates a person's learning. These opportunities should aim to maximise the potential for learners to explore, analyse and apply their knowledge in a variety of contexts. This is about enabling learners to develop their individual approach to critical practice, and in turn means that a very creative, active approach is adopted, whether your enabling role is that of a teacher, supervisor, mentor or coach. Learners will need to be exposed right from the start to the idea that there is no one way to practise if they are to be effective career-long practitioners, able to work independently and deal with complexity and change in a positive way.

As you can appreciate, providing suitable learning opportunities that incorporate the ideals of partnership and self-direction and which enable the type of learning and professional development that generates competence and capability is not a goal that is achieved by being given a complete checklist of learning theories, set teaching methods or learning activities. Instead, this part of the book offers a range of ideas that will enable you to understand your learners' learning, consider how to present learners with diverse ways of thinking and acting, and allow a critical review of these learning processes.

Chapter 5
Understanding learners

The first stage in enabling the learning of others is to understand their needs, requirements and behaviour.

Taking a critical approach

Obviously, learners will have prior learning experiences that influence their expectations and assumptions, and getting to know them is a key part of planning and organising learning. However, you will also have previous learning experiences that have influenced your expectations and assumptions. You may unconsciously adopt a particular teaching style because it is the only one you have been exposed to, or believe that learning happens in a certain way because that is the only way you have learnt. Therefore either party may bring incorrect assumptions or expectations to the new learning experience.

Let's start with you. Before you begin to enable others, it is a good idea to understand more about yourself as a learner and ensure you have already developed yourself to be the type of learner who is independent and self-directing. If you have not done this, it will be relatively difficult for you to enable anyone else to take this type of approach. It is clear that no learning occurs in a vacuum. As an adult learner you bring a wide range of prior learning and experience to this new learning situation. Your previous experience, as well as your beliefs and values, will play a major part in how you view learning and how you 'naturally' teach or enable others. You should have reflected on and explored previous learning experiences to be fully aware of your beliefs, values and style concerning learning, teaching and enabling learning. This will help you define your role as an educator as well as your role as a learner for your own studies and should be an ongoing process. Chapter 12 provides further advice and guidance on this reflective progression for continuing learning and development.

Let's move on to the learner. The process of getting to know the learner may well have started in the planning stages of a placement or in early contact meetings. However, understanding the learner and valuing their perspective is an ongoing and inherent feature of enabling learning rather than a one-off event. As the learning experience gets under way, learners' behaviours, styles and approaches to learning will become more evident and you need to be aware of this. Another key point is that part of your role is to enable the learner to know themselves, but not all learners will have enough insight, self-awareness or life experience to do this effectively. For example, a second-year qualifying student may be used to a school or university style of learning environment and know how to learn only from lectures and seminars. It is important to allow time throughout the learning experience, for example as a planned supervision item, for reflection and to encourage learners to have a greater awareness of their own limitations and their particular barriers and motivations for learning via activities and/or discussion. The issue of diagnosed, or indeed undiagnosed, additional learning needs may also become apparent. If already diagnosed then the student's university should be able to help with support. In the latter situation it might be appropriate to mention to the student any patterns that you have noticed within their written work and to see if they thought a learning needs assessment at their university would be worthwhile. By adopting a critical, open and flexible attitude, items such as learning contracts and planned learning schemes can be revisited to take account of emerging needs or changes where necessary.

Having seen the importance of not only understanding and developing the learner but also yourself, as well as the necessary ongoing nature of this task, we can look more closely at the areas you will need to consider.

What do you need to know about learners?

Some of the key factors that can affect a learning experience are:

- motivation;
- anxiety;
- views of knowledge and learning;
- approaches to learning;
- learning styles;
- awareness of competency.

We will look at each of these in turn to see how to develop a more complete understanding of people as learners.

How motivated is the learner?

Motivation is the compulsion that keeps a person within the learning situation and encourages them to learn (Rogers, 2002). Adult learners are assumed to be 'internally' motivated by factors such as one's own hopes, desires and needs (Knowles, 1990). However, work-based learners will also be externally motivated to some extent by factors such as incentives, rewards and professional requirements. Internal factors have been argued to be the stronger and more enduring force, but external ones can become internalised (e.g. ambitions for promotion leading to personal development), and it is perhaps inappropriate to distinguish the two as entirely separate. For instance, we know of practitioners who express personal fulfilment from undertaking post-qualifying programmes.

Pink's (2010) work on people-centred motivation, suggests three key motivators:

- *Mastery* – the desire to get better and better at something that matters.
- *Autonomy* – the urge to direct our own lives.
- *Purpose* – the yearning to do what we are doing in the service of something larger than ourselves.

These can be linked to an adult learning approach. As adults are usually more motivated to learn about things that interest them or have relevance to what they want to do (Knowles, 1990), motivating elements can be enhanced by making the learning environment as relevant and as useful as possible for the individual. Key factors appear to be how immediate, attainable and relevant the learning goals are. By taking a learner perspective and working in partnership with your learner, you will be discussing and agreeing upon a learning scheme together, producing goals that are meaningful and which can become the learner's 'own', i.e. internalised.

Working with more than one learner, for example when leading a multidisciplinary team workshop, can obviously make this more difficult to achieve, but any group of learners will probably have been brought together for a reason or with a particular aim. If you leave enough time in a group session to find out about individual motivations and make sure they are addressed in some way, it will reflect a more learner-centred approach.

The 'feel good' factor associated with motivation should be continually reinforced but it is also important to be aware of the demotivating factors in any learning situation, some of which may be beyond our control, such as lack of time for studying, unsupportive colleagues, unhelpful administrative procedures. Those that are under our control, however, need to be kept under constant review.

ACTIVITY **5.1**

List the factors which are likely to motivate or demotivate learners during their learning.

Comment

The range of factors should relate to the variables associated with a learning environment (Knowles, 1990): physical (e.g. desk space or other resources), cultural (e.g. team dynamics), psychological (e.g. learner's anxieties) and social (e.g. the relationship between you and the learner).

How anxious is your learner?

Anxiety is a key factor in learning. There are a number of reasons why learners may feel anxious.

- They are in a situation in which they are not competent.

- They are aware of their 'not knowing'.

- Becoming reflective practitioners means taking extra responsibility for what and how they learn rather than relying on knowledge from an expert.

- Their past and present personal and educational experiences may have a negative impact, making them feel fearful, vulnerable or intimidated in a practice learning environment.

- Social work itself is anxiety-provoking.

- There is the pressure to 'pass'.

Adapted from Horwath (1999)

A person may be confident and self-directing in their university, personal or work life but feel much less confident in a new learning situation. The point is that most people, when out of their comfort zone, will feel anxious and this can impair their ability to learn effectively. Anxiety for novice workers tends to make them over-reliant on procedures and rules to avoid making mistakes. Anxiety for more experienced workers is apparent when they enter new posts or when their organisation undergoes significant change and they are expected to let go of established ideas and methods. In this type of situation people who are used to being confident and competent in their work suddenly find themselves unsure and less knowledgeable and, as a result, they may become destabilised and disoriented learners (Horwath, 1999).

The loss of competence and morale therefore combine to make any learning difficult. If someone in a learning situation is feeling unsure and/or unsafe, they may:

- become defensive or angry;

- become 'needy';

- withdraw;

- start to demand the 'right' answers;

- try too hard to please.

The key issue is that a person in any of these modes of behaviour will not want to, or be able to, learn effectively, and so it is your responsibility to ensure not only that anxiety-making factors are lessened, but that any signs of anxiety like these are noted early on and the root cause uncovered.

Those with high workloads and course work to contend with will no doubt feel under stress and anxiety will be a natural feature of this. Resilience is dealt with later in Chapter 12 but it is important to recognise how stress and anxiety may feed into underlying conflicts and unmet needs of the learner. This situation can then effectively 'disable' a learner's ability to feel in control and to influence outcomes, to see new things as opportunities to learn, and to become involved in their environment and their learning. These are key 'resilience markers' or attitudes identified by Maddi and Khoshara (2005).

How does your learner view knowledge and learning?

One important underpinning factor associated with a person's view of learning is their view of knowledge (i.e. the material being learnt: ideas, theories, methods, etc.). People have different ways of viewing knowledge, ranging from believing that things are either right or wrong to building up valid knowledge for a particular situation but remaining open to other views (Hofer, 2002). For example, we may know people who believe that their choice in music is the right one and who scorn alternative views; whereas other people who like one particular style of music also expect others to have different tastes and actively listen to alternative styles of music to widen their appreciation.

RESEARCH SUMMARY 5.1

Baxter Magolda (1996) undertook a study of American students, interviewing them about their beliefs and ideas about knowledge and knowing throughout their college and early career years. She noted how their ideas developed over time and developed this range of beliefs into four stages of 'knowing'.

1. *Absolute*

   People at this stage think there are 'right' answers out there to be found, and knowledge is seen as certain or absolute. They become especially anxious with uncertainty and will be looking for anything that can be applied to solve it.

2. *Transitional*

   People at this stage have doubts over the certainty of knowledge. They can see that there are many answers but they still rely on others to tell them which is the right one for a situation.

3. *Independent*

   People at this stage have begun to have an opinion of their own and think through issues and express themselves, but there is little judgement of knowledge, opinions and beliefs so all views (informed and uninformed, relevant and irrelevant) may be considered equal and unchallengeable.

4. *Contextual*

   At this stage a person's knowledge is constructed for particular situations, considering the relevant conditions and using appropriate evidence. Their understanding is therefore based on evidenced propositions or reasons for that context but can still be challenged as the person remains open to other ideas and the changing context.

The last stage, looking at knowledge contextually, critically constructing valid meaning for oneself and being able to develop a confident 'knowing' for different situations, aligns well with the critical, questioning and open stance needed for professional capability. This is the level to which we aspire and to which we are enabling others to develop. Therefore understanding how learners view knowledge is an important factor for enabling learning in a work-based environment. A learner may be viewing knowledge in an absolute way because they are young and inexperienced, or because this is the way they were taught and have continued to think, or because they have become anxious. As seen earlier, being in a new or uncertain situation can affect a person's usual capabilities. Many learners are confident practitioners who usually hold a contextual view of knowledge, but anxiety makes them default to thinking that they need the one 'right' answer and the 'teacher' can give this to them.

How could understanding more about the stages of 'knowing' help you as an enabler of learning to work more effectively with your learners?

Can you suggest any ways that you could work with learners which would be more likely to help them to make the transition to a more advanced stage of knowing – for example, how would you enable a learner to move from absolute to transitional thinking?

Comment

Such understanding allows you to more fully appreciate the learner's perspective and the particular barriers that may be preventing development. You may have thought about some specifically designed activities which allow a learner to see a number of alternative but equally valid approaches to practice. Creating a safe environment that encourages and allows a range of answers and approaches to tasks will also be important.

As we have seen, if learners are at an absolute stage and believe that there is only one right way of doing something (e.g. interviewing a service user), they will be desperate for an expert to show them this one way. If an educator does this there is a particular danger that the learner will not learn to think practice problems through for themselves or try different methods. They may continue to practise with the one way that was shown to them and become entrenched in it. They may always be uneasy with new situations and feel anxious in them, and either become unaware of problems or look to others for solutions to them. They will find it difficult to develop their practice in the future as they will not have understood the fundamental issue about practice knowledge – that it is 'constructed' and 'reconstructed' in an ongoing, critical and developmental way, not 'given' as a complete, ongoing 'truth' from someone else.

Of course, many learners will need direction and support to scaffold their learning in order to achieve this more sophisticated level of thinking and we will explore how best to do this in Chapter 8. The point is that if you provide people with just answers, they may well come to believe that answers are 'out there', and rely on someone else for them. This is what 'learning' then becomes for them – someone telling them something, rather than them working a problem through for themselves with the help of others.

REFLECTION POINT

There is another side to this coin. Think about how you view and talk about types of knowledge (either practical or theoretical). If you discuss practice knowledge as 'right/wrong' ways to do things, it could give a learner the idea that your way is the only way to do it. If you discuss only one theory or model of practice (e.g. a task-centred approach), a learner may think this is the only one they need to consider. Think about the ways you could model a more contextual way of viewing knowledge, and help your learner move towards adopting this view as well and appreciating the complexity of social work practice and theory.

It is therefore important to understand these influencing factors concerning the way people view knowledge and to be very aware of how learners might exhibit them through their behaviour, for example the type of questions they are asking or the way they discuss a point with you. To help understand this further and see how we might consider a learner's language and behaviour in this way, we can use Säljö's's (1979) work, which classified learning into five levels or categories.

1. Learning as an increase in knowledge, acquiring information.

2. Learning as memorising or storing information that can be reproduced.

3. Learning as acquiring facts, skills and methods that can be retained and used as necessary.

4. Learning as making sense or abstracting meaning. Learning involves relating parts of the subject matter to each other and to the real world.

5. Learning as interpreting and understanding reality in a different way. Learning involves comprehending the world by reinterpreting knowledge.

By listening to learners as they talk about the knowledge, skills or values they are learning, it is possible to become aware of the level at which they are viewing them. For instance, I could say that I can still recall my times tables from rote learning them, or I may say that I did geography at school by acquiring the facts about different countries, or I revised for exams by noting down all the key details about a topic, memorising them and reproducing them. The language I am using in the previous sentence is very different from the language I use to describe my learning now. For instance, I would say I am applying and interpreting a range of ideas and values on the job and understanding and evaluating how well they achieve my objectives. Each type of language is associated with very different ways of viewing knowledge and with different levels of learning.

Each of Säljö's (1979) levels will be suitable in different circumstances but, as we can see, levels 4–5 are the more appropriate for developing critical practice and align with a contextual view of knowing and knowledge.

Which approach does your learner take to learning?

Looking at how learners not only view their learning and the knowledge they are dealing with but also at how they approach learning tasks and activities allows us to understand why the same task can be undertaken differently by different learners. Approaches to learning link closely with the levels of learning seen above; they are not personal attrib-utes and it is important to realise that learners are able to adopt or choose any approach. There are two main approaches taken (Marton and Säljö, 1976): surface and deep.

- The surface approach focuses on the acquisition and memorising of information, and on facts and concepts in isolation. Learners cannot distinguish more general principles from examples, and they tend to be unreflective. Learning is largely driven by external motivators such as assessment or employer demands. In social work, these principles align with a limited view of the way people might learn professional competences for assessment purposes, i.e. the tick-box notion. As you will have realised, this matches Säljö's's (1979) levels of learning 1–3 above.

- The deep approach matches Säljö's's (1979) levels 4–5, i.e. meaning, understanding and application of knowledge; relates previous knowledge; connects to other knowledge; relates and distinguishes evidence and argument; and can relate practice to theory. Learners tend to be self-motivated and reflective. In social work these principles align with a more developed notion of learning professional competencies where a more cohesive and integrated view allows for professional capability to be developed as well.

Entwistle and Ramsden's (1983) work on students' approaches to studying found a third (strategic) approach.

- The strategic approach – the motivation here is to get the best marks or rewards. The exercise of learning is construed as a game so that acquisition of technique improves performance and involves adopting well-organised and efficient study methods. The learner focuses on assessment criteria and the teacher's preferences. Here we see where a learner might 'get away' with a tick-box approach if the assessment methods take account of only the more mechanistic processes, rather than allowing for the transferable skills necessary for capability as well. However, if the learner perceives that the teacher and/or assessment criteria require something more deep and critical, then learning can be driven in this direction.

As a deep approach is more able to take account of uncertain and complex situations, learning and assessment opportunities should be designed explicitly to align with this approach (Biggs, 2003). These ideas will be developed further in the following chapters within this part of the book. However, the approach learners choose or adopt will be related to their perception of learning, perception of the task, motivation and previous experience.

Individual learners will view learning activities differently and will approach them in different ways. For example, you may have arranged for two qualifying students to shadow you in order to appreciate the complexity of a case review meeting and discuss it afterwards. One student may just watch the proceedings, the other may think about what is happening as they watch and therefore be much better prepared for the discussion. It is what the learner does that counts in the end (Biggs, 2003). The point is that you need to be explicit about what you are expecting from learners but also understand the ways they are interpreting this, rather than make assumptions; otherwise their approach may not be what you intended. To enable a deep approach to be adopted whenever possible, you will need to understand what is happening from the learner's perspective, be able to work from this starting point and help the learner develop where necessary.

ACTIVITY 5.3

What would encourage you to learn in a deep or surface way?

What state of mind would a learner need to be in to adopt a deep learning approach?

Comment

Deep learning can be encouraged by the right style of learning and assessment opportunities, i.e. the ones which align more with Säljö's higher levels of learning. Of course, it can also be dependent on having the necessary respect, safety and space to engage in critical thinking and open discussion. In contrast, learning environments in which an educator only tells the learner about things and imposes their own thoughts and ideas will encourage surface learning. With regard to a learner's state of mind, the bottom line is that the learner is responsible for their own learning. Having a firm partnership based on mutual respect, being motivated and feeling safe are therefore key underpinning factors which may allow a learner to not only appreciate the level of learning required, but want to engage in it.

Which is the learner's preferred learning style?

Most learners will also have preferences for learning in a certain way, i.e. using certain methods or strategies. This learning style will be the way they learn most naturally as individuals, either through habit or preference. There are many different styles. Honey and Mumford's (1982) model, based on Kolb's (1984) experiential learning model, identifies four main learning styles.

- Activist

  - Enthusiastic for new experiences and may rush into them.

  - Can get hooked on what is happening in front of them.

  - May get bored by having to stop and consolidate ideas.

  - Can centre everything on themselves – even group discussion.

- Reflector

  - Observes and evaluates experiences from several different perspectives.

  - Collects data and considers evidence before deciding on action.

  - May be overly cautious and distant.

  - Likes to fully understand a discussion before making their point.

  - May seem distant but tolerant.

- Pragmatist
    - Enjoys experimentation and practical application of ideas and theories.
    - Can get frustrated by open-ended discussion.
    - Prefers active problem-solving.
    - Sees opportunities as a challenge.
    - May also rush into action.
    - Tends to look for better or more practical ways of doing things.
- Theorist
    - Will usually think problems through logically and systematically.
    - Can be a perfectionist.
    - Likes to analyse.
    - May not be able to think laterally.
    - Can prefer certainty to subjective judgement.
    - May be detached and analytical.

This is one of the best recognised models, but there are other types of learning style that have been identified, such as those associated with the notion of 'multiple intelligences' (Gardner, 1993), i.e. intelligence involving auditory, visual and kinaesthetic (body movement) skills and abilities. There is, however, considerable debate surrounding the reliability of learning styles and their use (Smith, 2001; Coffield et al., 2004), but they may still have a place in helping both learners and educators understand more about their methods and preferences.

It is important to realise that no one learning style is better than any other; all have strengths and weaknesses. Some people have a strong preference for one particular style while others are more balanced. Knowing a learner's preferred style can be useful because it can indicate how a learner may learn most effectively. A good match between the style of a learning activity and a learner's preferred style should maximise learning potential, but if there is a mismatch between the two, learning may be hindered.

However, learners need help to learn different skills and abilities (and therefore learning styles) in order to achieve certain outcomes. The question of whether you match a learner's preferred style with a learning activity or alternatively design the activity to stretch the learner to become more versatile would need to be judged for each individual and situation. For example, if a qualifying student, Nadir, is more naturally 'activist' but you require him to reflect critically on case notes and apply and justify social work methods and models with you in supervision before he acts, he may need extra support to see the importance of this and to find a process of reflection and application that works for him. It may be relatively easy to think of single active or more reflective activities for a student to engage in, but to try to make an active task more reflective and a reflective task more active may be more challenging.

Another issue is that we all tend to teach as well as learn in our preferred style and this may not be appropriate for an individual learner or all learners within a group. Your preferences for learning in a certain way will affect your assumptions about others too. For example, you might assume that Nadir would want to think and reflect on case notes first before meeting a service user, but as he has a preferred activist style it may seem like wasting time to him. As noted earlier, if you are enabling the learning of another you should have reflected on and explored your previous learning experiences in order to be fully aware of your beliefs and values concerning learning and teaching, and this should include knowledge of your preferred learning style. This point also reinforces the need to continually work towards understanding learners and their perspective, work in partnership with them and allow their input into the learning experience.

CASE STUDY 5.1

Tom met the newly-qualified social worker he was mentoring, Yasmin. She was a mature, confident practitioner, having been a care worker with children before qualifying; she was also dyslexic. Tom gave consideration to Yasmin's learning style and they looked at how Yasmin learnt in practice. Yasmin told Tom she learnt best from observing, doing and then reflecting on what had happened. Therefore, in order to promote Yasmin's learning, Tom decided she would observe him in practice preparing and carrying out a reassessment with a service user who was recovering from a stroke, as this was a piece of work Yasmin was to carry out. Afterwards, they used a supervision session to reflect on the intervention that had occurred, what had gone well or not and what had been learnt. In this discussion Tom could see that although Yasmin was an effective practitioner she was not asking the right level of questions which would have shown a more developed understanding of the service user's condition and needs. A lack of specialist knowledge was preventing her from appreciating the service user's capabilities.

Tom knew Yasmin would also need to undertake some independent reading/study into the subject of strokes to give her a wider breadth of understanding. However, Yasmin said she found textbooks and journals difficult to read. Tom encouraged her to gain the necessary knowledge in ways she found more appropriate. She contacted the hospital social work team to see if she could shadow a ward round/meeting on the stroke ward to gain a greater understanding of the effects of strokes. She also contacted the Stroke Association for literature and information and also looked at the internal training manual for relevant courses.

By allowing Yasmin the flexibility and freedom to self-direct her learning at this point, Tom ensured that the most effective learning took place.

Is the learner conscious of their competency or incompetency?

The 'conscious competence model' (unattributed, cited in Atherton, 2009b, and Chapman, c. 2009) shows four stages associated with learning new skills. The stage at which a learner may be within this model may be another factor that affects their learning ability.

Stage 1: Unconscious incompetence

This is the 'ignorance is bliss' state where we do not know what we do not know. Making learners aware of their ignorance will probably create anxiety, but it is an important stage in developing motivation. For example, you may have been unaware of the 'stages of knowing' or 'stages of learning' theories looked at earlier in this chapter but hopefully this hasn't made you feel too anxious as they are being introduced to help you to understand the issues at hand, not to make you feel inadequate. However, if your learner has a vested interest in not doing certain things or in doing things only in their established way, this will also involve another stage of 'unlearning', which will need to be fully supported in partnership.

Stage 2: Conscious incompetence

We are aware of what we don't know. This should engender greater motivation towards finding out more, but only if what needs to be learnt is seen as relevant and useful. We also hope that you will be motivated to find out more about the stages of knowing and other theories in this book and to start applying them as you can see their significance and usefulness for yourselves.

Stage 3: Conscious competence

We are aware of what we do know. In many circumstances after learning has taken place this stage may be perfectly adequate, at least for a time. For some skills, especially advanced ones, we can regress to previous stages if we fail to practise and exercise them. How many of us have learnt to do something on a computer and then completely forgotten how to do it a couple of weeks later if we did not have the chance to redo it?

Stage 4: Unconscious competence

We can use our knowledge without thinking about it. For example, this easily applies to basic skills such as driving or swimming, i.e. the kind of thing we can do without thinking. However, this can also refer to a situation where we know something but do not know how we know it and probably cannot express it (e.g. our more intuitive understandings and hunches). If we are asked about a good piece of practice our answer will fail to do justice to the complexity of what we have done. By encouraging at least some articulation of it, an educator will enable learners to claim credit for what they know and can do, making it meaningful and relevant.

Remember, practice educators commonly assume learners are at stage 2 and aware of the existence, nature and benefit of any new skill (just like they are), and therefore aim towards achieving stage 3. In fact learners may be only at stage 1 and have none of this awareness. The challenge for you is to make them aware in a learner-centred and supportive way. They may think they know all they need to know and, of course, this means you will also need to address their motivation too. Not doing this can be an underlying reason for the lack of success of a lot of training and teaching, especially for more mature or experienced practitioners.

REFLECTION POINT

Again, there is another side to the coin here. If you are at stage 4 in certain areas of your own practice, how can you teach the things you are unconsciously competent at? For example, imagine you are helping a student to develop their practice and you instinctively know how best to encourage an abused child or adult to talk to you. Would you be able to explain to the student the subtle signs you are looking for as well as the techniques you use? Do you ever review these more tacit parts of your practice?

Some authors have suggested the addition of a fifth stage. Baume (2004) says this is a stage of 'reflective competence' where he is:

> ... additionally looking at my unconscious competence from the outside, digging to find and understand the theories and models and beliefs that clearly, based on looking at what I do, now inform what I do and how I do it. These won't be the exact same theories and models and beliefs that I learned consciously and then became unconscious of. They'll include new ones, the ones that comprise my particular expertise. And when I've surfaced them, I can talk about them and test them.

At this fifth level, practitioners are consciously aware of some of the unconscious or subconscious abilities they are using, and are able to analyse, adapt and enhance their activity. They understand why they are doing something and make mindful but subtle changes in light of this understanding. This, of course, aligns very neatly with critical thinking, capability and critical practice. There is an interesting debate and some clever applications of this feature on the **www.businessballs.com** website.

ACTIVITY **5.4**

Make a 'mind map' or 'spidergram' to note down and connect your understanding of the ideas presented to you so far, for example views of knowledge and learning, approaches to learning and conscious competency. (Search for 'mind maps' on the internet, e.g. using Google, if you are unsure of how to do them.)

Comment

The common features associated with higher levels of knowing and learning, deep learning and reflective competence appear to all relate to our notions of active, independent, reflective and critical thinking.

Chapter 6
Developing learning objectives

Obviously, understanding learners, their views about learning and knowledge, their approaches to learning and their learning styles, etc., are underpinning factors to enabling learning. However, if we don't, as well, have a thorough understanding of what learners will be able to do as a result of their learning, and can explicitly state this, then we cannot effectively plan to help them achieve it or know when they have. This is our next stage in enabling learning. Before we can begin to design an appropriate learning opportunity we need to find out (in partnership with the learner) what the learner already knows or can do (to build on strengths) and what they still need to learn or develop (linked to the PCF/ Knowledge and Skills Frameworks as appropriate).

The 'constructive alignment' approach (Biggs, 2003) allows the design of a learning scheme to begin with the question *What do we want the learner to be able to do as a result of learning?*, and aligns all learning, teaching and assessment strategies to these outcomes in order to optimise the conditions for learning. Such outcomes or learning objectives will at some point be discussed with your learner and this will be where the learner's own goals will be taken into account properly. Again, a critically reflective and flexible approach can be taken to these objectives to ensure you can review and change them where necessary as the learning experience progresses.

General principles

Learning objectives should include:

- content;
- level;
- clear terms;
- support and review points.

Specify the content

It is important to identify the overall content of the learning scheme early on. This may be set to a large extent by other bodies, for example the Professional Capabilities Framework (CSW, 2012a). In other circumstances the needs of the team or the organisation may dictate the topic area of a team development session; for example, the specific requirements of a new piece of legislation or policy. By mapping out the areas to be covered it is easier to prioritise, focus and then plan the learning scheme(s). There may indeed be a long list of professional competencies, outcomes or standards to be aware of and 'cover' for learners undertaking a degree in social work or for newly-qualified workers, and therefore you may need to collate and prioritise the most relevant areas first.

Once this is done, analysis of the particular area of practice can be undertaken with the three domains of knowing, acting and being, or 'head, hand and heart', so that a holistic view of that area of practice is established at the outset.

- The learner should know about ... knowledge (the theory, research, policy, legislation associated with the area of practice).

- The learner should know how to ... skills (the related, specific procedures, processes, practice abilities, e.g. clear communication).

- The learner should be aware of ... values (anti-discriminatory practice, ethics, etc.).

Setting out these areas early on in the process can ensure the development of practice capability as well as competence right from the start and ensure that important but less measurable aspects such as values are not just added on later.

CASE STUDY 6.1

Aida worked in a community drop-in centre and was allowing Laura to shadow her as a first-year placement. Aida wanted Laura to see ways to approach and talk to the people using the centre. Later on, after a discussion, Aida was hoping Laura would be able to introduce herself and start to chat to them by herself. Aida's initial attempt at writing a learning objective began with a general statement: 'You will be able to communicate well with people using the centre.' She soon realised that it was ineffective as it did not tell Laura anything about what she needed to do: for example, the type of behaviour, words, or actions that would be acceptable. The objective needed to be broken down further and related to this situation.

This was not an easy exercise to do. Communication covered such a wide range of skills and abilities, for example open questioning, eye contact, appropriate contact. How could she put all this in one objective? Aida realised it required a sharp focus on one particular aspect. She decided to use their discussion after the shadowing experience to hear what Laura thought 'good communication' was and the areas she felt less comfortable with, and to concentrate on developing this as a learning objective. One of the things Laura highlighted was the need for firm but sensitive refusal when service users made inappropriate requests, but felt she might be too unassertive to do this. So Aida decided to develop a learning objective with Laura that included understanding more about the nature of assertiveness, its relationship to social work values and being able to apply this knowledge using appropriate verbal and body-language skills at the centre when necessary. By doing this Aida was able to develop a holistic and meaningful learning objective in partnership with Laura.

Indicate the level of learning

The overall features of any learning can usually be categorised according to a hierarchy like the one seen earlier (Säljö, 1979). For example, the level of learning required to understand a particular section from the direct payments scheme is lower than that required to be able to use and critically apply parts of the scheme to deal with the needs of a vulnerable service user. Here we can now use Bloom's (1956) hierarchy to show that learning involves different cognitive (thinking) processes, from simple to more mechanistic levels of remembering to then being able to break knowledge apart, put it together and subsequently to judge or measure it:

- Recognition and recall – memorise, identify, recognise.
- Comprehension – understand.
- Analysis – break down into parts.
- Synthesis – putting together with other knowledge to form new concepts.
- Evaluation – assess the value of the new knowledge in respect of needs and aim.

The model above is still accepted, but the revised version below adds the important new category of creating knowledge (an extremely relevant addition when we think about professional capability) and moves from using nouns to more active verbs (Anderson and Krathwohl, 2001). These verbs are:

- remembering;
- understanding;
- analysing;
- applying;
- evaluating;
- creating.

It is suggested that the 'higher' levels of learning cannot be addressed effectively until the 'lower' ones have been achieved. For example, if you want learners to use and critically apply direct payments guidance to a particular service user who is disabled, they will first need to have read and understood it. This will need to be built into the learning scheme in ways appropriate to their situation and particular needs. There are also implications here for the way learners perceive learning. As we have seen, a deep learning approach and a contextual way of knowing are both associated with higher cognitive levels: understanding, evaluating and applying knowledge, and constructing individual meaning. However, without first developing underpinning awareness and understanding, or having the ability to analyse, critique and synthesise ideas, your expectations for a deeper approach may not be able to be achieved by the learner.

The best way to approach this issue is by designing the 'lower' levels or more basic stages of learning as part of an overall deeper approach. Reading and understanding can be presented as necessary starting points but in order to align with a deep rather than a surface approach you can ensure they are 'taught' in constructive, critical and active ways. This is an important point that has implications for the way you write the learning objectives, structure the learning tasks, use a learner's prior experience and support learning.

Ensure clarity of terms

Learning objectives need to state what learners will be able to do as a result of their learning and you can use the language of Bloom's (1956) hierarchy to express this. Using the direct payments example mentioned above, the objective might be: 'To apply the direct payments guidance to a particular case'.

As you will be requiring learners to demonstrate their understanding of these outcomes, the criteria used should also be clear, that is identifying key aspects to show how well you want this to be done. This will also enhance the motivational aspects as detailed above; goals or outcomes need to be explicit, achievable and relevant. Learners therefore need to know what the behaviour or skill 'looks' like in practice so they can compare what they are doing with what is required, identify any gaps and engage in appropriate action to close them. In this way, learners become more empowered and enabled to take control of their learning and work towards greater self-direction.

Also, by knowing how well a learning outcome needs to be achieved, the educator and the learner will be able to tell more accurately if and when the learner is achieving it and have a tool by which to identify any problem areas more directly. This has the benefit of taking the onus off the learner as a 'person' and placing it onto the 'task' instead, making feedback less personal and more useful, an important point we will return to later. This also impacts on other aspects of the learning process, such as assessment and facilitation, as outcomes provide the criteria to judge levels of achievement and to see where learners are going wrong. Learners have a fundamental need to know exactly what they are aiming for in order to know how well they are doing and how to do it better.

In the direct payments example, the level of analysis and type of evaluation required could be stated as follows.

- Read and analyse the guidance.

- Identify the aspects that are relevant to the case notes for Mrs X.

- Generate a number of options for action that can help Mrs X.

- Evaluate each in respect of social work values.

Include support and review points

Having explicit learning objectives and criteria, being aware of the level of learning expected, and also the knowledge, skills and values involved within the objective allows you to develop a more detailed structure for learning. This, in turn, allows for fuller understanding of the learning process and for an explicit learning scheme to be developed. The support associated with each stage within the scheme can also be identified and is, of course, judged in respect of the learner's level, particular needs, etc., and their previous experience.

As we have seen, previous knowledge and experience are key components of adult learning and need to be taken account of when planning a learning scheme. This allows for key skills and requirements to be built in as necessary and ensures the scheme is aligned to, and is useful for a learner's needs. For example, in the scheme above the discussion of options for action in stage 4 could highlight similar examples the learner has dealt with in the past.

However, there are a number of dangers to be aware of. First, although prior experience (whether learning, knowing, or doing things) can be of enormous value as a building block or starting point for any learning programme, it can also act as a barrier. A learner will feel safer with material they already know and may be reluctant to question it even though it is incorrect or inappropriate for the new situation. Second, we may mistakenly expect or assume that learners already possess the necessary knowledge, skill or values to learn in a particular environment. If learners are not achieving a learning objective, the problem may lie with an aspect of their previous experience, or the lack of it. There are a number of scenarios.

- They don't have the appropriate knowledge.

  - They may be unable to proceed with a piece of work because of a lack of information to tackle the problem. In our example the case notes may simply not be accessible.

- They don't have the skills to work with knowledge at the appropriate level.

  - They will not be able to deal with the complexity of linking theories to practice if they cannot analyse the situation in order to find some general principles. In our example the learner may not know how to analyse the written information in the documents.

- They don't have the background, the practical skills or understanding of the appropriate value base to undertake the task.

  - They may understand the theory behind interpersonal communication but have no practical experience of actually talking to a service user or may not have seen it from a service user's perspective. In our example the learner may not understand the personal experience behind the case notes and the implications that has for the range of options that might be suitable.

The stages in our example can be more fully articulated to show the appropriate type of support and the review points.

- Supply the learner with the national and local direct payments guidance and direct her to the Directgov website.

- Ensure the learner knows how to access the service user's case notes as she uses the same software. However, ensure passwords work.

- Let the learner practise analysing the guidance with more basic examples first.

- Review point – the parts most relevant to Mrs X's situation need to be identified. Discuss Mrs X's situation in supervision first to ensure it has been understood on a more personal level before the next stage.

- Tell the learner she can generate at least three ideas to help Mrs X using lists or mind maps. Tell her she will be expected to explain and critically reflect on them by herself before they are discussed together in supervision.

- Final review – in supervision let the learner explain and reflect on each option without interruption before discussing them together.

Chapter 7
Considering learning theories

We can now consider theories about how learning occurs and look briefly at the ways they can inform practice. Even though human beings are always learning and developing in some way, the activities and processes involved are complicated and are still not fully understood. Consequently, there are a number of theories about how learning occurs; they are all valuable, but there is no one overarching theory. Therefore, when designing ways learners may be enabled to achieve their objectives, it is important to recognise the limitations of using learning theories and to think more critically about their use and application in practice.

Because none of the learning theories fully explains learning, they will all be deficient for your needs in one way or another and should not be used exclusively or uncritically. The point is that any concept or model will rarely fit a specific process completely, especially one as unclear as learning. However, critically thinking through any aspects of a theory with the needs and requirements of the learner, and with ideas for particular methods, is useful in itself. It will help you notice any mismatched areas, and your own learning becomes a little deeper as you check your understanding. Presented below is a small selection of learning theories that appear to align with our notion of practice-based learning and a few ideas for their use in practice. Further ideas and theories for consideration may be found in Merriam and Bierema (2014), Beverley and Worsley (2007) and Walker et al. (2008). A range of learning opportunities is considered in Chapter 8.

Constructivist learning

Views associated with deep learning and contextual knowing particularly align with constructivist learning theories (e.g. Bruner, 1960), which state that there are only individual perceptions of reality, meanings and knowledge rather than external, objective realities. Learning is therefore an individual's active construction of new perceptions, an act of self. If you base learning activities on this theory you would be stimulating and assisting the development of the learner's construction of their own awareness and insight.

Ideas for practice

- Let learners unpick and try to resolve case studies by questioning, thinking and testing out their own ideas.

- Encourage acts of active self-search and discovery rather than input or transfer your ideas to learners.

Humanistic learning

The idea of being learner-centred follows very humanistic principles (e.g. Rogers, 1980) and places learners and their desire to fulfil their potential at the heart of the learning process. Aspects such as involving learners in as much planning and design of their learning as possible align with humanistic principles. Your role here is to increase the range of experiences so the learner can use them to achieve their own desired changes.

Ideas for practice

- Let learners set their own personal goals alongside their professional ones.

- Allow learners to use but also extend their existing abilities by designing tasks which challenge them in some way.

- Allow learners to develop their own learning contract.

Social and situated learning

The idea of 'learning on the job' through a type of apprenticeship aligns well with social (e.g. Bandura, 1977) and situated learning theories (e.g. Lave and Wenger, 1991). Social learning theories explain that within any social context people can learn from one another, from observation, imitation and modelling. Situated learning theory argues that learning is usually unintentional rather than deliberate and is embedded within activity, context and culture. Learners become involved in a 'community of practice' which embodies certain beliefs and behaviours to be acquired (Lave and Wenger, 1991). If work-based learners are learning the language, attitudes, values and practices of the workplace (not just knowledge and skills) via contact with you and other practitioners, then this may need monitoring. Your position will automatically be that of a mentor or role model to many learners, providing inspiration and models of good practice, but there may also be another part to play in ensuring that a student or novice worker is not picking up inappropriate attitudes or practices from colleagues.

Ideas for practice

- Ensure learners can observe and follow practitioners as they undertake their tasks.

- Monitor the beliefs and attitudes, as well as the practices, a learner is acquiring.

- Encourage learners to take part in all team activity and meetings.

- Develop your coaching and mentoring skills.

Experiential learning

Experiential learning provides a general acceptance that experience and observations form the basis of learning. It can, however, mean different things to different people.

- Learning from current experience – the experience creates a need for further learning.

- Using past experience for learning – challenging the present.

- Learning by doing – actively engaging in the learning context.

Here, we focus more on 'learning by doing' so that encouraging experiential learning means guiding and facilitating the learner through various elements of the experience, ensuring they become part of the overall learning scheme. As we shall see, most experiential learning models contain a reflective element. The aim of reflection is to draw out the 'learning' from these experiential processes by analysing, identifying and linking the significant incidents to ideas and theories that shed light on them (Beatty 2003, cited in Parker, 2004, p47), and to inform future action.

Ideas for practice

- Develop simulations or games for learners.

- Let learners become involved in and reflect on 'live' cases.

- Develop problem-based learning activities.

- Act out and reflect on role play scenarios with learners.

Experiential models

Kolb (1984) developed an explicit model around the key characteristics of learning from experience, based on the work of Dewey, Lewin and Piaget, known as the experiential learning model.

In his model, the process of experiential learning is described as a staged, cyclical process involving the four learning modes. The process of learning may be entered at any stage and it perpetuates itself. Concrete experience is followed by reflection on that experience, then by the identification of general ideas or theories describing the experience, then by the planning of the next experience, leading in turn to the next concrete experience. The key point is that all four stages of the cycle should be apparent within a learning scheme in order for it to be an effective process where knowledge is created through the transformation of experience. As the learner needs to move from being an active participant to an observer, to an analyst and then to an experimenter in order for deeper learning to take place, you would plan for each stage to be a specific part of the learning experience. You would also enable the learner to undertake various processes within each of the stages to maximise the learning. These include designing the learning experience in the first place, encouraging use of reflective models and questioning techniques for the reflective phase, encouraging theory to practice links for the analytical phase and then promoting the use of action plans for the next phase.

Kolb's (1984) model is criticised for being a rather 'technical', staged approach (Miettinen, 2000; Coffield et al., 2004) and does not take into account the more emotional aspects of learning. Race's (2010) model, although less theoretical, does include these aspects and his elements interact with one another like ripples in a pond rather than progressing through a cycle (Figure 7.1). This creates an integrated, interacting 'whole' that constitutes successful learning and is made up of:

- wanting/needing (motivation);
- doing (trying out, action);
- digesting (making sense);
- feedback (outcomes; reactions).

The ripples of 'wanting' filter out from the centre through the surrounding layers. From the outside, 'feedback' sends ripples back into the model from the various sources that provide it (e.g. instructors, fellow learners, assessment). 'Doing' and 'digesting' intersect with each other and are influenced by 'needing/wanting' and 'feedback'. By working with this model, any learning opportunity you design will be driven by the learner's motivation so that the 'doing', the opportunities for 'digesting' or reflecting and 'feedback' are all positively engaged with. Here, your role may be slightly different than if you were following Kolb's model as you may be considering the design of the learning task from a much more motivational angle.

Figure 7.1   Adapted from Race's (2010) 'ripples' model of learning

---

ACTIVITY 7.1

Think about how you 'learn by doing'. Design a model (e.g. a diagram or picture) that contains the elements you think are most important and shows how they are connected.

Comment

The way you portray the process will be very individual (we have seen everything from pictures of trees to 'snakes and ladders' in our workshops). The most common elements that are used are, of course, 'doing' and 'reflecting' but a range of personal as well as social elements can be included, for example, planning, discussing, team involvement. In order for any experiential learning to be maximised, though, the processes need to be made explicit and reinforced.

> ## CASE STUDY 7.1
>
> *Practice educator Kate wanted Joe, a third-year qualifying student, to critically analyse and evaluate his practice more holistically. Joe was a good practitioner in many ways, but he was adopting a paternalistic attitude to the service users (older adults) which, although caring, was in effect denying them a voice. Kate could see that the compliant responses of a particular service user, Albert, had been more to do with submission than actual agreement with the plans being offered for his future.*
>
> *Kate discussed a number of reflective activities with Joe, who admitted to being a more activist type of learner than a reflector. The idea of keeping a written journal had a completely demotivating effect on him. They tried other reflective activities such as case discussions and critical questioning but they were ineffective. Joe was still unable to become fully aware of the effect his overprotective stance was having.*
>
> *Kate decided to take a different approach and set up a 'game', the object of which was to encourage 'Albert' to speak his mind. Kate wrote down on a set of cards some key enabling phrases but also some of the more disabling phrases Joe had used in practice when discussing Albert's future with him. Joe had to actively role play the part of Albert while Kate, playing the part of his social worker, read out the phrase on each card. Joe, as Albert, had to rank each phrase between 1 and 10 to show how enabled he felt in being able to express a different view from that being offered. Joe soon began to realise that the phrases and language he used were the more disabling ones because he now heard them with different ears.*
>
> *Kate had realised that following an experiential learning cycle with Joe meant starting with an active experience from the service user's perspective rather than from his own. She could then sensitively help him reflect and learn from this.*

Reflective learning

Reflection and reflective learning theories are, of course, very important to practice learning in their own right, as well as being part of an experiential learning process. We consider certain aspects of reflective learning here, but also develop a number of ideas further in the next chapter when we consider how reflective practice can be enabled within a range of broader learning opportunities.

Schön (1983) suggested that learning can emerge from the analysis of practice through the process of reflection in two ways: reflection-in-action (while doing something) and reflection-on-action (after doing something). Even though Schön has been criticised for not describing the process of reflection adequately (Ixer, 1999; Moon, 1999), there is now an increased emphasis on learning through reflection and an acknowledgement that 'becoming a professional' is more than the simple acquisition of knowledge and development of skills. For Boud et al. (1985, p19) reflection is an activity in which people *recapture their experience, think about it, mull it over and evaluate it.* They focus on the key aspects of returning to an experience, attending to or connecting with feelings, evaluating the experience and integrating the new knowledge. It is a process that involves, among other things, the consideration of 'self' and one's own experiences of practice (Doel et al., 2002).

Limitations and issues – a number of questions to consider

- The lack of clarity over what reflection actually is can make it a difficult activity to explain and assess.

  - We may indeed be thinking about what we are doing while we are doing it in practice, and making or reviewing on-the-spot decisions: for example, when undertaking an assessment. This is a very different type of thinking and reviewing from that which we do on an event after it's happened, say in supervision – should they both be called 'reflection'?

  - Are reflective processes and outcomes distinguishable?

- Not all experiences are open to analysis and reflection; we have all had intuitive, perceptive or insightful moments that defy explanation and are difficult to articulate.

  - Is the thinking or deliberating we do in action actually able to be 'recovered' and articulated, or is it too tacit?

  - When we reflect on practice, can we really re-create the situation honestly and our thoughts exactly as they were, or is the reconstruction necessarily something different, and if so, in what ways?

- Emotions influence moral decision-making and so a social worker should be aware of, and be able to reflect, on their own value system and accompanying emotions (Keinemans, 2015). However, the connections are unclear and there is a danger of a 'tick-box' approach to this.

  - How can we examine the value of emotions to the process of moral decision-making in the broadest sense and encourage the development of professional identity?

- Not everyone 'reflects' in the same way.

  - Do you reflect better on paper or in your head, with questions or by considering ideas?

There are many ways people reflect and, indeed, it is a very individual activity, rather like learning. There also seems to be a range of different possible outcomes. We would not like to prescribe any one method over any other, but there are a few principles relating to the nature of reflection to take note of.

Principles of reflection

- Reflection should be active.

  Ensure that the reflective process leads to learning or active output. Atkins and Murphy (1994, cited in Rolfe et al., 2001, p24) point out the need for action in order to fully support reflective practice:

  For reflection to make a real difference to practice, it is important that the outcome includes a commitment to action. This may not necessarily involve acts which can be observed by others, but it is important that the individual makes a commitment of some kind on the basis of that learning. Action is the final stage of the reflective cycle.

- Reflection should be holistic and meaningful.

  One of the most important aspects of learning through reflection identified by Ruch (2000) is the idea that there is no attempt to split personal experiences from professional and educational experiences; it is holistic in nature. In other words, reflective learning acknowledges and values the fact that when adults learn something new, all kinds of information from other parts of their lives help to shape that learning and place it in the context of what is already known. Reflection is therefore likely to play a large part in making personal and deep meaning for a learner, and encourage the integration of learning across all three required areas for professional capability – a learner's knowing, acting and being.

- Reflection should be developmental.

  Reflection can be seen as a developmental process in a number of ways (Knott and Scragg, 2016; Rutter and Brown, 2015).

  - The more explicit methods and outputs of practice usually need to be identified before more implicit aspects such as assumptions and intuition can be unearthed and evaluated for their 'fitness for practice'.

  - Learners may need time to recognise and explore their own particular methods of reflecting.

  - These methods may need to be improved in order to become deeper and more critical.

- Reflection should be critical.

  There is a need for reflection to be inherently critical. This is not about you or the learners criticising their practice, rather it means that reflection is able to examine and analyse practice in order to objectively evaluate strengths and weaknesses. Being critically reflective means being able to measure, assess and appraise all aspects of practice so that the learning can enhance and change practice for the better in more fundamental ways. Essentially, a deeper critical thinking approach to reflection is needed so that enhanced capability as well as competence is achieved, i.e. it is not just skills or knowledge that are 'reviewed', rather a new view of practice is achieved as the assumptions or 'givens' associated with certain methods or practices are also scrutinised.

REFLECTION POINT

Critical reflection is necessary for all professionals because on a day-to-day level there are some dangers associated with the development of practice expertise and with a more sur-face approach to reflection. We can all fall under the very real danger of unquestioningly applying standardised responses in complex situations (Thompson, 2000). These are the purely intuitive or routine methods of practice that help us survive large workloads. Think about your own routines and 'rules of thumb' – are you able to identify and evaluate these habitual practices?

As we can see, an alignment with deep learning and capability means that learning through reflection is a very seductive idea for professional learning and development. However, it is not the only way people learn and may not be suited to more mechanistic skills. As stated earlier, there is no one overarching learning theory.

Enabling critical reflection

Critical reflection can also create doubt, uncertainty and sometimes, like any deep learning, negative reactions. When people are encouraged to reflect on their own learning and practice by others they may experience a very real fear that they will be exposed and demonstrate a lack of knowledge or poor practice through the discussion. This fear can become ever more real in situations where they feel that their practice is under particular scrutiny. Enabling critical reflection is therefore a difficult balance between providing a safe and supported but also appropriately challenging learning situation.

The quality of the relationship between a learner and their practice educator can therefore have a very significant impact on the depth of critical reflection and learning that takes place. Each relationship will be unique and will evolve over time (Beverley and Worsley, 2007), but developing a partnership allows trust and respect to build, which in turn helps alleviate the more negative effects of any power imbalance, past experiences or difference.

There are a number of core elements to be aware of when enabling critical reflection, which we can consider by means of an example, the supervision of Rebecca, a newly-qualified social worker who is displaying elements of oppressive practice towards mental health patients by believing they are all at risk if they return home.

- Be sensitive and non-threatening, and keep the focus off the person and onto relevant issues around the task, knowledge or skills.

  You could ask Rebecca about the process for assessing risk factors associated with a mental health service user returning home in order to show the wide range of aspects that can be considered.

- Ask open but specific questions which encourage a shift in perception.

  You might ask Rebecca how someone with a mental health issue might be thinking about living back in their own home.

- Ask questions which sensitively challenge and test assumptions and preconceptions and check for prejudice.

  Together you could discuss which particular risks are likely to be more prevalent for people who have had a mental health diagnosis and why.

- Use active listening techniques.

  Pay full attention to the speaker, repeat back what they have said in your own words, summarise, check emotions to show that you understand what they have said and their emotions.

  You might begin to notice Rebecca's underlying anxiety around taking responsibility for such decisions.

- Ask for concrete examples to test assumptions and clarify understanding.

  You could ask Rebecca whether she has actually seen a particular type of behaviour she is worried about and whether there is evidence of it for this client group.

- Encourage self-evaluation but keep it strengths-based.

  You would allow Rebecca to voice her real concerns around her own accountability in this issue and her unease regarding service users' safety.

- Avoid being judgemental or offering solutions.

  You would challenge Rebecca's thinking but not tell her she is wrong or devalue her opinions. You would work with Rebecca's ideas and assist her to broaden them to look at possible alternatives and outcomes that acknowledge the safety aspect but which do not oppress service users.

The role of others in reflective learning

Reflective learning usually needs to have other people involved to make it more purposeful and more critical. There are limits to how much people can learn from experience if they are reflecting on their own (Ellstrom, 2006, cited in Boud et al., 2006).

- *Other people can encourage different and more balanced perspectives. Reflecting alone can become self-justifying or self-pitying. Argyris and Schön (1978) talk about the importance of supporting others to confront their own ideas and explore their unconscious assumptions.*

- *Other people can provide emotional support through facilitator or peer input. As reflection will involve personal elements and professional risk, facilitators and peers should not only provide explicit and jointly agreed expectations and have modelled the process, but should also be sensitive to key signs of anxiety and distress.*

- *Other people can ensure the necessary space and time for a learner to undertake such activities. Reflecting on casework can allow the time to slow down and think about different alternatives as well as the potential dangers of 'rushing in' to act in certain cases.*

Ideas for practice

Critical incident analysis

Critical incident analysis techniques allow reporting on specific situations and events, and will therefore provide appropriate material for reflection. However, in order to align with our key principles, you and your learner should be clear about (and have agreed on) which elements of the reflective process are appropriate for the situation and the expected outcomes.

Using frameworks or models

Most reflective frameworks offer a series of elements or steps to explore practice experience more fully and critically, providing the structure, focus and scaffolding for learning.

They should move a learner away from mere description of events and actions (although this is a necessary starting point), through an examination of particular aims, reasons and decisions within those actions and events to an evaluation of the outcomes and further, to identification of the learning that occurred for practice plus any changes or actions that are needed. Links and connection with theory, research, policy and legislation can be made where appropriate.

A framework for reflection

Description – What happened?

Feelings – What were you thinking and feeling?

Evaluation – What was good and bad about the experience?

Analysis – What sense can you make of the situation?

Conclusion – Is there anything else you could have done?

Action plan – What was learnt? If it arose again, what would you do?

Based on Gibbs (1998), cited in Rolfe et al. (2001, p32)

There are two key points to be made here. First, the most common elements within reflective models such as these, i.e. description, analysis and evaluation, are all necessary for maximising the learning that such reflection can achieve. Second, reflection can encompass a deeper level of criticality within each of these elements as follows (Rutter and Brown, 2015; Brown et al., 2010):

- *Description*

  More details than the ones that were initially noted need to be identified so that significant but less obvious features are not lost or ignored. Example – after an observation a student might be asked: *Did you notice what the siblings were doing while you were watching the child and mother?*

- *Analysis*

  Deeper questioning about what happened and why it happened needs to show not only the inherent assumptions of the person reflecting, but also the 'givens' associated within the reflective situation itself, and any connections or links between aspects of the event. An open view on the experience or situation is also required by seeking other perspectives and by exploring a wider range of alternative ideas, decisions, interpretations, actions, etc. Example – at a peer supervision meeting or an action learning group a practitioner might ask. *Do we automatically reject the medical model and how does this affect our attitudes to the people who work with it?*

- *Evaluation*

  Judgements on processes and outcomes need to go beyond what worked or didn't and what was learnt, to a deeper level of understanding about the importance, quality and appropriateness of the experience for self and others. This is about judging not only whether something was done correctly but whether it was the correct thing to do and also, perhaps, a reconsideration of how it is decided what is 'correct' in the first place, i.e. triple-loop learning as described by Argyris and Schön (1974). This level of criticality is unusual as most of us lack the power to challenge the parameters in which we work. However, sometimes we do need to re-examine fundamental areas of practice that we take as a 'given'. Students have a particular knack of asking naive questions which make us stop and rethink things. Example – a first-year student on a shadowing experience may ask: *How have we decided it is right to take children and place them in a care system where they could be at risk of a different kind?*

The 'Me, My, More, Must' approach

A values-based model of reflection designed for health and social care students in practice-based learning settings is the 'Me, My, More, Must' approach (Wareing, 2017) (see box below). This has been designed to help learners consider who they are and what impact their personally-held values might have before they describe a particular experience, situation or incident. The reflective exploration is around how their value system determines the professional judgement they have made arising from an event, and as such incorporates the idea of a more reflexive approach in the context of relational ethics.

Me

- Who am I?
- What values are important to me as a person?
- What values are important to me as a healthcare worker?

My

- What are my thoughts and feelings regarding this learning experience, situation or incident?
- What concerns do I have regarding myself?
- What concerns do I have about other people involved in this experience?

More

- What questions have been generated from this experience, situation or incident?
- What ideas have been generated from this experience, situation or incident?
- What has surprised or puzzled me about this experience, situation or incident?

Must

- What must I do now to identify my learning needs?
- What must I do to identify my learning goals?
- What values must I explore in order to become the healthcare worker I wish to become?

Recording reflections

The aim of reflective writing is to enable learners to identify, evaluate and personalise their learning and possibly develop and employ strategies to improve this learning and apply it to day-to-day practice. Encouraging the recording of reflective output (either written or via alternative media) can help to ensure the descriptive level is as accurate as possible and encourages deeper learning from this material (Moon, 1999). Of course, a traditional form of journal writing will not suit everyone's learning style and so the method for recording should not become an imposition.

The issue of trust is also important here. It is inconsistent with our main principles, and decidedly oppressive, to insist on learners following specific and prescriptive instructions to 'make' them reflect and to focus only on negative aspects. Rather, you can make the process and the content the outcome of joint decisions focusing on the wider reflective learning aim, and provide appropriate support and guidance. Learners should also have the right to keep any recordings private, with relevant sections being chosen by the learner to share or use to show their processes. Moon (1999, pp199–202) gives some particularly useful exercises for the process of recording and for giving it a focus, for example writing from different perspectives, SWOT analysis and imaginary dialogues.

ACTIVITY 7.2

Think about how critical reflection has played a role in your own learning and in developing your practice. Research various models of facilitating reflection and develop your own model which incorporates the features you think are most important.

Comment

Any model needs to ensure safety for the learner as well as challenge, the opportunity to include successful as well as less successful events, and the enabling of a deep and also critical approach to reflective learning.

If the aim of critical reflection is to evaluate our thinking and actions, it plays a key role in developing critical practice. This will be considered in more detail in the following chapter.

Chapter 8
Designing learning opportunities

Once you have understood learners' needs and perspectives, established the learning objectives and considered the principles behind certain types of learning and associated activities, you can start to make decisions about how best to design and manage the learning opportunities. In other words, you are now asking which learning events are most appropriate for learners and their needs, and how they can achieve the level and approach to learning required. Opportunities can include instructional as well as facilitative methods, but they all should align with our ideals of partnership and self-direction and enable competence and capability, again linking to the Professional Capabilities Framework and Knowledge and Skills Framework as appropriate. We can first revisit our ideas about critical practice and a critical approach to enabling learning and ensure an appropriate approach is taken from the outset.

Developing critical practice

Critical practice is a requirement to work with uncertainty, risk, diversity and difference in a way that recognises oppression and works to empower and promote the needs and rights of colleagues and fellow workers, as well as users and carers (Adams et al., 2002). Critical practice is therefore not about 'being certain' (the 'certain' thing is not necessarily the 'right' thing). It is about being able to deal with uncertainty using sound, valid and accountable processes and, where appropriate, maintain a position of 'respectful uncertainty', or at least hold on to doubt for longer and seek out other possible versions (Taylor and White, 2006). This requires the development of a practitioner as a 'critical being', i.e. a person who not only reflects critically on knowledge but also develops their powers of critical self-reflection and critical action (Barnett, 1997). In order to achieve this, learners need directed but risk-free opportunities to critically analyse and evaluate practice, explore alternative approaches wherever possible and develop their own ways to deal effectively with the continuing complexity of practice.

Structured learning opportunities as planned and structured pieces of work should therefore contain three elements in order to ensure that reflection is encouraged throughout the experience:

- preparation – an activity/activities to support reflection before the experience;
- a practice learning experience;
- consolidation – an activity/activities to support reflection after the experience.

By planning and designing learning opportunities in this way critical practice can be modelled effectively for the learner as they are encouraged to undertake a more in-depth and meaningful approach to reflective learning.

Ideas for practice

The key point is that you can encourage a deeper, more meaningful approach to learning in most situations. There are some basic but very practical methods that help to facilitate this which you could use within a wide range of learning activities:

- ensure exploration and discussion from the learner's viewpoint;

- encourage critical and evaluative comments;

- allow choice in learning;

- build on personal knowledge and experience;

- ensure application to the learner's situations;

- allow the learner to draw out general principles from specific learning so they may be used in other contexts;

- give and discuss formative feedback;

- allow time for reflective opportunities.

It comes back to our initial principles of 'constructive alignment' or 'joined-up thinking' and a clear understanding of learners and what is required from them. If there is a continued mismatch between the input from the educator and the learning approach required, the learner is in effect being taught to either fail or underachieve. Knowing that you are aiming for the learner to adopt a deep approach to their learning will guide the design of learning opportunities in an appropriate direction.

Instructional input

In some situations a basic level of knowledge use or learning is required – for example, the acquisition and recall of facts or simple procedures, establishing basic knowledge and understanding – before more complex tasks can be undertaken. Even if certain knowledge or skills need to be accepted for the most part unconditionally, or presented in a particular or very simple way, the learning opportunities you manage or design can still encourage learners to develop understanding for themselves.

Let's think this through in more detail with an actual learning opportunity in mind. You may be looking at the assessment process with a student, Mike. You will first need to tell him 'what' it is about, describe the form and the process and allow that description to make sense and be understood. You may show Mike what the assessment form looks like and go through the process of filling one in. You may then allow him to see 'how' the assessment is done by letting him observe you undertake an assessment of a service user and allow him to practise it.

However, these 'stabilising' features of learning need to be achieved within an overall 'deep approach' rather than a surface one. In order to develop a deeper approach to learning, any stabilising features should be part of a more complete package of learning that develops Mike's individual insight and meaning-making as well as his awareness of alternatives. You need to be incorporating more than the 'what' or 'how' by looking at the 'why?', 'what else?', 'how else?' and 'so what?' In this example, it may also mean asking Mike how he really feels about the assessment process and its budgetary constraints, or ensuring he is able to see a variety of different methods by shadowing other social workers, or letting him think of alternative ways to ask assessment questions. This can obviously be done when you judge the time is right for Mike, but it will move any discussion and thinking beyond mere reproduction, description or explanation to more critical and evaluative understanding and interpretation.

REFLECTION POINT

The problem, as we have described earlier, is that many learners may actually prefer to be just told things and given answers. Nevertheless, your role as an educator is about challenging and developing learners' thinking. Think about the abilities and skills you already possess that can help achieve this sensitively.

The amount of direct input, structure and material you provide for a learner will probably be dictated by the complexity of the information and the level of self-direction and independence the learner is capable of or needs encouraging in. In general terms, if a learner is very inexperienced and anxious or the material extremely complex, your input will be as instructive as necessary to provide a solid framework of understanding and confidence. If the learner is self-directing and confident with the topic, or the topic or skill is relatively simple, the educator's input may be more facilitative and guiding as the learner 'instructs' him or herself. Obviously, this is not a simple equation and the way you choose your methods is very much a contextual and relational process, dependent on the situation. The balance you are trying to achieve is in developing competence and as much capability as appropriate for the learner but with minimal risk to the learner, service users and the organisation.

Ideas for practice

When using a more instructional type of input there are some general principles to be aware of (Atherton, 2009a).

- Advance organisers

  These are simply devices used in the introduction of a topic which enable learners to orient themselves to it so that they can locate where any particular bit of information fits in and how it links with what they already know. These devices may be outlining handouts, statements of objectives or introductory orienting remarks. They give learners confidence that the educator knows where they are going. They also help learners to get a handle on the session and to see when new material is being introduced.

- Scaffolding

  The educator provides the external structure within which the learner can build their building. This includes engaging learners' interest, demonstrating, progressing from the simple to the complex, organising material, summarising, providing feedback, and so on.

- Models, metaphors and analogies

  With simple models the starting point is the simplest possible case of something, and then it is elaborated and moved on to those models that are closer to the real world. Using analogies ('something is like something else because …') needs care because they can be so powerful that learners get hooked on them and may not see where an analogy doesn't fit. Using metaphors needs even more care as you are saying that 'one thing is something else' to suggest the similarity, although not literally.

ACTIVITY *8.1*

Use the internet or other sources to find a range of other ideas to show you how to present information and instruct others using various methods (e.g. PowerPoint, handouts, whiteboards). Make a list of key tips and ideas.

Comment

Ideas for stimulating interest and enabling understanding, for example using diagrams, clear headings and points, should be useful in all areas of your work, from meetings to report writing.

Work-based learning activities

There are a number of established work-based learning activities that are more suited to enabling the holistic development of practice values, knowledge, skills and abilities. They will obviously be active and learner-focused in their design, linking to the key characteristics of the learner and their preferences as seen in Chapter 5. As established earlier, learning activities need to encourage learners to critically analyse and evaluate their practice and provide opportunities to explore alternative approaches wherever possible.

In general, active, experiential and reflective methods appear to be most appropriate for adult learners and to be more effective for developing professional capability. They help reinforce learners' understanding that there is usually more than one possible approach to working in a complex situation and can ensure that integration takes place between all three of Barnett and Coate's (2005) domains of knowing, acting and being. Your role as an educator is to find out more about work-based learning activities and critically evaluate them with the information gathered so far in this process, to ensure the ones you choose are aligned with the learner's needs, etc., and then review your own skills for delivering them. Some broad examples are presented below and further ideas and theories for consideration may be found in texts such as Doel and Shardlow (1998), which provides a wide range of engaging ideas and activities.

Shadowing

Shadowing, the practice of accompanying others to see and learn from their practice (Gould, 2000, p588), is a well-used method of promoting such learning on placement. By shadowing and observing an experienced social work practitioner, some implicit abilities and processes become more visible and so the content of practice becomes more open and accessible (Shardlow and Doel, 1996). Observing a number of practitioners in this way will provide much raw material from which a novice practitioner can develop their own approach.

Demonstrating/modelling

Learning by modelling takes the shadowing activity one step further so that, as well as observing an experienced practitioner complete a skill, a student or novice will imitate the practitioner's behaviour at a later time. As such, it is used as a method for learning very complex behaviours and is one of the more holistic ways to ensure readiness for practice (Shardlow and Doel, 1996).

Role play

Role play is any activity in which you either put yourself into somebody else's shoes or you stay in your own shoes but put yourself into an imaginary situation. This is an effective method of making more theoretical material come alive and also for developing interpersonal skills in a safe situation. Role play can also flag up certain features of a situation more clearly than in real life, which can get bogged down in unnecessary detail.

Case-study work

Case studies can range from simple 'stories' illustrating issues in practice to complex sets of documentation that may require analysis and evaluation. They work well for developing problem-solving skills and abilities.

Simulations

Simulations set up particular scenarios. It does not have to be the external circumstances that are simulated – the simulation can also be created from the decision-making, skill and practice of the practitioner working with these circumstances. This can allow a 'safer' and less anxiety-provoking environment than working with a real-life case but still allows a sense of urgency for decision-making.

Critical incident analysis

These procedures collect direct observations of human behaviour that have critical significance in a particular arena. These observations are kept track of as incidents, which are then used to solve practical problems and develop broad principles. The analysis should pick out the key parts of the event so that the importance of the processes (actions and responses rather than just outcomes) is understood.

Coaching, mentoring and supervision

Broader types of learning opportunities such as coaching, mentoring and supervision are able to provide the appropriate space, freedom and lack of risk which enables learners to reflect critically on their thinking and actions, as well as on alternative approaches and choices. They can allow learners to at least hold onto doubt for longer and seek out other possible versions, helping to reinforce understanding that there is usually more than one possible interpretation or approach to a complex situation, and that there is often no 'right answer' or 'right way' to do something in professional practice. They can also help develop the type of reasoning, deliberation and judgement needed to deal with the complexity of practice.

Supervision, mentoring and coaching all use learning through experience and critical reflection (explored in the previous chapter) as key development tools (Brockbank and McGill, 2002) and they all rely on dialogue and questioning as a means of enabling learning.

Dialogue – the role of critical questioning

Dialogue, and in particular critical questioning, is a fundamental part of coaching, mentoring and supervision. Recent research shows that practitioners value 'continuous conversations' in 'learning workplaces' for their professional development (Beddoe, 2009).

The role of discussion and questioning was examined in the previous chapter when we considered how best to enable deeper reflective learning. The aim was to move beyond description to more meaningful analysis and evaluation. McGill and Beaty (1995) recommend the use of questions that are open (e.g. how …? why …?), affective (e.g. how are you feeling?) and probing/checking (e.g. when …? where …? in what way …?). Remember, there are no 'right' questions to ask learners because there are no clear-cut answers. 'Certain' reasons and justifications are not always appropriate when talking about professional knowledge. In fact, as with many conversational situations that aim to enable learning and development, success depends on listening correctly too (i.e. actively, without interruption or judgement) and on reflecting back what you think you have heard for clarification.

Critical questioning (Brookfield, 1987) takes the dialogue process one step further in drawing out not only assumptions and underlying thoughts but also personal givens and accepted public truths. Questioning someone to elicit self-scrutiny of such issues must not become, or be seen as, behaviour that insults, threatens or attacks their self-esteem. As we now know, it is not what you do as an educator but how learners perceive that action which will lead to their response. If learners perceive your questioning techniques as threatening in any way, they will retreat or attack and the learning experience will become a negative situation.

Critical questioning therefore involves very skilful framing of insightful and empathetic questions to encourage analysis and challenge thinking. This is a skill that may need training and subsequent practice and refinement for educators but many skills may be transferred from the type of work undertaken already with service users. Brookfield (1987, pp93–4) suggests general guidelines including:

- *be specific* – relate questions to particular events, situations, people and actions;
- *work from the particular to the general* – exploring a general theme within the context of a specific event helps people feel they are in familiar territory;
- *be conversational* – informal, non-threatening tones help people feel comfortable.

We would add another suggestion: be aware of the effect your questioning is having and watch for any negative signs, such as non-response, a defensive position being argued too aggressively, brooding resignation.

We can now explore coaching, mentoring and supervision in turn to show the particular approaches, techniques and methods of each. Of course, we can present only overall ideas here but you can use the further reading lists to explore these methods in more detail.

Coaching

There are a number of circumstances where short-term coaching can help people to be more effective in their roles. For example, we all know workers who qualified many years ago and are stuck in habitual ways of working. For instance, John has become fixed on using a task-centred approach and he says it has 'done him well' over the years. Coaching can help to challenge John's habitual thoughts and actions by allowing him to safely explore and evaluate alternative approaches away from people he knows. Coaching is not necessarily provided by someone who is an expert in the subject, but rather by someone who has an expertise in coaching techniques. If you were John's coach and from a different department to him, you could easily play devil's advocate in your discussions, getting John to re-examine some more fundamental issues, and thus increase John's capability to think more flexibly.

Coaching is not about telling someone how to do their job. Any teaching and advice are generally aimed at developing the person's skills, knowledge and confidence to enable them to find their own solutions. You would not be 'judging' John's practice or telling him how to adopt a different social work method. One of the fundamental tenets of coaching is that the person being coached is the 'expert' in their subject or practice area and has the capability to achieve their goals with the support of the coach. You would be developing John's confidence and motivation to look more openly at other practice approaches. This should be a very non-threatening learning environment, and for John it could mean some very transformative learning.

Coaching is therefore a deductive process, one of 'drawing out' the necessary change or development from the person being coached, helping them to learn, enabling them to be more analytical, think more critically and problem-solve more effectively. The remit of a coach, however, is quite narrow. Coaching is most commonly time-limited, a one-to-one process which is set up to enable the person being coached to achieve specific goals or targets; it focuses on results and how those results can be most effectively achieved. It is often about supporting change and helping people to move on, so when it is done well it is a very empowering technique.

Below are some of the methods used in coaching:

- challenging assumptions, prejudices and habitual thinking;
- supporting problem-solving and decision-making;
- supporting metacognitive development (skills such as learning how to learn, improving critical thinking, etc.);
- enabling people to recognise and empathise with other perspectives;
- enabling the transfer of learning/skills/knowledge from one situation to another;
- negotiating, agreeing and monitoring the achievement of objectives;
- identifying the need for new learning;
- planning and facilitating the new learning.

Mentoring

Mentoring is generally considered to have a wider remit than coaching. Mentors are often provided for newly-qualified workers or workers taking on new areas of responsibility to help them develop the specific skills and knowledge required to undertake their new role. Although mentors are always more experienced members of staff than mentees, the mentor relationship should not be hierarchical. It is sometimes described as a 'learning alliance' to demonstrate that the relationship is about working in partnership to support learning, principally of the mentee but also of the mentor (Thompson, 2006).

One of the most significant differences between coaching and mentoring is that mentoring should always be provided by someone who is skilled and experienced in the mentee's field of work and is able to provide direct support with the development of knowledge, skills and confidence (Neary, 2000; Mullins, 2005). Familiarity with the mentee's work environment is also very important. Mentor arrangements are normally longer term than coaching relationships and will often involve more frequent contact, including access to the mentor's support in between any formal mentoring sessions that take place. The objectives for the relationship are likely to evolve over time as the mentee develops skills and confidence and shifts their focus from one area of their practice to another.

Below are some of the methods used in mentoring:

- direct teaching through the provision of information;
- clarification and explanation of policies, procedures and legislation;
- working through case studies to develop understanding;
- sharing material such as reports and records to help the mentee understand the organisation's requirements;
- shadowing by the mentee of the mentor's work;
- joint working to aid the development of skills and confidence;
- reflective discussions in mentoring sessions;

- objective setting;

- recommendations for reading and research;

- setting of learning and development tasks.

CASE STUDY 8.1

A newly-qualified social worker, Beth, makes a routine home visit to a long-term service user of the agency at the request of the regular worker who has been called away urgently. Although the service user is told that Beth will be coming, he refuses to open the door to her but shouts through the window and tells her in no uncertain terms to get lost. Beth is very upset at the incident – she describes anger, frustration, helplessness and embarrassment. Ali, her mentor, thinks of some questions which may help Beth move on from her feelings and uncomfortable position in the situation to examine broader issues regarding her own practice and why the situation might have occurred. Ali knows the importance of examining case notes thoroughly before any visit to understand what might be going in a service user's mind (e.g. suspicion, privacy issues) and can see why this service user may well have reacted in the way he did. Ali gently leads Beth away from a negative emotional view of what happened by focusing his questions on key practices that Beth can easily improve on for more positive future outcomes.

Mentoring is a means of ensuring that knowledge and skills are passed from experienced members of staff to those who are less experienced, and can be an effective way of supporting a culture of learning within the workplace.

Supervision

The supervisor in an educational role supports in-depth exploration and analysis of work processes from their initial allocation through to completion of tasks, helping the supervisee to test their assessments, explore and uncover assumptions, prejudices, alternative perspectives and gaps in knowledge and consider alternative approaches. See Chapter 12 for further information.

According to Smith (1996, 2005) and Hawkins and Shohet (2000), supervisees may be helped to:

- understand the client better;

- become more aware of their own reactions and responses to the client;

- understand the dynamics of how they and their client are interacting;

- look at how they intervened and the consequences of their interventions;

- explore other ways of working with this and other similar client situations.

Effective supervisors can help learners reflect and gain an in-depth understanding of a situation and facilitate analysis to enable learning and decision-making processes. They can also encourage learners to adopt a more independent role and take responsibility for management and self-evaluation of their own learning during this process. These approaches support the development of more transferable skills, such as creativity, critical thinking, problem-solving and decision-making, which will enhance professional capability. As seen earlier, the right balance between supervisory authority and supervisee autonomy needs to be thought through for each individual learner.

Supervisors can also ensure there are effective learning outputs from the process. They can help learners to scaffold and integrate the knowledge and understanding that result from critical reflection and place it into a work-based context for future use. With these aims in mind, Davys and Beddoe's (2009, p932) reflective learning model might be used to provide *parameters, guidelines and information* in order for supervisees to *begin to construct their own sense of mastery of the skills and interventions required by practice*. The model describes four sequential stages that can be revisited at any time in the process: event, which involves description and clarification; exploration, which involves reflection of impact and evaluation of implications; experimentation, which concerns implementation or moving forward of ideas so they are not lost; and evaluation of the whole agenda.

Of course, supervision enables all levels of workers; in some situations younger staff may be supervising more experienced workers or vice versa. Managing the various power and experience issues can be difficult to judge, but following the principle of working in partnership allows for a more egalitarian and humanistic approach, i.e. a supervisor does not need to adopt the role of an expert.

CASE STUDY *8.2*

Velma is supervising Joan, an experienced worker. Velma's patience is being challenged by Joan's entrenched, negative views of young, unmarried mothers. Velma knows she has to question Joan in a very critical but sensitive manner so that Joan does not end up taking a defensive and negative position by feeling threatened or exposed. She also wants to avoid damaging their relationship. Velma knows there are many similarities between critical questioning and effective counselling skills. She endeavours to transfer these skills by thinking through ways to empower Joan to reflect and develop her own thinking on this issue. She needs a way in that is safe and unobtrusive and which does not set her up as the 'expert' or perfect social worker, which will only alienate Joan. She decides to discuss with Joan the course she recently attended, which had introduced the stages of knowing to her. She explains the ideas to Joan and professes to still being an 'absolute thinker' in many ways. Joan finds it difficult to believe this but Velma shares an example of how she feels so angry about male car mechanics who always seem to treat her with disdain, which then makes her believe they are all arrogant, brash young men out to rip her off. As the conversation develops, Joan begins to relay a story about a recent encounter she had with a teenager and her baby – this is the way in and together they unpick how and why their feelings and attitudes to certain others become so negative and how they can try to remedy this.

These are some of the methods used in supervision:

- case-work discussion;

- critical questioning;

- critical incident analysis;

- role play;

- imagined scenario building;

- reflective journals.

Enabling theory–practice connections and evidence-informed practice

Making connections between theory (and/or research) and practice is an important aspect for developing critical practice, and supervision is a perfect place for it to be enabled. The more traditional way is for the learner to consider theory first and then use it to explain or inform practice and predict the outcome. This view has been criticised (Margetson, 2000, cited in Nixon and Murr, 2006, p807) as it can develop fixed 'templates' which do not fit more complex cases. More specific details or information about cases or service users may become ignored or manipulated to fit the theory which distorts true understanding. For example, when working with children and applying attachment theory, it is important to recognise the limitations of its classifications and be aware that individuals who are securely attached can nevertheless display aspects of either avoidant or ambivalent behaviour.

We can see that theory and research findings can only inform – they cannot predict or control exactly what will take place. Research evidence can be extremely useful material for social workers (especially those newly-qualified) to gain more information about issues, possible interventions and outcomes, but it cannot be taken 'off the shelf' as an unmediated solution or be seen to exactly 'match' a specific situation. In fact, it would be difficult to reduce the complex, uncertain and unstable situations we work with to something that a standardised theoretical body of knowledge, or a set of specific research findings, can answer (Adams et al., 2002). To apply or base practice on any type of evidence without moral or ethical sensitivity or a wider assessment of context, individual circumstances, situational requirements or risk assessment of possible implications would be deemed 'uncritical' practice and is unacceptable (Brown and Rutter, 2015).

A learner can also undertake more inductive problem-solving where the detail of real situations is analysed first before looking at which theories or research findings relate to this. This enables learners to start to interpret practice and in turn allows for complexity and creativity to be taken into account. (Note how neatly and effectively this fits with our notion of professional capability.) However, there are dangers here too. For example, when discussing particular cases it would be important not to become fixed on one set of prominent issues (e.g. behaviour) and then fail to notice other aspects (e.g. culture) which theory or research might show are significant.

As discussed earlier, a student or novice practitioner with less practical experience may want more direction and 'rules' to follow and look to more formal knowledge to provide it. This type of practitioner will need to be enabled to start reflecting on the practice situation first, i.e. to describe, analyse and evaluate the significant aspects for themselves and develop their professional judgement. Collingwood (2005; Collingwood et al., 2008) provides some practical ideas for use in supervision which encourage theory–practice integration.

A review of thinking in this area (Nixon and Murr, 2006) concludes that professional knowledge is created by combining and recombining more explicit formal knowledge with an understanding of tacit knowledge from professional processes. Kondrat (1992) talks about the practitioner being able to move from the subjective perspective to an objective view of that perspective and back again. Consequently both deductive and inductive reasoning are likely to be taking place and the fundamental need for professional judgement and evaluation is an essential part of both processes.

Bringing it all together

ACTIVITY 8.2

Think about your learner:

- *agree a learning objective;*

- *note particular learning needs, i.e. what they already know or can do (to build on strengths) and what they still needs to learn or develop (linked to PCF/KSF);*

- *note how they learn (preferences, approaches, anxiety, etc.); take into account limitations in the learning environment and the resources that are available.*

Now start to design/map out a structured learning opportunity that takes this information into account and plan which experiences/activities should be included to ensure their specific learning needs are addressed – be creative!

As seen earlier in the chapter, a structured learning opportunity should be a planned and structured piece of work which has three elements to ensure deeper, more critical and reflective learning occurs before and after a learning opportunity.

- *preparation – an activity/activities to support reflection before the experience;*

- *a practice learning experience;*

- *consolidation – an activity / activities to support reflection after the experience.*

You are aiming for deep, reflective, experiential learning. You want this learner to critically analyse and evaluate their practice, i.e. to think about different perspectives on the situation they are working in and to critically explore a number of different approaches they could have taken.

Comment

By creating tailored learning opportunities which allow learners to approach their learning in active, questioning and critically reflective ways, you should be enabling the development or the enhancement of critical practice.

Of course, you also play a key role in all these learning situations not only by ensuring that learners have access to a wide range of practice experience and opportunities to critically discuss and reflect on their own practice, but by modelling a critical, reflective approach to practice as well. Part Four will look at this in more detail by considering your continuing professional development, but before then Part Three will focus on managing the assessment of learning.

Summary of Part Two
Domain B

- The key guiding principles for enabling work-based learning are: establishing an effective working relationship and partnership with the learner; valuing the learner's perspective and adult learning principles; following an aligned approach.

- The main areas involve understanding the learner, developing learning objectives, considering learning theories and designing appropriate learning opportunities.

- It is important to review the learning schemes you design, involve the learner and link to how well they are doing – be flexible, and adapt and change if necessary.

- There is no one overall definition of 'learning'; it is a very complex and situated phenomenon.

- Work-based learning activities should encourage learners to critically reflect on, analyse and evaluate their practice as well as provide opportunities to explore alternative approaches wherever possible.

- The reflective process should be active, holistic, meaningful and critical.

- Coaching, mentoring and supervision all provide ways to develop critical practice through dialogue and questioning.

FURTHER READING

Brockbank, A and McGill, I (2002) *Facilitating reflective learning through mentoring and coaching.* London: Kogan Page.

Provides background information together with a helpful section on practice skills.

Cartney, P (2000) Adult learning styles: implications for practice teaching in social work. *Social Work Education*, 19 (6), pp609–26.

A practical and also critical look at using learning styles in social work practice education.

Doel, M and Shardlow, S (1998) *The new social work practice: exercises and activities for training and developing social workers.* Aldershot: Arena.

This book offers very creative ideas to think about and some excellent practice learning activities.

Fook, J and Gardner, F (2007) *Practising critical reflection: a resource handbook.* Maidenhead: Open University Press and McGraw-Hill Education.

An in-depth look at critical reflection in practice, offering skills, strategies and tools for personal and educational use.

Johns, C (2017) *Becoming a reflective practitioner*, 5th edn. Chichester: Wiley Blackwell.

A classic guide to developing a reflective approach to care in everyday practice, outlining a process for developing one's own reflective and holistic approach to care.

Kadushin, A and Harkness, D (2002) *Supervision in social work*, 4th edn. New York: Columbia University Press.

A basic text covering the challenges of supervision for social work educators, practitioners, supervisors and agencies.

Keinemans, S (2015) Be sensible: emotions in social work ethics and education. *British Journal of Social Work*, 45, pp2176–91.

This article argues that emotions are relevant for moral decision-making and therefore social work ethics training and education should pay attention to them.

Knott, C and Scragg, T (eds) (2016) *Reflective practice in social work*, 4th edn. Los Angeles: Learning Matters.

An accessible and introductory text that explores a range of approaches to reflective practice that aims to help students become more confident in answering key questions.

Wareing, M (2017) Me, my, more, must: a values-based model of reflection. *Reflective Practice*, 18 (2), pp268–79.

This paper describes a new model of reflection designed for health and social care students in practice-based learning settings and qualified professionals engaged in work-based learning.

Part Three
Domain C: Manage the assessment of learners in practice

The material in this part links to the following domain standards.

Domain C: Manage the assessment of learners in practice

Practice educators at Stages 1 and 2 should:

1. Engage learners in the design, planning and implementation of the assessment tasks.

2. Agree and review a plan and methods for assessing learners' performance against agreed criteria.

3. Ensure that assessment decisions are the outcomes of informed, evidence-based judgements and clearly explain them to learners.

4. Evaluate evidence for its relevance, validity, reliability, sufficiency and authenticity according to the agreed standard.

5. Use direct observation of learners in practice to assess performance.

6. Base assessment decisions on all relevant evidence and from a range of sources, resolving any inconsistencies in the evidence available.

7. Encourage learners to self-evaluate and seek service users', carers' and peer feedback on their performance.

8. Provide timely, honest and constructive feedback on learners' performance in an appropriate format. Review their progress through the assessment process, distinguishing between formative and summative assessment.

9. Make clear to learners how they may improve their performance. Identify any specific learning outcomes not yet demonstrated and the next steps. If necessary, arrange appropriate additional assessment activity to enable them to meet the standard.

10. Ensure that all assessment decisions, and the supporting evidence, are documented and recorded according to the required standard. Produce assessment reports which provide clear evidence for decisions.

11. Ensure that disagreements about assessment judgements and complaints made about the assessment process are managed in accordance with agreed procedures.

12. Seek feedback from learners on their experience of being assessed and the consequences of the assessment programme for them. Incorporate the feedback into future assessment activity.

(Continued)

(Continued)

13. Contribute to standardisation arrangements and the agreed quality-assurance processes which monitor the organisation's training strategy.

14. Using professional judgement and drawing on appropriate support, demonstrate the ability to make difficult assessment decisions around areas of development, which may include marginal or failing students.

Additional learning outcomes for practice educators at Stage 2

1. Where appropriate and drawing on support, demonstrate the ability to mark students' academic work.

2. Demonstrate an ability to use a range of assessment methods including recording, reports and the feedback of people who use services and carers, professionals and other colleagues.

Introduction to Domain C

We have already established that becoming – and indeed remaining – an effective social worker is not a simple process. Social work practice is a challenging activity that must be underpinned by an understanding of the complex relationship between knowing, acting and being, described by Barnett and Coate (2005) as professional capability. In Parts One and Two we looked at how practice educators can facilitate learning to support the development of processional capability and in Part Three we will move on to consider the challenging subject of how social work practice can be assessed. As part of this discussion we will introduce and discuss the concept of holistic assessment and show how assessment standards, such as the Professional Capabilities Framework (BASW, 2018), can be used to benchmark and support the development performance at different stages of a social work career.

When asked to reflect on early experiences of making assessment judgements in a professional context, most people recall feelings of uncertainty and anxiety. It is not uncommon for even the most confident of social workers to experience similar feelings when faced with the responsibility of assessing a student for the first time. Practice educators are often called the gatekeepers for the profession because they have an important role to play in deciding whether or not students and newly-qualified social workers are able to move on to the next stage of their career (Lafrance et al., 2004). This can quite reasonably feel like a heavy responsibility, as preventing the progress of someone who has already invested a large amount of time and money is not an easy thing to do, while passing a learner who could pose a danger to service users is every practice teacher's worst nightmare (Finch, 2017; Walker et al., 2008).

This section of the book will provide information and ideas that will help develop your confidence in the assessment of learners. It will encourage you to evaluate your existing skills, knowledge and attributes and consider how these can be transferred and developed to enable you to make holistic judgements that are fair, reliable and accurate. We will be focusing mainly on the assessment of social work students, but many of the principles and strategies that you will encounter in this part of the book can also be applied to the assessment of other learners in the workplace and will be particularly useful in work with NQSWs.

Part Three is divided into three chapters. Chapter 9 provides an introduction and overview to the assessment of learners in the workplace. It refers back to earlier chapters and explores links between assessment and learning. Chapter 10 looks in more detail at the assessment process, breaking it down into seven stages and exploring each stage in turn. Chapter 11 provides you with examples of specific tools that you can use to assess learners, and helps you to consider how you can apply these strategies in your own workplace.

Chapter 9
Understanding the assessment of social work practice

So far in this book we have looked at what professional learning is and why the concept of capability is important when we are considering what social workers need to learn. In this chapter we will explore the relationship between learning and assessment in greater depth. This will give us a better understanding of the reasons why we assess and enable us to think more deeply about the wider role that assessment plays in the development of professional practice. We will start by addressing the fundamental but deceptively simple question – why do we need to assess social work practice in the first place?

Why do we assess?

This appears to be a very straightforward question and is one we often ask at the beginning of assessment workshops. Responses generally fall into the following broad categories:

- to find out what learners know or what they can do;

- to judge whether or not learners are good enough to qualify or move on to the next stage of their learning;

- to give learners feedback on their learning and/or their practice;

- to give practice educators feedback on how effective their teaching has been.

These are all valid and important justifications for undertaking assessments, but they do not tell the whole story. If we look more deeply at the connections between learning and assessment we will see that the relationship between the two is far more complex than the above list suggests and that understanding this relationship is a fundamental prerequisite for effective teaching and assessment (Biggs, 2003).

RESEARCH SUMMARY 9.1

It has been shown that what people learn is strongly influenced by the way that they think their learning will be assessed. Ramsden (1992) found that the primary goal for many learners was not the learning itself, but the achievement of a good assessment outcome. Because of this they tend to focus on the parts of their course that will help them do well in their assessment tasks – often to the detriment of other aspects of their learning.

(Continued)

RESEARCH SUMMARY **9.1** *continued*

Earlier research had already shown that the approach taken by learners could be influenced by the assessment strategies used by their teachers. Marton and Säljö (1976) found a clear link between the design of assessment tasks and the adoption of deep/surface approaches to learning (see Chapter 5 for more details on deep and surface learning). Biggs (2003) investigated this link further and found that when students thought a surface approach would enable them to do well in an assessment task (e.g. when the assessment involved simple recall of facts) they were much more likely to adopt a surface approach. Conversely, when an assessment task was designed to test for deeper learning (e.g. seeking to establish levels of understanding or the ability to transfer knowledge and understanding from one context to another), students would more frequently adopt a deep approach to their studies.

It would seem, therefore, that assessment is not just a tool for measuring achievement and providing feedback about performance but an integral part of the learning process, with the power to exert a great deal of influence over what and how people learn. Badly designed and inappropriate assessment strategies have repeatedly been shown to skew learning and change priorities towards what will be assessed rather than what actually needs to be learnt (Singh, 2001). By contrast, well-designed assessment strategies not only enable learners to demonstrate their achievements but ensure that learners' attention is directed towards fully meeting their intended learning outcomes. So, we can see that in order to give a more accurate description of why we assess we need to add a further point to the above list at the beginning of this section:

- to direct and shape learning – by helping learners to understand exactly what they need to learn and how they can demonstrate achievement of their objectives.

In the following case study we will show just how much assessment can influence the depth of learning achieved in a practice situation and how significant this can be in terms of professional development.

CASE STUDY **9.1**

Jenny and David are social work students in the early stages of their placements in the same busy children and family team. As part of their induction their practice educators decide they need to understand how Attachment Theory (Bowlby, 1969) informs the team's approach to practice.

Both students are given books and articles to read together with the opportunity to shadow an experienced worker undertaking an initial assessment. Individual follow-up supervision sessions are arranged to provide an opportunity for their practice educators to assess the learning that they have achieved.

CASE STUDY *9.1* *continued*

Both practice educators give clear information to the students about how their learning will be assessed before they embark on their learning experience:

- *Jenny's practice educator tells her that in her follow-up supervision session they will be doing a short quiz about Attachment Theory to enable Jenny to demonstrate her knowledge and understanding of the theory.*

- *David's practice educator explains that in his follow-up supervision session they will discuss what David has learnt from his reading and his shadowing opportunity. She asks him to bring his reflective notes to the session to help him critically explore how he believes Attachment Theory has informed the experienced worker's practice.*

The two students have good academic records and have both already demonstrated to their practice educators that they are naturally reflective practitioners. However, clear differences emerge in the way that David and Jenny approach this particular learning task.

To succeed in her quiz Jenny realises she simply needs to learn some basic facts about Attachment Theory. She meets this learning objective the day after the task is set by memorising key ideas, significant dates and research data from the resources she had been given by her practice educator. Although she observes an experienced worker undertaking an initial assessment she doesn't link the observation with Attachment Theory in the way that her practice educator intends. She hurries away after the observation without discussing what she has seen and although she later makes notes in her reflective diary, they are about procedural issues relating to the assessment, with no specific mention of attachment issues or Attachment Theory.

David, by contrast, is forced to take a different approach to his learning because he knows that to succeed in his assessment task he needs to demonstrate an understanding of how theory can inform practice. David reads the material he has been given but he doesn't spend much time memorising facts. Instead, he notes questions to ask before the shadowing experience to help him understand more about Attachment Theory and how and when it is likely to be used in the intervention. During the observation David focuses mainly on the areas of practice that the worker has indicated will be most relevant to his learning and afterwards asks more questions to ensure that he understands what he has observed. David's reflective diary entry is sharply focused and includes a detailed analysis of both his observations and his discussions with the worker. David is able to make clear links between theory and practice and is also beginning to think about some alternative theories that could have been useful in the intervention he has observed.

Despite the differences in approach, the students perform well in their respective assessment tasks. As a consequence both practice educators are satisfied that they have enabled the students to learn about Attachment Theory and feel justified in making positive comments in their final reports about knowledge relevant to practice.

In Case Study 9.1 that we have just considered, it is undeniably true that (a) both students have been enabled to learn about aspects of Attachment Theory, and that (b) both have provided evidence that can be used as part of their overall assessment. But it is worth pausing to consider what has actually been achieved by David and Jenny and to review the links between their learning and assessment.

Although both David and Jenny were set the same objective and were offered similar opportunities, they chose to use the opportunities differently. Because the students wanted to impress their practice educators and be successful in their placements, it seems likely, based on the research evidence we considered earlier, that the assessment strategies adopted played a role in influencing the learning decisions that they made. Jenny appears to have been driven towards surface learning – with a focus on gaining superficial knowledge and understanding – while the more complex and demanding assessment strategy adopted by David's practice educator appears to have encouraged and supported much deeper learning to take place. This will almost certainly have led to very significant differences in the learning outcomes for the two students, with David in a much stronger position to use his learning to inform his own future practice.

However, it is not just the learning outcomes that are different. The differences in the assessment strategies adopted also mean that the quality of assessment evidence available to the practice educators varies widely. Jenny's assessment task has only generated evidence of her knowledge and understanding of one specific theory while David's practice educator has far more evidence to draw on. He is able to assess not only David's knowledge of Attachment Theory but also David's ability to use his knowledge critically to analyse and inform practice. And because of the approach that the assessment strategy encouraged towards learning, he will also be able to make some judgements about David's wider capabilities, for instance his ability to take professional responsibility for his own learning, communicate with other professionals and use supervision effectively.

The concept of professional capability

So now we need to begin to bring some ideas together and think about how they can help us understand more about the development and assessment of professional capability. In Chapter 1 we introduced the concept of professional capability and discussed some of the reasons why the Professional Capabilities Framework (PCF) (BASW, 2018) has been developed as a benchmark for social work practice. We looked at the fact that social work is a complex activity and considered how the introduction of the PCF attempts to capture that complexity and provide practice educators, assessors and managers with a tool that can be used to guide learning and judge performance both in initial social work education and in continuing professional development. We also discussed the more recent introduction of the Knowledge and Skills Statements (KSSs) (DoH, 2015; DfE, 2018) which set out the minimum required standards of knowledge and skills that must be achieved by social workers once they are employed in specific statutory roles.

Case Study 9.1 shows just how important it is to use assessment strategies that shape the 'right sort' of learning (deeper learning) and enable us to measure professional performance effectively. The College of Social Work hoped that the introduction of the PCF in 2012 would accomplish both of these objectives by offering a framework that not only set out what social workers should be achieving at different stages in their careers but also provided guidance on how the complexity of the task could be captured and judged. The ongoing relevance of the PCF as a way to benchmark social work capability was confirmed during the refresh process completed by BASW in 2018. This is important because, unlike the National Occupational Standards (TOPSS, 2002) that it replaced, the PCF (CSW, 2012c; BASW 2018) does not just focus on the component parts of practice but encourages educators to take into account the way that those parts are brought together to form professional expertise. This was a very important step forward in social work education because, for the first time, there was formal recognition that an oversimplified assessment system not only fails to measure practice capability but can actually drive social workers to develop a fragmented view of their practice that inadequately prepares them for their complex role in society. If used in isolation, the KSSs (DoH, 2015; DfE, 2018) could be seen as a retrograde step – a move back towards a more competence-based system. But the KSSs were not introduced to replace the PCF but to add another layer to the assessment of social work practice – giving more detailed guidance about what the government in England expects social workers undertaking specific social work roles and in specific practice settings to know and be able to do (BASW, 2018). Both the PCF and the KSSs are therefore considered to have an important role to play in ensuring the quality of social work practice. In the final part of this chapter we move on to explore the concept of holistic assessment. This is the approach to assessment that underpinned the development of the PCF and which enables practice educators to integrate both the KSSs and the PCF in the assessments that they make.

Work to explore ways in which the PCF and KSSs can be most effectively used within a single overarching framework has started. This was formalised in a joint statement made by BASW and the Chief Social Workers in England in March 2018, but at the time of writing is still ongoing. For the latest developments check the BASW website (**www.basw.co.uk**) and from spring 2019 it will be important to look out for announcements made by the newly formed professional regulatory body, Social Work England.

In the final part of this chapter we move on to look at holistic assessment – the approach to assessment that underpins the PCF and enables practice educators and assessors of practice to take an integrated approach to the use of the KSSs and the PCF.

What is holistic assessment?

Holistic assessment is not a new idea in social work – it is a process that most workers will be very familiar with from their assessments of service users and carers. In an educational context holistic assessment needs to be used in situations where learning or performance objectives are interrelated and complex. This clearly applies to the assessments that practice educators are now being asked to make against the nine domains of the PCF (CSW, 2012c; BASW, 2018), in which the focus is not on making judgements about performance in individual elements of the framework but rather on measuring the development of professional expertise as a whole. Although the process of holistic assessment places a much greater emphasis on the professional judgement of the practice educator, it does not mean that these judgements are no longer required to be backed by evidence. The evidence required will, however, be different, as it will need to show not only what social workers know and can do (evidence of occupational competence for assessment against the relevant KSS) but also how social workers bring their skills, knowledge and values together across the domains of the PCF (to provide evidence of a broader and more generic professional capability).

One of the fundamental principles of holistic approaches to complex work contexts is that there is rarely a single 'right' way to practise. In every social worker's 'toolbox' there will be a wide range of 'tools' in the form of skills, knowledge and values and each time the worker reaches into that box to undertake a piece of work they make a decision (conscious or unconscious) about which combination of tools they think will work most effectively for them in that particular context. Two different workers approaching similar tasks may choose a different combination of tools and will almost certainly use the tools that they do select quite differently. However, despite the differences, both practitioners could be equally effective in terms of the process and outcomes of their work. Because of these wide-ranging differences in the approaches that effective practitioners can take and the complex interactions between different elements of practice, it is important that the people assessing practice develop skills in judging the whole of practice and not just its component parts. To more fully capture practice capability it is also important to undertake holistic assessment over a period of time – judging performance not just on the basis of one piece of practice but on practice across a range of contexts and with different types of service users. This will enable judgements to be made about the transferability of skills and knowledge – including in untaught situations.

At the beginning of a professional career a worker's toolbox is fairly empty and their lack of experience means that it can be hard for them to know which tools to use and how to use them. With time, experience, education and support, professionals gradually add (and remove) tools to and from their boxes and become more confident in their ability to use them to approach complex tasks. This process of growth is sometimes described as the development of professional expertise and it is this overarching capacity to undertake professional tasks effectively that practice educators need to attempt to measure through holistic assessment. Because this capacity develops throughout a career it is clearly inappropriate to attempt to use a single set of standards to measure social workers at different stages of their development. It is therefore important that holistic assessment takes into account what could reasonably be expected at a specific stage of a social worker's career.

Although the main focus in holistic assessment is on taking an integrated approach, it would be wrong to suggest that there is never a need to look more deeply at specific aspects of a social worker's practice. At times practice may fall short of expectations and under such circumstances it can be useful to look at the component parts of practice as well as at the practice as a whole. The individual capability statements that make up the domains of the PCF (CSW, 2012c) can help practice educators to drill down into practice, identifying gaps and areas for development or concerns. In their guidance on holistic assessment the College of Social Work (2012c) uses the analogy of eating a meal in a restaurant. They suggest that we make a holistic judgement based on the overall taste, quality and presentation of the meal but point out that if we are unhappy with the final product we may want to look more closely at the details of the preparation and ingredients to see what could have been improved. This process of drilling down is explored further in Chapters 10 and 11.

Principles and conditions for holistic assessment against the PCF

The BASW (**www.basw.co.uk**) and Skills for Care (**www.skillsforcare.org.uk**) websites contain a wide range of useful resources for practice educators undertaking holistic assessment. The following principles are drawn from the College of Social Work guidance on holistic assessment which is now available at **www.basw.co.uk**:

- assessment is progressive over time;

- assessment must be consistent with the appropriate level descriptor;

- evidence must be sufficient and provide depth across all nine domains;

- the assessment process must be trustworthy, reliable and transparent;

- the learner will contribute evidence for assessment but the professional judgement of sufficiency must be made by an appropriately qualified practice educator.

In the remaining chapters of Part Three we will explore some of the practical challenges that you will face undertaking a holistic assessment and consider some of the approaches that you can adopt to ensure that you are able undertake your assessment role effectively, accurately and fairly.

Chapter 10
The assessment process

In the previous chapter we established that assessment is a complex process which is an integral part of the learning process. We introduced the Professional Capabilities Framework (CSW, 2012c; BASW, 2018) and the Knowledge and Skills Statements (DfE, 2018; DoH, 2015) as benchmarking tools. Although we saw that it is normally considered best practice to assess social workers holistically, with evidence being naturally generated from the work being undertaken as part of the placement, it became clear that it is sometimes necessary to 'drill down' in a more structured way into areas of concern.

In this chapter we will look at assessment in greater detail and explore a range of strategies that will help you tailor your approach to the needs of individual learners and specific assessment contexts. This will include some strategies relevant to good quality holistic assessment and others more specifically aimed at helping with the more in-depth analysis and evaluation of practice required when capability is not being readily evidenced.

1. Planning assessment – working in partnership

When a student begins a placement or a NQSW starts their first job, they will already have some specific learning and assessment objectives in place (arising professionally from the PCF and/or KSSs and personally from their own development needs). One of your first steps as their assessor is to ensure you understand these objectives and have a plan in place for how they can be met. You can do this by talking to the learner, attending any meetings arranged for practice educators by the learner's course and by carefully reading available guidance such as programme handbooks and assessors guides. Consider the early inclusion of any other people that you intend to involve in the learner's assessment, such as colleagues, your manager and the people who are receiving your services and their carers, to ensure that they understand how they will be expected to contribute to the process (revisit Part One of this book for more ideas on what you may need to do in this planning phase). Seek clarification if there is anything that you are unsure about – the student's university-based tutor or your organisation's workforce development team should be able to help.

In Part One, we established the importance of encouraging and enabling people to take responsibility for their own learning and suggested that the development of an effective partnership was one of the ways that this could be facilitated. Partnership working is particularly important in assessment, as it enables you to address (but not solve) the inevitable power imbalance that results from your role as the learner's assessor (Walker et al., 2008). It also provides an opportunity to negotiate and agree reasonable adjustments for any additional needs that a learner may have. By encouraging and supporting the learner to make decisions about how and when they are assessed, you will enable them to retain some control which will hopefully increase the chances of a successful outcome (Knowles, 1980). This can be developed further by ensuring that you provide frequent opportunities for self-assessment and establish and facilitate a right to reply to your assessment judgements. Ensuring that self-evaluation and the critical analysis of feedback received are an integral part of assessment will not only address power issues but will also support the development of self-awareness and critical practice – essential components of professional capability (Barnett and Coate, 2005; BASW, 2018).

In most social work learning situations the learner will carry ultimate responsibility for ensuring they provide the evidence needed by the end of their placement or learning experience. However, you will need to facilitate this process by providing appropriate opportunities for assessment to be carried out. The planning and organisation of the assessment process should therefore be seen as a shared responsibility between the learner and the practice educator with early discussion important to ensure that the learner understands their responsibilities within the process (see Part One for more on planning and organisation and Part Two for planning learning activities).

2. Deciding what you need to measure or assess – agreeing objectives

In simple terms, what you need to assess will be determined by the learning objectives that are agreed with a learner or have been specified by the course that they are undertaking. Some of these will be mandatory and will be clear from the beginning (e.g. meeting PCF/KSS standards) while others will be identified as the placement unfolds. It is widely agreed that it is important that the process for assessing learners is transparent and that assessment outcomes are clearly linked to agreed learning objectives (Biggs, 2003). In Chapter 6 we looked in detail at how to work in partnership to develop tailored objectives that reflect what is known about a learner and their learning context. We established that doing so would ensure you develop objectives that are achievable, relevant, understood by the learner, take into account any additional needs that they may have and reflect the stage of development that they have reached.

However, because the professional assessment frameworks for practice placements (e.g. PCF and KSSs) and are far too detailed and complex for individual learning objectives to be agreed for every requirement, it is normal for the learning objectives agreed for placements to be fairly broad. This can cause some difficulties once the placement begins because, while broad objectives provide a general direction of travel and highlight certain experiences that need to be provided, it is not always clear how the work a learner is doing will specifically enable them to meet all of their professional requirements. It is therefore important that early discussions clarify how the experiences that the learner will be having in the placement link to each of the domains of the PCF. Using a case study or having a detailed discussion about a shadowing experience may help with this process. Ongoing discussions using the PCF/KSSs within each supervision session will then normally be enough to ensure that evidence is identified, discussed and evaluated in an organic and collaborative manner as the placement progresses.

However, there will be occasions when this organic process of learning and evidence collection does not work so well. This may be because there is a misunderstanding or disagreement about what has been achieved or because there are specific areas of practice where evidence is not being generated at an appropriate level. Through the following case study we will explore how a practice educator and learner can work in partnership to address this type of difficulty by agreeing more specific learning objectives which clarify expectations and improve the learner's chances of success.

CASE STUDY **10.1**

Leah is a final-year social work student who still needs to demonstrate to Arvind, her practice educator, that she is able to manage risk. The relevant part of the PCF that Arvind is concerned about is in the Intervention and Skills Domain where the following example of relevant practice is provided – to recognise the factors that create or exacerbate risk to individuals, families or carers, to the public or to professionals, including yourself, and contribute to the assessment and management of risk (BASW, 2018).

Leah and Arvind have spent time in supervision thinking about how Leah can provide evidence relating to this important aspect of her professional capability. They both agree that she would have the opportunity to do so through her work with Mr and Mrs Smith, who are both 93 years old and are currently living in their own home with some support from their daughter, Jane. Jane is worried about the risks faced by her parents at home and wants them to consider a move to sheltered accommodation. Mr and Mrs Smith have always said that they want to stay in their own home and Jane finds it difficult to express her concerns to them.

Arvind arranges to observe Leah in a meeting with Mr and Mrs Smith and their daughter. Before the meeting Arvind and Leah discuss her proposed approach and jointly identify some behaviours and actions that would enable Leah to evidence her capability. As a result of this discussion they agree the following list of objectives, related to the more generic PCF standard, for Leah to meet. During the meeting Leah will:

- *provide an opportunity for Jane to honestly and openly express her concerns to her parents and identify the exact nature of the risks she feels that they are facing;*

- *accurately and clearly summarise Jane's concerns and check that Mr and Mrs Smith understand why she is so worried;*

- *provide Mr and Mrs Smith with the opportunity to honestly and openly express their perception of the risks and benefits associated with staying at home;*

- *accurately and clearly summarise Mr and Mrs Smith's views and check that Jane understands their views;*

- *propose an action plan which includes an independent assessment of risk by an occupational therapist.*

These specific objectives enable Leah to understand exactly what she needs to do in the context of this current case to demonstrate her capability in the Intervention and Skills Domain of the PCF (BASW, 2018). They will also help Arvind to focus on specific and agreed aspects of Leah's practice in his assessment.

---

3. Deciding how to assess or measure it – applying standards

Knowing what to assess is of course important, but it can only give you a starting point for making a judgement about practice capability. Once you have agreed what you need to assess, you have to plan with the learner how you will go about gathering the information you need to reach a decision. In the next chapter we explore some of the tools and methods that practice educators regularly use to gather evidence, but before you can decide which of these tools you would like to use, you need to know a little more about how to judge their strengths and weaknesses.

There are a number of different definitions of 'good' assessment that can be used to critically evaluate the methods we use to gather evidence about practice (e.g. Brown, 2001; Singh, 2001; Doel et al., 1996). The Practice Educator Professional Standards (CSW, 2012a) require practice educators to ensure that any assessment that they undertake is based on evidence which meets the following standards:

- Relevant

  Does the selected assessment strategy enable the learner to demonstrate achievement of their learning outcomes?

- Valid

  Does the evidence presented demonstrate competent practice that is appropriate to the particular requirement being assessed at the time?

- Reliable

  Will the same results be achieved if the learner was assessed again in the same situation? Will different students with similar levels of competence be assessed at the same level in similar assessment tasks? Will different assessors achieve the same assessment results?

  What are the sources of bias? Have any assumptions been made that cannot be justified?

- Sufficient

  Is the evidence drawn from a large enough sample to ensure accuracy (e.g. from a whole interview not just a brief conversation)? Evidence should not just come from a one-off event but should be drawn from several occasions across the placement showing that the skill or knowledge has been learnt and can be applied at different times and in different contexts.

- Authentic

  Is the evidence presented definitely the work of the individual being assessed? If joint working has been involved, the assessor should be aware of the level of support provided for the learner and how much of the work was actually done by the learner.

Few assessment methods are flawless and it is particularly difficult to undertake good qual-ity assessment in work-based learning situations where so many variables are outside the direct control of the practice educator and the learner. However, careful assessment design and using a combination of methods can minimise the inaccuracies and improve the quality of the outcome. See Chapter 11 for more details of how this can be done.

Ideas for practice

- Increase the relevance of the evidence you gather by using a method that is appropriate to the learning objective. For instance, if you want a learner to demonstrate that they have a particular skill such as communication, use a method that enables you to see the learner applying the skill (e.g. direct observation) rather than a method which will test theoretical knowledge of a skill (e.g. an assignment) or ability to reflect on their use of a skill (e.g. reflective log).

- Increase the reliability of your evidence by employing a range of different methods to gather evidence – learners may perform better in some types of tasks than in others or may have additional needs that make some activities particularly challenging.

- Increase the reliability of your evidence by sampling sufficient practice or knowledge so you can be confident that any judgements you reach are based on an accurate picture of the learner's capability (Singh, 2001). Sample performance in different settings and on different days to avoid 'fluke' assessment judgements.

- Increase the relevance and validity of the evidence you gather by ensuring that learning objectives are clear and measurable. For example, assessing a learner's 'good communication skills' would be much more subjective and difficult to judge than specifically assessing whether a learner was able to communicate a particular message to a service user and be understood.

4. Agreeing what you will be looking for – using assessment criteria

Once you have decided what you need to assess and the methods you are going to use, you need to start the process of collecting evidence. This is not always as straightforward as you may initially think. There is plenty of scope for misunderstanding if those involved in the process of gathering evidence have not explicitly agreed what type and quality of evidence is needed to make a judgement about whether requirements have been met or not. While it will not be necessary or even possible to have a very detailed discussion about how you will be assessing every aspect of a learner's practice, there will be times that you do need to use a more structured approach to increase the transparency of the decision-making process. This is particularly important when there is any disagreement about the evidence that is being collected.

If we return to the case study from earlier in this chapter, Arvind and Leah agreed that one of the learning objectives that Leah would be assessed against was to *provide an opportunity for Jane to honestly and openly express her concerns to her parents and identify the exact nature of the risks she feels that they are facing.*

Unless Leah and Arvind agree assessment criteria that explicitly set out what Arvind is expecting to see before the observation takes place, there is a danger that they may have a different understanding of which aspects of practice are most significant and what good-enough practice is expected to look like.

Examples of assessment criteria relating to this objective that could be agreed include the following.

- *Very poor/unacceptable practice.* Leah does not ask Jane in the meeting how she feels about the risks that her parents are facing and after the meeting claims that Jane obviously didn't have any concerns because she didn't raise them herself.

- *Poor practice.* Leah asks Jane to describe how she is feeling about risk but does not support her or provide any encouragement when her parents disagree with her views.

- *Good-enough practice.* Leah asks Jane to describe how she is feeling about risk and provides some limited support when her parents disagree by suggesting that her parents listen to everything she has to say before they have their say.

- *Good practice.* Leah talks to Jane before the meeting and helps her to identify the key points she wants to raise and the evidence that she has to support those points. She suggests that Jane writes down her points to help her remember them and give her confidence in the meeting. In the meeting Leah provides support to Jane by asking questions which encourage her to fully and honestly express her concerns.

ACTIVITY 10.1

Write some of your own assessment criteria for Leah's learning objective 'to provide an opportunity for Jane to honestly and openly express her concerns to her parents and identify the exact nature of the risks she feels that they are facing'. Make sure you are particularly clear about where the border falls between pass and fail. You could focus on body language or communication skills and think of what you would expect to see Leah do to demonstrate her competence in this area of practice.

Comment

There are many different assessment criteria that could be agreed. The focus of the criteria developed will depend on a number of factors including the specific nature of the work being undertaken and the individual needs of the learner (this could be based on a previous observation of their practice). When you are completing this activity the criteria you use can be tailored to reflect the specific learning needs of an individual student who you may have in mind.

5. Judging or weighing evidence – reaching an assessment decision

So, we have agreed what to assess, how we will be gathering evidence and what specifically we will be looking for during the evidence-gathering process and now we need to reach a judgement about a learner's practice capability. This is hopefully the point at which we can go back to the PCF and/or the KSS for some clear guidance about whether the learner has met the requirements or not. However, despite the clear improvements that they offer over previous assessment frameworks, the PCF and the KSSs still cannot tell us with any degree of certainty what good-enough professional performance will look like in practice. This is because what is considered to be 'good enough' varies from context to context, learner to learner and practice educator to practice educator and is therefore dependent on too many interacting factors for any assessment system to be detailed enough to take away an assessor's doubts about the validity of their judgements. As a consequence, any decision that you reach about the evidence a learner generates will be based on your own views about expected standards and approaches to practice – and that will inevitably be highly subjective. For example, a social work student in a day centre for older people might be expected by their practice educator to take responsibility for planning and running activity groups in order to demonstrate their capability. However, a similar student working in a drug rehabilitation programme may only be expected to be involved in a support role in similar groups because their practice educator might think that the facilitation role was too complex for a student to take on. In the second case, the practice educator could quite legitimately think that capability could be demonstrated by the student providing appropriate support in the group and by demonstrating a clear understanding of the processes involved.

Subjectivity not only affects what learners are expected to do but the standards they are expected to achieve. Shardlow (1989, cited in Shardlow and Doel, 1996) noted very wide variations in assessment judgements made about the same piece of practice by different practice educators. According to Cowburn et al. (2000), this is because the assessment of social work competence can never be measured in absolute terms as the people carrying out the assessment are not neutral and are unable to act as value-free collectors of evidence.

To add to this already complex picture, as we will see in the next chapter, much of the evidence available to practice educators relies heavily on learners' self-evaluations. This type of evidence adds yet another layer of subjectivity to the decision-making process, raising some very real questions about the reliability of any judgements that practice educators are able to reach about practice!

To overcome some of the difficulties described above, Shardlow and Doel (1996) encourage practice educators to triangulate their assessments. This suggestion is based on the hypothesis that when two or more pieces of evidence from different assessors, assessment methods or contexts correspond with each other, it is more likely that an accurate judgement has been reached. Triangulation involves practice educators and learners working together to identify, collate and compare evidence from different sources (e.g. direct observation, self-assessment, feedback from a service user, feedback from colleagues). When this triangulation exercise is carried out, assessment judgements are no longer based on the opinion of a single individual or from a single event. The strength of evidence produced will therefore be increased and the practice educator can be more confident that their assessment judgement is both accurate and fair.

So, we have established that you will face a difficult task judging evidence that you gather because of the complex and context-dependent nature of the assessment decisions that you are being required to make. Considering the following questions may help you to think more analytically about the context and be more confident about reaching judgements about the holistic evidence presented to you by learners.

- What level is the student at with their development and what can you reasonably expect a learner at this stage of development to achieve in the specific area of competence? (Bear in mind previous experience of undertaking this type of work as well as the stage they have reached in their course.)

- Does the learner have any additional needs which should have been taken into account either in the way they are being assessed (method) or when judging the outcomes they have achieved. For example a student with dyslexia may need material that is going to be discussed in supervision sent to them before the session to enable them to perform as well in a reflective discussion as a peer without dyslexia.

- How complex or challenging was the specific piece of work that the learner was undertaking at the time of the assessment – was this more or less challenging than a learner at their stage of development would normally expect to undertake? Do you need to make allowances for this in reaching your judgement?

- What impact did assessment anxiety or the assessment method have on the learner's performance? Do you need to take this into account or provide further opportunities for the learner to demonstrate competence?

- How good is the quality of each piece of the evidence you and other assessors have gathered – is it relevant, valid, reliable and sufficient?

- Has triangulation helped to confirm your assessment decision because the evidence agrees or are there disagreements between different pieces of evidence?

- If you have anomalous results, can you justify or explain them? Do some of the results need to be given greater emphasis than others? Should some be disregarded?

- Where there is a disagreement between pieces of evidence, has the learner's performance improved over time and does the most recent evidence demonstrate competence at a good-enough standard? Will you need further evidence or are you confident that performance has reliably improved in this area?

So you can see that when it comes to assessing practice there can be no short cuts to answering the question: *What is good enough?* One of the ways that you will develop your confidence is through talking to others, either in a support group for practice educators or by working with a mentor or a colleague. Through this type of discussion, you will begin to be more confident about defining minimum standards of practice in your own workplace.

REFLECTION POINT

What opportunities already exist for you to discuss standards with other practice educators or a mentor?

If opportunities are currently limited, what will you do to ensure that you create opportunities to support your role?

6. Discussing the evidence with the learner and providing feedback

Throughout this book we have stressed the importance of working in partnership with learners to ensure that, wherever possible, they take responsibility for their own learning. Many supporters of reflective learning see self-assessment as a core skill in the development of professional practice and as an important part of the wider assessment process (Barnett and Coate, 2005; Knott and Scragg, 2010).

> *We cannot expect students to become competent professionals unless they learn to be actively involved in constructing and reconstructing notions of good practice as they proceed.*

(Boud, 1999, p122)

Including self-assessment in your overall strategy and openly discussing assessment decisions with learners will help them to develop skills in making critical judgements about their own performance and encourage them to take more control and responsibility for their own learning (Crisp et al., 2006). Self-assessment should not, therefore, be considered an alternative form of assessment but rather as an integral part of most other assessment methods (Cree, 2000, p30). For instance, you can encourage a learner to self-assess their practice after you have observed their practice or to self-assess a letter sent to a service user. In such situations, the self-assessment will be part of the overall learning and assessment process, allowing both learners' and practice educators' perspectives to be incorporated into final assessment judgements.

Despite the potential value of self-assessment, there are a number of problems with its use in practice. Learners can lack the self-assessment skills required to make meaningful contributions and may not have the expert knowledge needed to assess their practice (particularly at the early stages of learning). They can even feel resentful that they are being asked to do the assessor's job (Boud, 1999). You may need to provide support to the learner to build the skills and confidence they need to enable them to actively engage in meaningful self-evaluation. You will also need to help them understand the breadth and depth of analysis and evaluation that are appropriate.

To do this, the learner will need to learn how to:

- ask themselves challenging questions;
- critically appraise new information;
- identify their knowledge and skill gaps;
- compare their actual performance with the standard required for the outcome and be able to take action to close the gap.

Modelling critical reflection and self-evaluation in your own practice may significantly assist learners with this process.

Discussing the evidence you are drawing on with the learner before you reach an overall decision about their capability is not only a good idea from adult and professional learning perspectives, but also makes sense if we want to ensure that our assessment would stand up to scrutiny if judged against the standards for good assessment outlined earlier in this chapter. This is because:

- you will see only snapshots of the learner's practice – the learner can help you understand more about the context and the reasons why they have taken a particular approach;

- your judgements are subjective and the learner will have a different perspective – you need to understand how they perceive the situation in which they are practising as a check to your own interpretations and judgements;

- you will find out more about the learner's feelings, anxieties, perceptions of the task they have been given and the context in which they are working and how this may have impacted on their performance;

- you will be able to gauge the learner's levels of self-awareness about their performance – they may have made some mistakes, but if they can identify the mistakes for themselves and are clear about how they would do things differently next time, your overall assessment would be more positive than one you might make about someone who was not able to see that something had gone wrong;

- you can check that if you and the learner have been working to the same learning objectives and assessment criteria – this may help if there is a mismatch between your assessment and the learner's self-assessment.

So, we have established that encouraging and supporting self-assessment is an important part of discussions with learners about evidence gathered but it is of course only half of the story. Feedback from experienced practitioners, including from you in your practice educator role, is an essential part of the learning process and will help to shape learning and provide detailed feedback on the evidence you have gathered from assessment activities. One of the key skills to develop in your practice education role is the ability to give feedback in a way that actively supports learning and development.

> *Feedback is the process of relaying to a person your observations, impressions, feelings or other evaluative information about that person's behaviour for their use and learning.*

> (Ford and Jones, 1987, p74)

The processes of assessment can generate feedback information that can be used by learners to enhance learning and achievement. Good-quality feedback on performance should therefore have a central role in aligned learning, teaching and assessment strategies. If learners are going to make use of feedback for development they should:

- know what standard they are aiming for (clear and agreed assessment criteria);

- be able to compare what they have achieved with the standard they are aiming at;

- understand what they need to do to close the gap and achieve the required standard.

> Sadler (1989), cited in Juwah et al. (2004)

Providing good-quality feedback will empower learners to take control of their own learning. However, it is not enough to simply tell learners about the strengths and weaknesses of their work and hope that they will be able to understand how to use the information for development. Try to help learners to work out how they can make use of the feedback and bridge the gap between what they are currently achieving and what is expected.

As stated in Part Two, if you have a thorough understanding of what someone will be able to do as a result of their learning (learning objectives), then you can effectively plan to help someone achieve it. More importantly, by knowing how well you need it to be done (assessment criteria), you and they will be able to tell more accurately if and when they are achieving it.

Good-quality feedback, both positive and negative, maintains self-esteem and provides learners with choice. Destructive feedback leaves learners feeling demotivated with nothing to build on. There is always an element of nervousness about giving and receiving feedback but it can be lessened if there is a shared intent and awareness that it may be a creative process leading to personal and professional development by both sides.

Obviously the feedback should be helpful and understandable. It may have to tackle awkward or difficult areas. By concentrating on the practice issues/behaviour, the work or the learning outcomes (i.e. the tasks, processes) rather than the learner's personality, attributes or abilities, you should be able to avoid it becoming 'personal' (i.e. being seen as a criticism of the learner as a person).

For example, as lecturers marking an assignment we might say that *the text lacks a critical analysis of the main issues* rather than *you lack critical analysis.* By focusing on what is being produced it is much easier to see what extra input, skills or knowledge is needed to help develop that area of work. It is also less discriminatory – it does not assume that the person is or isn't something. In our example, the person may be very critically analytical in their practice; it is just that at this time they are unable to articulate it in their writing.

Principles of good feedback:

- *Specific rather than general.*
- *Refers to behaviour rather than the person.*
- *Clear – one message at a time, not too much information.*
- *Provided promptly to minimise unnecessary stress.*
- *Comes quickly to the point, without losing the message.*
- *Descriptive rather than evaluative.*
- *Recognises positive aspects, but does not apologise for addressing negatives.*
- *Is confident.*
- *Consistent – check feedback has been understood.*

- *Appropriate – linked to criteria and competences.*

- *Recorded so that the learner can take the information away with them.*

- *Positive – this is the beginning of the solution.*

Adapted from Sharp and Danbury (1999)

ACTIVITY 10.2

You have to give feedback to a learner who does not make eye contact with people when she is talking to them. What is wrong with the following statement? How can you improve it?

You look strange and distant when you are talking to people; no one likes people who can't make eye contact.

Comment

To complete this activity you need to think about how you can depersonalise this feedback – removing the focus from the learner and their characteristics and instead concentrating on the impact of their practice at the time. Consider how you can use your feedback as a starting point for discussion which encourages the learner to consider how values, personality traits and cultural norms are linked to their use of eye contact and the importance of using eye contact appropriately to meet the needs of the person being communicated with in professional practice.

Learning outcomes will generally be improved when there is effective encouragement and support for the learner to self-evaluate as well as receive feedback in a constructive manner, enabling the learner to extend their learning and build confidence in themselves on their route to becoming critically reflective practitioners.

7. Reaching and documenting an assessment decision

So far we have looked at how you can decide what needs to be assessed and we have explored ways in which you can assess aspects of practice. We will now consider how you can bring the elements of assessment together to reach an overall assessment decision. In the case of a social work student or NQSW this will normally involve making a pass/fail decision. In doing so it is important that you refer to the specific guidance produced by the learner's programme and seek support if you are unsure about procedures or need advice with regard to your assessment decision. The guidance provided should clearly set out the expectations for learners with regard to meeting standards in each placement or practice learning situation.

Although you will need to have a general feel for overall progress at all times during the placement and ensure that the learner keeps good records of progress towards meeting objectives, there are specific points where you and the learner will formally be required to bring evidence together to enable you to make judgements about performance. In the case of a social work student these will normally be:

- at the mid-point of the placement where you will probably need to provide an interim review;

- at the end of the placement when you will need to provide a final report and make a pass/fail recommendation.

Individual programme requirements will vary with regard to documenting and reporting final assessments. Many programmes now give the majority of the responsibility for documenting and evaluating evidence to the student, with the practice educator's role limited to supporting the student in the development of their portfolio of evidence and the provision of a brief summative report. However, it is very important that you bear in mind that if a student/NQSW is failing or marginal, you will be required to justify your assessment decision with detailed references to specific evidence of lack of competence in relation to the PCF (BASW, 2018) and/or the relevant KSS (DoH, 2015; DfE, 2018). For this reason supervision notes and written feedback provided to the learner should contain enough detail to allow you to draw evidence together and make specific references to examples from practice if required.

Although you will have taken the views of others, such as the learner, your colleagues, service users and carers, into account in your assessment journey, the responsibility for the final assessment decision will rest with you as the practice educator. However, even at this point the importance of partnership with the learner is still strong. If you have worked collaboratively throughout the placement, your assessment decision should hold no surprises for the learner but it is still important to give the learner an opportunity to read and comment on your report. Many programmes will have a formal requirement for this to happen.

In your final assessment report you should ensure that your decisions/recommendations are linked to the PCF (BASW, 2018) or other relevant standards such as the KSSs (DoH, 2015; DoE, 2018) and can be supported by clear evidence either from the learner's portfolio or through examples that you provide from the placement experience. A balanced report will highlight both strengths and areas for future development. Don't shy away from highlighting these learning needs – they do not indicate a weak learner but rather provide an indication of a commitment to ongoing development.

The final report can emerge naturally out of an effective collaboration. Work with the learner and encourage them to highlight their most valued learning from the experience, their strengths and their development needs. If you agree, incorporate the learner's ideas into the report. If you disagree, base the report on your views but actively support the learner to honestly express their different views in their comments on your report. The report and the report development process are further opportunities for meaningful learning to emerge from the assessment process and form the end point of the seven stages of assessment.

In the next chapter we will look in greater depth at some of the methods that you can use to assess learners in the workplace.

Chapter 11

Assessment methods and their use in the workplace

Assessing professional performance in the workplace requires a flexible and creative approach. As we have already discussed, the way that a learner is assessed will have a major impact on the quality and direction of their learning and it is therefore important to give careful consideration to the methods that you use to gather evidence and to reach judgements about practice competence. They should:

- be aligned with your intended learning outcome;

- be relevant, valid, reliable, sufficient and authentic;

- take into account your work environment, service users and the learner.

In this chapter we will explore a range of methods including:

- supervision discussions;

- logs, diaries and reflective journals;

- critical incident analysis;

- case studies;

- projects;

- direct observation of practice;

- indirect or informal observation of practice;

- evidence from practice or from artefacts;

- feedback from service users;

- feedback from colleagues and other professionals.

Because of the limitations of space and of our own creativity, this should not be considered a comprehensive list – when you gain more experience and confidence in your role you will adapt these methods and will be able to develop and explore alternative approaches. All of the methods included here provide opportunities for learners to play an active role in the assessment process and will help you to assess a learner's ability to complete specific tasks or functions as well as make judgements about their overall capability. As you read about each of the methods, reflect on their relative strengths and weaknesses using the standards for good assessment provided in the previous chapter. As well as considering each method individually, you could consider how they could be combined to triangulate evidence and overcome any weaknesses that you have identified.

Supervision discussions

Supervision discussions are one of the main sources of evidence that can be drawn on when you are assessing work-based learners. You can find out what a learner has been doing and what they plan to do, as well as gaining an insight into their thoughts and feelings about practice. You will also be able to test many aspects of capability such as their level of resilience, emotional intelligence and ability to transfer knowledge and skills from one context to another and to apply theory to practice. Because discussions are normally frequent, wide-ranging and formally recorded they can help you to assess holistically both across the domains of the PCF (BASW, 2018) and/or the KSSs (DoH, 2015; DfE, 2018) and over time.

Although supervision discussions are undoubtedly a rich source of assessment information, it should be remembered that any evidence you gain regarding practice is provided by the individual learner and is therefore selective and subjective (Singh, 2001). Learners may choose not to share aspects of their experiences with you, might focus on the positives to create a 'good impression' or get stuck in an analysis of the mistakes they feel they have made. Their inexperience could lead to significant aspects of a situation going unnoticed or being misinterpreted and they may not understand what needs to be reported and discussed. It is also likely that by the time learners come to supervision, there will be a great deal that they no longer remember accurately enough to make discussions meaningful (Martin et al., 2010; Newell, 1992). Taking all of these factors into account we can see that the information available to you in a supervision session may not be an accurate or complete account of practice and will, of course, always be presented from the learner's own perspective.

Because evidence collection in supervision depends on the interaction between you and the learner, you need to remember that the quality and quantity of the information you gain will be partially dependent on the learner's reporting and reflective skills. It is worth bearing in mind that a person who is good in practice will not necessarily be able to talk confidently and comprehensively about what they have done and a weak practitioner may tell a very good tale! You need, therefore, to use objectives and criteria to ensure that you and the learner understand whether it is their ability to describe, analyse and evaluate practice, the practice itself or both that will be the focus of your attention. Your skills as a facilitator are also relevant – skilled questioners elicit more accurate and detailed information (positive and or negative) than less skilled questioners. Skilled questioners are also more likely to gain more information about overall capability by employing techniques that provide appropriate challenges to learners which enable judgements to be made about, for instance, their depth and breadth of understanding. In supervision you will be a key part of the learning environment and you need to remember that the relationship you develop and the style and quality of questioning you adopt will have a significant impact on the performance of the learner (Moon, 2002; Davys and Beddoe, 2010). You should therefore take this into account when you judge any evidence gained from supervision discussions – reflecting on the role you have played and the support you have provided. It may be useful, for instance, to ask yourself questions such as 'was the learner able to analyse their own response to that situation because they have good levels of emotional intelligence or was it because I asked a series of leading questions that enabled them to give me the answers I wanted to hear?' Another issue with using supervision for assessment purposes is that the complexities of many sessions make it impossible to agree specific assessment objectives and criteria for the discussions that take place. This means that any judgements reached could be open to criticism on the basis of both fairness and accuracy because learners would not have known when and how they were being assessed (Shardlow and Doel, 1996). Telling learners they are being assessed 'all of the time' would not solve the problem. At any point in time, learners would still not know what was being assessed or which standards you were using to judge their performance. This could leave them in a constant state of anxiety and uncertainty, reducing the likelihood of open and honest reflections and undermining opportunities for learning in supervision sessions. Although all of the difficulties described above could theoretically be overcome by agreeing that supervision would not be used for summative assessment, this could never be a satisfactory solution. Practice educators could not agree to disregard evidence of poor, dangerous or unsound practice disclosed in a supervision discussion. Therefore, while some assurances can be provided that learners can openly discuss less-than-perfect aspects of their practice without penalty, it is important that they understand that supervision discussions can and will be used as a source of assessment material. A working agreement between yourself and the learner should be reached on how this will be managed, with a particular emphasis on the limits that are set around confidentiality.

ACTIVITY **11.1**

You are planning to discuss a piece of legislation within a supervision session with a social work student. You would like to use this discussion as evidence that the student has a good understanding of how the legislation can be applied in practice for inclusion in their final report. It should be possible for you to do so both fairly and accurately, but what will you need to do before the session to make sure that this is the case?

Comment

In order to make this a fair and accurate assessment you would need to consider agreeing learning objectives and assessment criteria with the student before the supervision session takes place. The learning objectives should clearly indicate that the learner needs to focus on how their knowledge will be applied in practice. It may be helpful to also give the learner an example of how you are expecting them to meet the learning objective – modelling this yourself when you are talking about a case with them or using a case study in supervision.

Logs, diaries, reflective journals

Reflective recording is widely accepted as a valuable learning and development tool in professional education (e.g. Rutter and Brown, 2015), but care will be needed when you use reflective recordings for assessment purposes. Reflective recordings, like other indirect assessment methods, are highly subjective and can provide an incomplete picture because learners select what they include and what they leave out (Hobbs, 2007). Nevertheless, Moon (1999) believes that reflective material can be used for assessment purposes, as long as appropriate assessment criteria are agreed in advance between practice educators and learners. As with supervision discussions, it is particularly important to be clear about whether it is the practice itself, the quality of the reflection on the practice or both that is being assessed when the criteria are set. Learners who know they are primarily being assessed on the quality of their reflection will be able to confidently record examples of their practice that need further development. However, learners who know that they are being assessed purely on the outcomes of their practice will not want to include less-than-perfect examples in their records.

It is a good idea to openly discuss the conflicts that could arise from using reflective recording for the purposes of both assessment and learning with the learner from an early stage and agree a strategy for how this will be managed. You could, for example, agree to share some, but not all, of the learner's reflective recording. As part of your discussion with the learner you should stress the value you place on reflective recording for learning and provide reassurance about the way that you will interpret and evaluate the material that they chose to share with you. For example, if the learner includes evidence of poor or weak practice alongside a clear analysis of what went wrong, together with the steps they have taken to develop practice for the future, make it clear that you would consider this to be positive evidence of their ability to critically analyse, evaluate situations and take responsibility for their own learning. Doing so will show the learner that poor or weak practice within a developmental context can still provide valuable evidence of professional competence and capability. It may also be worth considering sharing some of your own reflective recordings to model good practice and demonstrate the importance of identifying areas for development.

Critical incident analysis

Critical incident analysis methodologies have been developed to enable social work learners to explore significant incidents from their practice experience and to use the learning from this exploration to inform future practice (Davies and Kinloch, 2000; CSW, 2012b). They can also be useful assessment tools as they can give you an insight into a learner's skills in analysis, problem-solving and evaluation in practice situations. They also give an indication of a learner's levels of self-awareness, emotional intelligence and ability to reflect on their own practice. Critical incident analyses can be completed either as a specific piece of reflective writing or as verbal activities within supervision sessions. This means that the issues that were raised above in our explorations of supervision discussions and reflective recording are all relevant when considering the use of this assessment tool.

Critical incident analyses can be based on both positive and negative experiences, but should be used to explore situations in which significant learning has taken place. When asking learners to complete a critical incident analysis, you should ask for:

- a brief description of context;
- a description of what the learner did;
- an exploration of how theory influenced what the learner did and thought;

- an account of the outcomes of the intervention;

- what alternatives were considered and why they were rejected;

- how the learner would tackle the same incident differently on another occasion;

- what learning the learner took away and how it will influence their future practice.

ACTIVITY **11.2**

Using the headings given above, write a critical incident analysis of an incident you were involved in during the last month. How could your analysis be used to assess your practice against either the PCF (BASW, 2018) or the KSS that is relevant to your area of practice?

Comment

Writing your own critical incident analysis will help you to be more confident using this method with others. Consider adding the critical incident analysis that you produce for this exercise to your practice educator 'toolkit'. You can share it with learners to illustrate the value of the tool in practice and provide an example of a critical incident analysis relevant to the workplace the student/learner is in.

Case studies

Case studies can be used to enable learners to apply professional knowledge and understanding to specific material provided by the practice educator in a safe environment (often within supervision). Material for case studies can be written specifically by the practice educator (like the case studies included in this book) or can be drawn from anonymised case records. It is even possible to use videos, soap operas or documentaries as sources, as these often deal with some challenging scenarios and can bring case study work to life. Learners are presented with case material and are asked to work through it, analysing issues, making assessments and exploring solutions to presenting problems. This can be done either independently or in partnership with you or another experienced social worker.

This type of learning and assessment tool enables the learner to explore options, take risks and make mistakes with no danger to either themselves or service users. Through either a supervision discussion or the preparation of a written report, the learner can demonstrate the way that they would approach the case, apply theory to practice, take decisions and so on. This can provide good material for assessment and may be particularly useful in deciding whether a learner is ready to take responsibility for working alone with service users.

Case study material can also be used to assess knowledge and understanding that cannot be directly tested in a particular learning environment: for instance, case studies that involve working with people with cultural backgrounds not generally encountered in a particular service.

As with the other methods we have discussed, it is important that there is a clear understanding about what will be assessed, how it will be assessed (assessment criteria) and the purpose of the assessment (formative or summative). Because case study work allows safe experimentation, its most useful role is probably as a learning tool and a way of formatively assessing a learner's knowledge, skills and attributes. However, case studies can be used quite effectively as a way of summatively assessing knowledge and values that may be difficult to test in other ways.

It is worth considering that for a variety of reasons learners can perform very differently in a simulation such as a case study than they will in a real-life situation, so assessments based on any form of simulation would ideally need to be triangulated with more direct forms of evidence.

ACTIVITY 11.3

Prepare a case study using some of the ideas above and think about how you would use this to assess a learner.

Comment

Having selected some material for use as a case study with the learner, you need to think about what learning objective the case study could help a learner meet and what assessment criteria you would use. How would you involve the learner in developing learning objectives and assessment criteria?

Projects

A project is a specific task that a learner is asked to complete, either on their own or in collaboration with others. Examples of projects sometimes given to qualifying students in placements include setting up new groups for service users or carers, undertaking consultations with service users, carrying out pieces of research such as feasibility studies, designing induction programmes and developing publicity materials for services.

Because projects can be quite time-consuming and can take on a life of their own, it is important that focus is maintained on the learner's overall learning objectives and that you and the learner clearly establish that they will be able to demonstrate appropriate achievement throughout the project. Assessment criteria should be agreed at the start of the project to enable the learner to understand how and when they will be judged. Particular care should be taken to establish whether the assessment will look at the outcomes of the project, the way that the outcomes were achieved, or the way that the project was evaluated by the learner – or a combination of all three.

Project work can give learners a degree of autonomy and provide an opportunity to see a piece of work through from beginning to end, but to be a relevant and reliable assessment method it is important to be sure that the project is feasible in terms of resources and achievable in the time available within the placement.

Can you think of any projects that a learner could undertake in your workplace? Which domains of the PCF/KSS would this project enable you to assess?

Comment

Consider developing a list of potential outline projects for discussion with students and other learners as this will allow them to choose a project that matches their interests and learning needs. Link the projects to professional requirements that could be met through the project. Think about how you could involve your team and service users and carers in this process.

Direct observation of practice

Direct observation of practice is a requirement for learners on qualifying social work courses and, in England, is widely used to assess practitioners during their first year in employment (ASYE). Regular observation is also now being introduced by many employing organisations as a way of checking that quality practice of is maintained throughout a social worker's professional career. The confident use of observation, as a method of assessing practice, is therefore a core requirement for all with responsibility for workplace assessment.

In its simplest form direct observation involves watching a task being undertaken, evaluating performance and providing feedback. Instinctively, we tend to believe that direct observation is an accurate assessment tool because we are able to see a person practise with our own eyes. However, it is important to bear in mind that observations can only ever provide a possibly non-representative snapshot of practice and without a fuller understanding of context and background it may be difficult to accurately evaluate what is seen. Another significant challenge is that because there is rarely one way to interpret a situation or one effective way to practise, any judgement that you make is highly subjective and needs to be opened up to critical scrutiny.

While little research has been undertaken to evaluate the effectiveness of observation in social work, large-scale research projects on the assessment of teaching practice have raised very serious concerns about the reliability and accuracy of the method (Gates Foundation, 2013; Murphy, 2013). A recent scoping review published by Research in Practice concluded that while observation does have a useful role to play in the assessment of social workers, it should be used with caution (Ruch, 2015). The report highlighted the crucial importance of the skills of the observer and reported that standardising methods, assessment objectives and criteria increases the reliability of judgements made. Important other key findings were that direct observation was considered to be most valuable (by both observers and observees) when it was experienced as developmental and constructive and when the process included opportunities for meaningful reflective dialogue.

Because the direct observation of even of a short piece of practice will potentially generate an enormous amount of data, it is a good idea to agree in advance some very specific objectives and assessment criteria. These objectives should relate to particular aspects of practice that either you, as the practice educator want to look at in more detail or that the learner would like feedback about. Try to keep the objectives very specific, e.g. not just how the learner uses communication skills but how the learner uses open questions, because this will help both you and the learner to be clear about what you are looking for. Both the practice educator and the learner should contribute to this process as this will make it more likely that the observation focuses on the learner's specific individual learning needs and that both parties are clear about the standards required. Having clear objectives and assessment criteria will enable the practice educator to focus on specific areas of the practice and to write detailed notes on these areas during the observation. This will help he practice educator provide good-quality feedback and increase the accuracy and fairness of the assessment judgement. It will also ensure that the learner has a clear focus for their self-evaluation and is able to retain some control over their learning and assessment. Although the objectives provide a focus for the observation they should not prevent you from noting and providing feedback about more general aspects of practice that are very poor or very good. However, where possible, the majority of the feedback you give should relate to the objectives agreed before the observation (University of York, 2000; Davys and Beddoe, 2015).

Direct observation of practice can provoke anxiety in some learners, which could have an adverse impact on their performance. To ensure that this type of assessment is as fair and accurate as possible, Doel et al. (1996) suggest an approach to observation that is integrated with learning. They say that, where possible, when observation is going to be used for assessment, practice educators should:

- discuss its use with learners early in the placement;

- discuss anxieties about the process openly;

- invite learners to observe their own practice (i.e. that of the practice educators) to build trust;

- evaluate their own practice openly with learners;

- enable the learner to move gradually from observer to participant to leader in practice situations as their confidence grows;

- undertake observations when the learner has reached an appropriate point of confidence and is used to taking the lead with the practice educator present.

Adapted from Doel et al. (1996)

ACTIVITY *11.5*

Ask a colleague to observe you making a telephone call/talking to a service user and give you feedback on your practice against the PCF (BASW, 2018).

How did this make you feel? Did you get any unexpected feedback? Can you learn anything from the way that the feedback was given to you?

Comment

Having recent experience of being observed will help you to understand how someone you are assessing may be feeling. However, as people respond differently to assessment situations, don't assume that your learners will feel exactly the same as you do. Reflecting on receiving feedback will help you to develop *your* own skills in giving feedback to others.

One of the biggest problems faced by practice educators when observing practice is separating their role as an assessor from their role as a practitioner (Humphrey, 2007). It is very hard to stay outside of the practice and observe as if you were looking through a one-way mirror. Agree with your learner in advance what your role will be in the observation and if and when you will intervene. You need to take care not to contaminate the evidence by acting as a co-worker rather than as an observer (Humphrey, 2007).

Indirect or informal observation

Where practice educators are working alongside a learner, there will be many opportunities for informal observation and assessment of their practice. Although this will be a rich source of evidence, there are some dangers associated with this method of assessment. If we think back to the criteria given in Chapter 10 for good assessment, we can see that it is important for learners to be clear about when, where and how they are being assessed. It will obviously be difficult to be transparent about the assessment process if there are no clear assessment objectives and if observation is taking place all of the time. This could be overcome by agreeing in advance that informal observation will be used for assessment and by discussing with the learner particular objectives for observations at different stages of their learning and development, for instance: *This week I will be particularly looking at your communication skills with service users.* You could then clearly set out the standards that you would be using in your assessment and agree relevant assessment criteria. The learner would then be aware that whenever you were in a position to observe them informally, you would be specifically looking at this area of their practice. You could provide feedback on your observations at agreed intervals and make clear links between your observations and assessment judgements (perhaps at supervision sessions).

Evidence from practice or artefacts

Learners can use material that they have produced as part of their professional practice for assessment purposes. Examples include letters, reports and assessments. It is particularly important when using this type of material to be clear about the assessment criteria you will be using, because requirements and expectations may vary between workplaces and between workers. Samples of work produced by experienced workers could provide learners with instances of good-enough practice. Unless there is a prescribed format for a task, a range of examples by different workers should be used to provide the learner with an insight into some of the different approaches that can be taken.

ACTIVITY 11.6

Write a list of criteria that you could use to assess a letter that a learner has written to introduce him/herself to a new service user. The criteria should provide a clear statement of what you would be looking for from the letter (content, quality of writing, appropriateness of style for audience, etc.). This will help the learner to know exactly what you think is good enough. It will also help you to assess the letter fairly.

Comment

Some of the criteria will reflect organisational procedures and policies but others may reflect your own preferred approach to the task. Be wary about imposing a particular way of working on a learner when other approaches could work equally well.

Ideas for practice

This is another area where collaboration with others in your team or organisation may be useful. Consider putting together a resources file with anonymised sample letters, forms, etc., that could be used by students and other learners. Incorporate a range of styles and approaches to enable the learner to understand that different approaches are acceptable (when this is the case).

Involvement of service users

It is widely accepted that the involvement of service users and carers in the assessment of health and social care learners is essential (Levin, 2004; CSW, 2012a; Croisdale-Appleby, 2014; Askheim et al., 2016). This is because, as experts in their own experiences, they are able to provide insights into a learner's practice which may otherwise go unnoticed. However, although most practice educators aspire to include the views of those in receipt of services, the challenges that arise from doing so can mean that the goal of achieving empowering and meaningful involvement are difficult to achieve (Askheim et al., 2016). According to Cabiati and Raineri (2016), a significant barrier to involvement is often the stigmatising attitudes of the professionals themselves, something they say that social work education still needs to work hard to address.

The concerns most commonly raised by the practice educators attending our workshops about the involvement of service users are:

- *Relevance and validity* – service users may be influenced by how much they liked the learner rather than by how effective they were, wanting to help the learners they liked with a good assessment and penalise those they didn't like with a poor assessment.

- *Reliability* – service users may not fully understand the criteria for measuring success and they may find benchmarking very difficult, particularly when their experience of social workers is fairly limited (expectations may be too high or too low).

- *Sufficiency* – it is not usually possible to engage with every service user and selecting a limited number to represent the whole user group can be problematic – it is impossible to know if the views of the selected few are representative of the whole group.

- *Authenticity* – people who have received a service may have their opinions shaped by the outcomes of the learner's work with them (which could be outside of the learner's control) rather than the learner's actual competence.

- *Practical difficulties* – service users in crisis may not want to participate, communication difficulties may make it difficult to ascertain views, etc.

Because of these concerns we are told by the practice educators that service user involvement is frequently limited to a one-way process of gathering information either through questionnaires sent out to selected service users or in a brief discussion following a direct observation. At this level there really is a danger that seeking feedback becomes a token gesture. If involvement is to be more meaningful, service users need to be valued as participants in the process, supported to understand their role and helped to feel confident about the criteria they should use to judge performance. Wherever possible, the way that contributions are made should be individually negotiated and directly linked to the PCF (BASW, 2018) or the KSSs (DoH, 2015; DfE, 2018), with consideration given to how information about overall capability can be gained through the information provided.

ACTIVITY **11.7**

Design a brief questionnaire to send out to users of your service to obtain feedback on one very specific aspect of a learner's practice.

Comment

Think how you could empower service users to make a meaningful contribution by providing information that would help them to understand what was expected from them, together with guidance on the criteria for the assessment. Remember to keep all guidance simple, straightforward and easy to understand.

Because feedback from service users will be an important tool, not just for assessment but also for learning, learners should be involved in deciding how and when service users are approached and should be fully informed of any responses received. It may also be worth thinking about other ways that this information could be gained more directly by learners to enable them to understand more about the impact of their practice on service users and to help them consider alternative approaches and methods – how about a three-way discussion (student, service user and practice educator) after a direct observation? What do you think are the benefits and barriers to this happening and how could you overcome them in your practice context?

Feedback from colleagues/other professionals

The final method we will consider is feedback from colleagues and other professionals. As with feedback from service users and carers, this is a valuable source of information and can provide insight and other perspectives on a learner's practice. However, it is worth bearing in mind that experienced professionals do not necessarily have the skills or knowledge to contribute meaningfully and fairly to the assessment of learners. Crisp et al. (2006) point out that willingness to participate in the process of assessment does not guarantee competence as an assessor. Anyone who is asked to provide feedback that will contribute to the assessment of a learner should be made aware of the learner's intended learning outcomes and must fully understand the assessment criteria that they should use.

It is a good idea to ask colleagues/other professionals to make a specific contribution to assessment rather than a general one, for example to comment on a particular aspect of capability or to undertake an observation of practice with negotiated assessment objectives. Some information, training and support may be needed to enable colleagues to participate in this way.

Summary of Part Three Domain C

- Making assessment strategies and methods, and the criteria used to assess them, clear and transparent is essential for the learner to progress.

- Getting the assessment 'wrong', i.e. misaligning it with the rest of the learning scheme, is likely to block learning and inhibit performance.

- While it is important for the safety of service users that social workers' competence is directly assessed in practice, it is also important to use assessment techniques that enable work-based assessors to gain an insight into the learner's transferable skills, such as the ability to construct and reconstruct knowledge and to think critically, because these are essential components of the broader professional capability.

- When designing an assessment strategy it is important to understand what you are aiming to achieve through the assessment process.

- 'Good' assessment is:
    - relevant;
    - valid;
    - reliable;
    - sufficient;
    - authentic.

- Assessing professional capability in the workplace requires a flexible and creative approach.

- Assessment methods. The tool that you choose should:
    - align with your intended learning outcome;
    - be relevant, valid, reliable, sufficient and authentic;
    - take into account your work environment, service users and the learner.

- To overcome some of the difficulties with assessment, practice educators can triangulate pieces of evidence.

- The nature of the assessment task that you will be facing is complex and highly dependent on the local circumstances of the learning experience you have provided.

FURTHER READING

Edmondson, D (2014) *Social work practice learning.* London: Sage.

This book is written for social work students and contains a very useful section on assessment which you could use with learners to plan their assessment strategy.

Cabiati, E and Raineri, M (2016) Learning from service users' involvement: a research about changing stigmatizing attitudes in social work students. *Social Work Education,* 35 (8), pp982–96.

Hughes, M (2017) What difference does it make? Findings of an impact study of service user and carer involvement on social work students' subsequent practice. *Social Work Education,* 36 (2), pp203–16.

Social Work Education (2006), 25 (4).

This is a special edition of this journal which explores and critically evaluates the involvement of users and carers in social work education. It contains papers written from professional, educational and service-user perspectives. Although it is now fairly old, it still contains some interesting and useful ideas.

Part Four
Applying learning from Domains A–C to address challenging practice situations

Introduction to Part Four

As you will have already discovered, the first three parts of this book have been developed to link directly to Domains A, B and C of the Practice Educator Professional Standards (CSW, 2012a). This has brought together the ideas and approaches most clearly related to each of the domains – helping those who are working towards meeting the Standards systematically build their knowledge and skills and generate evidence of practice capability linked specifically to the requirements. Although the authors felt that it was useful to approach the book in this way, we recognise that in the real world, dividing work-based learning into discrete domains can be a rather artificial thing to do. In Part Four, we will therefore, take a different approach – bringing ideas and principles together from all of the previous chapters in order to look more holistically at some of the most challenging aspects of being a practice educator.

In Chapter 12, we explore some of the challenges involved in forming and maintaining supervisory relationships and consider the impact of the quality of these relationships on learning in practice placements. The chapter includes some useful hints and tips for working effectively within supervision sessions and encourages readers to draw on their reflections on their own past experiences as a supervisee and current experiences as a supervisor as a foundation for future practice.

In Chapter 13 we consider the role of practice educators in supporting the development of resilience – arguing from a standpoint that a lack of resilience in the workforce is something that needs to be tackled as a matter of urgency by the profession. While it will become clear that more effective practice education is only part of a more wide-ranging solution, we will see that practice educators have a very important role to play.

In Chapter 14, we will move on to look at how the knowledge and skills from Domains A, B and C can be used by practice educators who are faced with a failing or marginal placement. We will consider the impact, on all involved, of being part of a learning experience where things are not going to plan. We will then explore a range of problem-solving strategies that can be adopted by practice educators to ensure they fulfil their vital gatekeeping function while treating learners fairly and with compassion.

Chapter 12

Applying learning from Domains A–C to develop an effective supervisory relationship

Introduction

There is a long tradition of managing and supporting social work learners through structured and regular one-to-one meetings – commonly called supervision sessions. In England it is expected that social work students will spend at least ninety minutes a week in formal meetings with their supervisor(s). These sessions provide opportunities for supervisors to monitor and manage learners' work, provide support, facilitate networking and enable and assess their learning (Morrison, 2005). Good quality supervision is seen as fundamental to effective service provision for social workers at every stage of their career, playing a central role in the promotion of reflective practice and accountable decision-making (SWTF, 2009a). The responsibility for providing supervision for students is a core part of the practice educator role and for many new practice educators the first placement that they support will also be their first experience of providing supervision. It is therefore unsurprising that most have at least some concerns about this aspect of their new role.

I know that although I was excited about the prospect of becoming a supervisor, I spent the first few weeks full of self-doubt – fearful that someone would find out that I didn't know what I was doing, worried that something would go horribly wrong. I felt ill-prepared and, at times, very alone with what felt like a significant new responsibility. I experimented with various approaches, based largely on my own past experiences as a supervisee. Although there were no disasters, nothing worked out quite as well as I had hoped. I applied models and ideas from books and from the practice teaching course that I was attending, but I often found that my well-meaning attempts felt awkward and contrived. Looking back, I can see that I worked so hard to follow other people's suggestions that I forgot to fully attend to what was going on in the room. After a while, I realised that supervising another person is more art than science and that it is the formation of an effective relationship and not the rigid application of a supervisory model that is fundamental to success.

While my own experiences both as a supervisee and as a supervisor have shaped my ideas about supervision, they are not the only views I am drawing on in writing this chapter. During each practice educator course, I encourage participants to explore their concerns about aspects of their new role. The following issues are among those that are most commonly raised about supervision:

- the speed with which supervisory relationships need to be forged;

- management of power and boundaries;

- the learner's emotional response to their learning experiences;

- working positively with difference;

- preparing for and managing supervision sessions;

- meeting the needs of the learner while keeping service users safe.

In this very short and practical chapter I have deliberately avoided analysing the purposes and processes of supervision, as this has been introduced in Chapter 8 of this book and covered very effectively in other excellent texts (e.g. Davys and Beddoe, 2010; Wonnacott, 2012; Kadushin and Harkness, 2014). My primary aim in this chapter is to focus on the fundamental importance of the supervisory relationship and explore how some of the ideas introduced earlier in the book can be applied to address the concerns outlined above. I hope that reading the chapter will give you some useful new ideas as well as encourage meaningful reflection on your own experiences, stimulate your curiosity and support further reading.

What sort of supervisor do I want to be?

As I mentioned in the introductory paragraphs of this chapter, I was influenced in my early days as a supervisor by the supervision that I had received as a learner. I remember picking my best supervisor and attempting, not very successfully, to replicate her rather inspirational approach. I was, of course, also affected by my less positive experiences and there were things that I knew from the outset I would never do to the people that I was supervising!

ACTIVITY 12.1

Reflect on your own experience of supervision (as a student or a newly qualified social worker). Has a supervisor ever made you feel good, inspired you or enabled you to think differently? Can you think of a time when supervision demotivated you or made you feel unhappy? Identify some factors from these experiences that you think were significant to these outcomes.

If possible, extend and develop this activity by discussing your ideas with other people and finding out if their experiences give you any new perspectives or ways of thinking about supervision.

Comment

The ideas that you have generated in the above activity will have helped you to explore your experiences of supervision and enabled you to uncover some of the beliefs about supervision that have developed as a result. While this is a good starting point in your journey to becoming a supervisor, you are likely to quickly discover that things that worked well for you will not work quite so well for others. Individual differences mean that each supervisee will have their own ideas about what they want and need from supervision and these ideas may differ substantially from your own.

Our past experiences of supervision are not the only things that influence the way that we think and act as supervisors. We each have a unique set of life experiences that affect the way that we interact with others, both personally and professionally. Taking a reflective approach to the supervisory role will help you to uncover the impact of these experiences and enable you to understand more about the roots of your behaviour and your expectations of others.

ACTIVITY 12.2

Consider the following questions and as you answer each one, think more deeply about why you are at the point you have reached now – reflect back on past experiences that may have influenced your thoughts and feelings; reflect forwards and consider the impact of your answer on your practice as a supervisor.

- *Do you have a number one priority for practice education supervision? How do you justify this?*

- *Which of your personal and/or professional life experiences are most likely to affect the way you act as a supervisor?*

- *How important is it that people like you?*

- *How do you feel and react when you know you have made a mistake?*

- *How do you respond to being challenged or told that you can do something better?*

- *How confident are you about challenging others?*

- *How confident are you about supporting people to explore their emotions?*

- *How confident are you working with someone whose cultural background is different from your own?*

- *How open are you to new ideas? What helps you to be more open to new ideas?*

- *How organised are you? Do you tend to leave things to the last moment?*

- *How do you deal with stress and how resilient do you feel right now?*

Comment

This is a general list of questions which is intended to trigger personal reflections. However, it will not necessarily include the questions that are most pertinent to your current situation so consider personalising the list by adding more of your own questions. You could also consider adapting this activity for use in supervision with a new supervisee. It may help them think about their approach to supervision and the supervisory relationship that you are in the process of forming.

Building a supervisory relationship

At the beginning of this chapter I said that new practice educators worry about the speed with which they have to build supervisory relationships. Student placements are short – a maximum of one hundred days in England – and this pressure on time can mean that both learners and practice educators are tempted to dive straight in and make a start on the activities that are most obviously and most directly linked to learning and assessment. But neglecting to build solid foundations for those activities is likely to be a mistake, and one which will almost inevitably reduce the quality of learning and assessment that can be achieved.

There is a strong consensus in the literature that the relationship between a supervisor and supervisee is a key aspect of effective supervision (O'Donoghue et al., 2018; Lefevre, 2005; Davys and Beddoe, 2010; Wonnacott, 2005). In this section of the chapter we are going to explore which aspects of a supervisory relationship are most significant, consider the consequences of a weak or harmful relationship (Beddoe, 2017a) and discuss ideas that may help you to initiate and develop an effective relationship with learners that you are supervising.

Earlier in this book, when exploring the importance of effective planning for placements, we discussed research by Michelle Lefevre (2005) in which students reported that the quality of the relationship with their practice educators was one of the most important factors in the success of their placement. This finding has been supported in a more recent study by Karpenko and Gidycz (2012), which showed that the quality of the relationship not only affected the student's evaluation of the placement but also their chance of making progress towards their objectives and the supervisor's ability to assess their capability. However, while there is general agreement that the quality of a relationship is important, it has been harder for researchers to pin down exactly what defines an effective professional supervisory relationship. One of the confounding factors is that there are almost certainly significant individual differences in the way that relationships are evaluated by those who are within them (Lefevre, 2005). It is also reasonable to assume that since supervisory relationships do not exist within a vacuum, other factors may come into play, for instance a weak supervisory relationship may be mitigated by strong collegiate alliances or by a more resilient, assertive and independent learner. The aspects of the relationship that are most important may also be affected by the stage that the learner is at or the learning that they need to achieve.

However, despite the challenges of reaching broad agreement about what defines an effective relationship, most writers in the field agree that feeling psychologically safe and supported is an essential requirement for supervisory success (O'Donoghue et al., 2018). If this basic need for psychological safety is not met, it has been reported that learners feel uncomfortable, lose faith in their ability and may be tempted to hide their mistakes (Karpenko and Gidycz, 2012).

REFLECTION POINT

What makes you feel psychologically safe and supported in a professional supervisory relationship?

Is your answer to this question always the same or are there differences between what you are looking for in different relationships? Would you have all the same requirements with someone you knew well as you would have in the early stages of supervision? Does 'who' the supervisor is make a difference to what makes you feel safe? Do any differences/similarities between you and the supervisor affect what you need to feel safe and supported?

Extend your reflections by talking to others and seeing if you can begin to identify common factors which are a requirement for you and your colleagues to feel psychologically safe and supported.

Comment

A recent review article (O'Donoghue et al., 2018) which brought together the findings of 26 research studies on supervisory alliances concluded that it was of central importance for supervisors to 'establish and sustain a constructive, considerate, culturally competent and caring relationship' with the people they were supervising. Features of such a relationship included trust, support, honesty, openness, the ability to collaboratively navigate power relations and respect for difference. In order to establish and maintain effective relationships the review found that supervisors needed empathy, emotional intelligence, professional expertise and relationship skills. Fairly predictably, poor relationships were more often reported when supervisors focused on administrative compliance and surveillance. In a powerful exploration of harmful supervision Liz Beddoe (2017b) identified that repeated disregard for power differentials, a focus on personal critique in feedback, the existence of micro-aggressions and an almost adversarial climate were often present in supervision that was so poor that it could cause harm.

Although it is relatively easy to spot when something goes seriously wrong in a relationship, it is not always so easy to notice the signs that a relationship is failing to thrive. This may be because of low expectations, lack of awareness or because the imbalance of power may prevent the learner from being open and honest about their needs.

Charlie is an experienced children and family social worker who has just completed a practice educator course. He is Sean's practice educator in a final placement in a fast-paced multidisciplinary assessment team. Charlie knows just how important it is to the success of the placement that Sean feels safe and secure within what can be a very challenging environment. Although Charlie and Sean have already booked weekly supervision sessions every Wednesday during the placement, Charlie often works from home and has identified this as a particular problem because he will not be available for Sean in the

(Continued)

office on a daily basis. To make sure that Sean is able to contact him he adds him as a friend on Facebook and tells him about regular Friday evening sessions at the pub round the corner from the office ('he can always be found there at 5.30 on a Friday even if it's hard to track him down elsewhere!'). He also gives Sean his personal telephone number to make contact during the evening because 'he knows how difficult it can be to get through on his work phone during the day'.

Charlie tells Sean that he hopes that setting up all of these channels of communication will be reassuring and help Sean to feel supported. Sean agrees that it all sounds great. However what Sean says and what he actually feels are quite different. This apparent flexibility makes Sean worry that he may not be able to talk to Charlie when he needs to. He also gets the impression that Charlie is so busy that it would be 'unreasonable' to try and talk to him too often outside of their Wednesday supervision sessions. As a young, single parent, Sean knows he will find it almost impossible to work after his normal hours and doesn't really think it is reasonable that Charlie appears to expect him to do so. However, although Sean is left feeling quite isolated in his day to day work, he doesn't feel confident enough to challenge what Charlie is suggesting.

Comment

This case study raises questions about maintaining appropriate boundaries as well as high-lighting the importance of spending time getting to know and understand the needs of the learners that you are supporting. In this case Charlie made assumptions that Sean would respond well to the kind of informal support that worked for him as an experienced worker. He did not take into account Sean's home situation and failed to understand the power imbalance. Spending more time getting to know Sean and giving him the opportunity to talk about how he would like to access support and guidance would have enabled Charlie to be more sensitive to Sean's needs.

Ideas for practice

Invest time in early supervision sessions getting to know each other, build on information that you gave and received in the pre-placement stage and gradually encourage a more open and reflective approach as trust begins to build. It is particularly important to spend time exploring and reaching agreement about any additional needs that the learner has identified and any past experiences of learning or supervision that may impact on their expectations or needs. Using appropriate self-disclosure may help the learner to feel more confident about opening up – maybe talk a little about how you felt when you were a student and the uncertainties that you had. However, don't make assumptions based on what you know would work for you or what has worked for students who have previously been placed in your team.

Consider completing an exercise together like Siobhan Maclean's (Maclean and Lloyd, 2013) 'Bring and Buy' exercise in which you support the learner to list the skills and attributes that they 'bring' to the placement and the things that they want to 'buy' or learn while they are working with you. This exercise enables both you and the learner to take a strengths-based approach and can help give structure to a conversation which starts with basic skills and knowledge and is extended to include discussion about key life experiences, personal values and the motivation to be a social worker. It is particularly important to give time, space and support for the learner to honestly talk about their hopes and fears for the placement and for you as the supervisor to provide reassurance that supervision is a place to explore, experiment, be challenged and sometimes get things wrong!

Negotiating a supervision agreement

Taking steps to reduce uncertainty, increase predictability and promote a sense of collaboration within the supervisory process can enhance a learner's feeling of psychological safety. Research evidence shows that supervision is both personally and socially constructed (O'Donoghue et al., 2018). This means that the individuals within supervisory relationships may have a different understanding of what supervision is for and how it will be managed, based both on the context in which the supervision is being provided and on past experience. Early informal discussion about what supervision will involve and what you are both expecting from the relationship can begin a helpful process of clarification that will reduce uncertainty and make supervisees feel secure. Formalising these discussions through a supervision agreement is the next important step, as this confirms that a shared understanding has been reached and documents the commitment of both supervisor and supervisee to the 'rules' that have been negotiated and agreed (Davys and Beddoe, 2010). This should not be rushed, because at an early stage it may be difficult for you both to know what you want from the relationship and how it is going to work. However, it is worth beginning the formal process of negotiation in the first supervision session with the aim of reaching an agreement within the first few weeks of the start of the supervisory relationship. The Social Care Institute for Excellence (**https://scie.org.uk**, accessed 17 April 2018) suggests the following headings and provides a template for download:

- Practical arrangements – venue, frequency, duration, cancellation process

- Arrangements for complimentary methods of supervision – e.g. ad hoc, telephone, etc.

- Link between supervision and other management processes – e.g. Assessed and Supported Year in Employment assessment, university processes and assessment, etc.

- Content of supervision sessions – standard items for discussion, how agenda will be set, etc.

- The expectations of the supervisee regarding supervision – including their past experience of supervision

- The expectations of the supervisor

- Preparation by supervisor – including familiarisation with work

- Preparation by supervisee – including issues they wish to discuss

- Factors that need to be taken into account in the development of the supervisory relationship – for example gender, additional needs, race, culture, age, sexual orientation

- Resolving difficulties – including how to recognise and resolve problems

- Recording supervision – who is responsible, how records will be shared and with whom.

Completing a standardised supervision agreement without full discussion sends the message that the learner has little power or influence over the supervisory relationship. Make sure that, even when your employer's policy requires you to use a standardised format, you provide genuine opportunities for discussion, personalisation and regular points of review.

Cultural competence in supervision

Most of us would agree that being respected, listened to and understood are basic human requirements for feeling safe and supported. However, genuinely understanding another human being is a complex and challenging task and something which will always be a 'work in progress'. Differences between a supervisor and a supervisee can to lead to misunderstandings which can then result in the sort of breakdowns in communication that we have just seen in Case Study 12.1. Sometimes differences between individuals are easy to spot but this is not always the case and human beings have a tendency to make the assumption that people who share an aspect of their background will think and feel the same way. Culture can be defined as the norms, values and traditions that shape the way that we think, behave and make sense of the world. Each of us participates in and are influenced by multiple cultures linked, for example, to our ethnicity, nationality, social class, gender, sexual orientation, age, physical and mental ability and religion. Cultural competence, in the context of practice education supervision, can be understood as the ability of a supervisor to flexibly shape supervision to take into account the cultural orientation, background and values of the person that they are supervising. Culturally incompetent supervision is the failure to respond respectfully, humbly and effectively to people of different cultures, classes, backgrounds, languages, identities and traditions. Recognising and working sensitively and effectively with difference in supervision is something that a significant proportion of the new practice educators that I work with worry about doing.

In Chapter 4 we began to explore the importance of understanding and acknowledging a learner's individual perspective as a key element in the provision of an inclusive learning environment. Lusk et al. (2017) argue that knowledge and appreciation of another's culture are not in themselves enough to meet a person's needs and promote a sense of safety. They suggest that supervisors need to:

- Incorporate critical cultural competence into their practice – actively analysing power differences between themselves and learners and seeking to reduce the impact of unequal power within the relationship.

- Take a strengths-based approach, seeing diversity as an asset and gaining an understanding of the learner's cultural background and values and the way that this will impact and relate to their experiences in the learning context. Discussions about how the learner sees the world and how their past experiences are likely to shape their opinions, feelings and actions help with the development of this understanding.

- Adopt cultural humility to level the relationship and reframe it as a peer professional partnership where both partners are learning.

Ideas for practice

There is a significant body of anecdotal and research evidence that suggests that black and minority ethnic (BME) students have lower levels of success and report higher levels of dis-satisfaction with practice learning opportunities than white students (Fairtlough et al., 2013). Although the reasons for this are likely to be complex and are still poorly understood, there is some evidence that racism and a lack of cultural competence within supervision can be a factor (Masocha, 2015; Tedam, 2013).

The Mandela model was developed by Tedam as a tool to support supervisors working with black African learners. Tedam had identified that the needs of black African students were often not being met as tools frequently used by practice educators were not tailored to meet their specific needs. The model is intended to act as a reminder for practice educators that they need to name and seek to understand differences and should be viewed as an ongoing process with the following elements revisited throughout placements.

- **M**ake time – to help the learner understand the work context and their role.

- **A**cknowledge needs – academic, professional development, practical, emotional.

- **D**ifference – name, explore and understand differences between the supervisor and learner.

- **E**ducational experience – explore past experiences, preferences and attitudes to learning.

- **L**ife experiences – discuss and understand the impact of experiences when the learner is comfortable enough to do so.

- **A**ge – acknowledge and discuss that for African students age and age differences can be particularly significant.

Although specifically developed for use with black African students, the way that this model supports an anti-discriminatory approach to supervision and the supervisory relationship means that it can very usefully be adapted and used with a wide variety of learners.

Preparing for supervision and providing structure in the session

Earlier in this chapter we explored some research that showed when a learner feels unsafe and unsupported they are less likely to make progress towards their objectives (Karpenko and Gidycz, 2012). We have also seen in previous chapters that learning is more likely to happen when people take responsibility for their own learning (Knowles, 1980) and we know that the PCF (BASW, 2018) makes it very clear that social workers need to be proactive in the development of their professional capability and need to understand how to use supervision effectively. Encouraging and undertaking good quality preparation for supervision helps us to use this knowledge to make supervision more predictable and controllable for both the supervisor and the learner. It also encourages learners to identify and articulate their support and learning needs, ensuring that they take responsibility for their own development and make more effective use of time in supervision.

As part of your informal discussions about supervision and within your supervision agreement you should have outlined the importance of good preparation for supervision and agreed, in general terms, what sort of preparation will be needed by both the supervisor and the learner. You may need to provide learners with help to understand what this actually means and how good preparation links to their overall learning objectives, particularly when learners have little previous experience of good quality supervision.

Ideas for practice

Consider sending agenda items to a learner at an agreed time before a supervision session is scheduled. Include information not just about what you want to talk about, but also what you are hoping you will achieve through each agenda item and what preparation you expect them to undertake before the session to support your discussion (consider designing a simple pro forma to help you with this process). Be very clear about any material that they will need to bring with them on the day and any preparatory work you would like them to complete. Ask learners to follow this same process and send you their agenda items with similar information about what they would like to achieve and what preparation it would be helpful for you to do. A well planned and detailed agenda can provide focus within a supervision session and can be used in conjunction with the reflective models introduced in earlier chapters e.g. the Davys and Beddoe (2009) Reflective Supervision Model or the Wareing (2017) Me, My, More Model, both of which help learners focus on emotions, values and self. Encouraging good preparation can help learners arrive more prepared to engage in deeper and more meaningful reflection.

Using creative approaches to engage learners in supervision

The single most important message that I hope has been conveyed throughout this chapter (and indeed throughout the book) is the fundamental need to take a learner-centred approach to supervision. I hope we have shown that it is only by doing so that you will be able to establish an effective supervisory alliance through which you can maximise opportunities for growth and development. However, this does not mean that supervision should always be a comfortable experience or that learners should never be challenged. Developing an effective relationship in which the learner feels safe, supported and understood makes challenge more comfortable and will hopefully even enable learners to welcome or even invite challenge as an essential part their learning experience.

Although, of course, I know how important it is to be learner-centred, I also know that I have a 'toolkit' of tried and tested approaches that I most commonly use within supervision sessions. While I hope that I always vary my approach in small ways to match the needs of each learner that I work with, it is often only when I encounter blocks to learning that need to be challenged or learners who lack an understanding of complexity that I start to think more much creatively. Thinking laterally and using more creative approaches within supervision can help learners to challenge established patterns of thinking and 'give permission' to safely explore new ideas. The more you know about and understand the learner, the more closely you can tailor the opportunities to meet their needs. Some of the approaches that are outlined in the following case study by an experienced practice educator have helped students to embrace new ideas and gain a deeper understanding of the people that they are working with.

CASE STUDY *12.2*

Once I have got to know students and have a clearer idea about the way that they are able to think and learn most effectively, I like to use creative approaches to engage with them holistically and encourage original thinking. For example, I recently applied Korthagen's (2004) onion model during a supervision session. We used paper and pens as we discussed a service user 'Ivy' in an active way, using the model to reflect in increasing level of depth. This particular student found it really helpful to visualise unpeeling an onion as we reflected and found the active process of capturing thoughts on large sheets of paper really beneficial. In another session I used Lego to support a discussion about social work values. With a few bricks each, we had to convey abstract ideas such as diversity, rights, justice and reflection. For this particular learner this was a fun activity in which bricks were a catalyst for imaginative dialogue, but I know that the approach would not suit all learners, particularly those who may feel this approach trivialised important issues. Another time I asked the student to bring in an item that was personal to them to prompt discussions about meaning and value. This enabled us to explore issues such as hoarding and self-neglect, and enabled the learner to develop a more empathic response to the people that they were working with.

Melissa Tettenborn,

Deputy Learning and Development Manager, Poole Borough Council

---

Adopting more creative approaches in supervision can feel a little risky because you are moving away from established, familiar approaches and embracing new ideas. However, we can see from the case study above that using carefully tailored and more creative approaches can be very worthwhile.

Chapter summary

- Good quality supervision is an essential part of effective social work practice.

- The formation of an effective supervisory alliance is fundamental to the achievement of supervisory success.

- Taking time to negotiate a supervisory contract helps strengthen partnership, reduces uncertainty and provides a framework for the development of an effective and safe relationship.

- Cultural competence is an essential skill for supervisors working with learners. A lack of cultural competence can undermine the supervisory relationship and prevent learning.

- Good preparation for supervision sessions reduces uncertainties and can rebalance power within the supervisory relationship.

- Taking a creative approach within supervision can help overcome learning blocks and encourage reflective thinking.

FURTHER READING

Davys, A and Beddoe, L (2010) *Best practice in professional supervision.* London: Jessica Kingsley.

Kettle, M (2015) *Achieving Effective Supervision.* Available at: https://www.iriss.org.uk/resources/insights (accessed 30 July 2018).

O'Donoghue, K, Wong Yu Ju, P and Tsui, M (2018) Constructing an evidence-informed social work supervision model. *European Journal of Social Work,* 21 (3), pp348–58.

Wonnacott, J (2011) *Mastering social work supervision.* London. Jessica Kingsley.

Chapter 13

Applying learning from Domains A–C to support the development of resilience in learners

Introduction

A recent survey indicated that 80 per cent of 2,000 participating social workers were considering leaving their jobs as a result of work-related stress (Community Care, 2015). There is little room for doubt that stress is a major problem for the profession, with unprecedented levels of burnout and an average career span of just eight years (Curtis et al., 2009). In the five-year period from 2003 to 2008, a fifth of the qualified workforce was absent for at least 20 consecutive days with symptoms of stress or anxiety (Grant and Kinman, 2012). Being a student social worker is no less emotionally demanding, with 40 per cent of respondents in a study reporting high levels of psychological distress (Kinman and Grant, 2011).

In 2009, the Social Work Task Force voiced serious concerns about the ability of practitioners to withstand the pressures they were experiencing at work. While these comments, quite rightly, placed a spotlight on the need for organisational improvements to leadership and supervision, many argued that without wider changes in areas like recruitment and education it was unlikely that substantial reform would be achieved. One of the more influential commentators at the time, Lord Laming, believed these changes were necessary, at least in part, to ensure that the professionals of the future were more effectively prepared for the emotional stress they would face in their future careers (Laming, 2009).

However, despite large number of changes in social work education and management over the last decade, anecdotal accounts from students and evidence, such as the surveys cited at the beginning of this chapter, indicate that there is still much to do. As practice educators, we are well placed to contribute to improvements in the quality of supervision for learners and to play a significant role in making the wider changes to education in the workplace aimed at enhancing resilience a reality. In the remainder of this chapter we will explore a range of strategies, informed by principles discussed in previous chapters, which can be used to support work-based learners to develop this vital aspect of their capability.

It is interesting to note that not everyone placed in a high-pressure situation experiences harmful levels of stress or burnout – some adapt well, even appearing to thrive on the challenge that work presents. The term emotional resilience is widely used to describe a person's ability to endure pressure, maintain positivity and 'bounce back' (Grant and

Kinman, 2012). Much recent attention has been given to the importance of resilience in the social work profession (Laming, 2009; SWRB, 2010; Munro, 2011). But while most commentators agree that it is a vital attribute for workers to possess, until recently, there has been little guidance on selecting more resilient recruits or on building resilience through the educational process (Rajan-Rankin, 2013).

Why are some people more resilient than others?

High levels of resilience have been found to be underpinned by the sorts of personal skills and coping strategies that enable people to manage their emotions and deal with the challenges of life without long-term negative effects. Relevant skills and strategies are thought to include:

- emotional intelligence;
- critical reflection;
- social competencies – e.g. assertiveness, communication;
- having an understanding that setbacks are part of life;
- believing that your actions can make a difference to outcomes;
- strong problem-solving and organisational abilities;
- being able (and willing) to ask for help;
- looking after yourself – physically, emotionally and socially.

Adapted from Grant and Kinman (2012)

Although research suggests that genetic, physiological and childhood experiences influence an individual's level of resilience (e.g. Buckner et al., cited in Grant and Kinman, 2012), there is clear evidence that relevant underpinning skills and strategies, such as those listed above, can be developed both through adult education and later life experience (Rajan-Rankin, 2013).

How can practice educators support the development of resilience?

Adopting the 'good practice' approaches explored in previous chapters on managing, enabling and assessing learning will help you support the development of the underpinning skills and attributes outlined in the previous section. The ideas we have included throughout the book about enabling critical reflection are clearly of particular relevance when considering how to support the growth of emotional intelligence, social competencies, problem-solving and reflective ability. However, of equal importance to the development of a learner's resilience will be the quality of the supervision you provide and the nature of the relationship that you develop with them. Good-quality supervision encourages a learner to take control of their own learning, assists with time management, builds confidence, helps develop an understanding that setbacks are part of life and supports independent problem-solving, while warm, open and supportive relationships help build self-esteem, promote positivity and make it easier for learners to express uncertainties and seek support.

You may find it helpful to explicitly discuss the significance of resilience with learners by sharing some of the ideas in this chapter with them. Although most will have been introduced to the concept of resilience at university, the realities of the workplace are likely to make the need to cope with stress become more significant. Helping learners to understand links between resilience and skills such as reflective practice, problem-solving and emotional intelligence will have the added benefit of enabling them to appreciate the relevance to practice of ideas and approaches that may previously have seemed quite abstract. Referring to the domains of the PCF (BASW, 2018) within your discussions will further reinforce the core significance of resilience to the assessment you will be making of their capability.

In the remainder of the chapter we will move on to explore how to:

- help learners to identify and understand more about the sources of their stress;
- help learners to understand and manage their emotional responses to stress;
- promote effective coping strategies; and
- promote self-care.

Each of these sections will include suggestions and practical ideas to help you promote resilience in the learners with whom you are working.

Helping learners to identify and understand more about the sources of their stress

Stress is a normal human reaction to being placed under pressure. While some degree of stress is both an inevitable and normal part of a professional career, potentially damaging stress (or distress) arises when there is a disparity between the demands that an individual perceives to have been placed upon them and their belief in their ability to cope with those demands (Collins, 2008). Seeking to understand more about the causes of a learner's stress is a good starting point for discussions about the emotional impact of their work-based experiences and their ability to cope with them.

Davys and Beddoe (2010) propose that it is helpful to think about the pressures on an individual as a complex 'stress system' made up of interacting factors that can be divided into the following categories:

- self (personal and career);
- practice;
- organisation;
- socio-political environment.

ACTIVITY 13.1

Using the concept of the stress system, described above, list some of the likely sources of stress for an NQSW or student working in your organisation.

Consider how understanding more about the gap between a learner's perception of the demands placed on them and their belief in their own ability to cope with those demands can help you to support the development of their resilience.

Comment

There can be no 'one size fits all' answer to this exercise as, at any given time, every work-place will have a unique mix of potential stressors and support mechanisms. This is significant because it is the individual's perception of the pressures they face, and their belief in their own ability to deal with those pressures, that is most relevant here. Each individual will interpret and respond to potentially stressful situations in a different way – for some, a particular type of pressure will result in 'distress', while for others, it may not. It is not always easy to understand why people react as they do. It is therefore important to avoid making assumptions about how learners are feeling as a result of the challenges that they are facing. The only way to gain a genuine understanding of their perspective is to support them to identify, analyse and discuss their reactions to the stress they are experiencing in an open and honest way.

Ideas for practice

Activity 13.1 you have just completed can be adapted and used with learners to help them understand more about the stress reactions they are experiencing.

Start by explaining the concept of the stress system (Davys and Beddoe, 2010) and then, using a large sheet of paper/whiteboard and pens, help the learner to capture their own stress system in a visual format. It may be helpful for you to start by drawing four large overlapping circles, labelling each with one of the four categories of the stress system (see above). Then, encourage the learner to list the factors that are currently contributing to their feelings of stress in each of the categories. Of course, not everything will fit neatly into one of the circles – use the overlaps when this happens and discuss the complexities of work pressures and their potential to interact with each other. You could extend the activity by asking learners to rate the impact of individual stressors and their ability to cope with them. Use the completed diagram as a starting point for a more developed reflective discussion. As part of this discussion you should aim to uncover sources of stress that are currently or likely to become 'distressing' for the learner. You can also begin to discuss the importance of strategies that will reduce the pressures being placed on them (if possible) and help them to cope with their feelings of stress. It may be useful to return to the diagram in a later supervision to see how their patterns of stress and coping behaviours have changed over time.

This method is a particularly good way of helping learners to recognise that some sources of stress can be moderated or changed through their own actions, but that many – such as workload, organisational policies, poverty and disadvantage, etc. – are beyond their direct or immediate control. Being able to identify and accept the difference between things that can be changed or influenced and things that cannot is often a significant learning experience and an important part of the journey towards building resilience.

Helping learners to understand and manage their emotional responses to stress

Emotional intelligence (EI) is widely thought to play an important role in resilience because it is an important factor in an individual's ability to understand and regulate their emotional response to stress (Grant and Kinman, 2012). Although EI has been described in a number of ways, most models include the following four elements:

- awareness and understanding of own emotions;

- ability to regulate and control own emotions;

- awareness and understanding of others' emotions;

- ability to manage relationships with others.

Morrison (2007)

REFLECTION POINT

Do you think that EI is an inborn characteristic or can it be learned and/or increased?

Research has indicated that it is possible to enhance an individual's EI through activities that promote reflective discussions on emotions and the role that emotion plays in human interactions (Clarke, 2006). Team events, peer support groups, informal discussions with colleagues and reflective supervision discussions all provide good opportunities for this type of learning. Ensuring that learners engage in reflective activities outside of supervision will maximise exposure to experiences that help them understand and manage emotion within their professional role. Reflective supervision provides further opportunities for this type of learning and can be used to highlight, explore and extend learning achieved in other contexts. To ensure that points of learning are not lost and that explicit links between emotion-focused discussions and overall professional development are made by the learner, it can be helpful to end reflective sessions by exploring what they have learnt through the discussion. It may also be a good idea to talk about how you will use the session to inform your assessment of a learner's capability – highlighting links to the PCF (BASW, 2018). The types of questions I have found useful include references to both resilience and emotion such as:

- 'Has anything we have talked about today made you feel differently about your ability to cope with your work with X?' or

- 'How do you think understanding how X may have been feeling when he shouted at you will help you to be more resilient next time you encounter a similar situation?'

Activities that enable learners to explore the way that they can control and use their emotions more effectively within professional relationships can also be helpful. You could, for instance, consider using role play in supervision to enable learners to explore alternative strategies for recognising and managing their own emotions and to practise responding to and controlling emotions in other people.

Don't always expect the process of uncovering and discussing emotion to be an easy one. Learners can be reluctant to openly discuss how they are feeling because they are afraid of appearing unprofessional or 'out of control'. Practice educators may also be reluctant to broach the subject of emotion – particularly when they are worried about having the time or capacity to deal with the outcomes of such a discussion.

Promoting effective coping strategies

People cope with stress in different ways. Collins (2008) identified two distinct types of coping strategies that can be adopted by people who are experiencing stress.

- *Problem-solving coping strategies* – which usually include behaviours such as:
  - planning;
  - seeking practical support and the involvement of others;
  - seeking advice, assistance or information.
- *Emotion-focused coping strategies* – which usually include behaviours such as:
  - venting emotion;
  - seeking sympathy and understanding.

An extreme version of either type of coping strategy is likely to be ineffective and may even reduce a learner's capacity for resilience in the long term. As we have already seen, opportunities to discuss emotion in supervision can be helpful and may enable a learner to make sense of a negative or stressful experience, but spending too long venting emotion is likely to reduce an individual's ability to critically reflect, cope and move on (Collins, 2008). Helping learners to balance the time spent in supervision between the two types of strategy will generally encourage the adoption of a more effective approach to dealing with their stress. To do this, you will need to get to know how the learner you are working with is likely to respond to a stressful experience. If they have a tendency to move straight to action without exploring the emotional impact of their experience, slow them down and encourage them to express and explore their feelings. If they get stuck with their emotion, give time for them to express their feelings, but then seek to move them on by shifting the focus of discussion to the promotion of problem-solving and action-planning behaviours. Modelling a balanced approach to dealing with stressful situations in your own working practices will be a helpful addition to their learning experience.

Ideas for practice

In the above section we discussed the importance of understanding a learner's reaction to discussing and dealing with stressful situations. A useful way of getting to know more about this aspect of a learner's behaviour, while keeping a focus on building resilience, is by adopting an empowering, strengths-based approach within the supervision session.

Questions you could consider asking to help you do this include:

- What sorts of things are most likely to make you feel distressed?

- How do you know when you are stressed?

- How will I know that you are stressed?

- What do you find unhelpful when you are feeling stressed?

- Tell me about a time when you were distressed and describe the strategies that you successfully used to manage your thoughts, feelings and actions.

- What can we put in place to assist you to avoid distress in pressured situations and strengthen your own good strategies?

Adapted from Davys and Beddoe (2010)

It will be important to introduce the topic of coping with stress at an early stage in any work-based learning experience. You could even consider including a specific section on dealing with work pressure in the learner's supervision or learning agreement. Sharing some of your own experiences and discussing ways that you react to and manage your own stress may be a helpful way of normalising the 'stress reaction' to pressures at work. This type of disclosure can be an effective way of making learners feel safer talking about the stress they are feeling and will hopefully encourage them to be more open about any feelings before they become a serious problem.

Promoting self-care

When social workers fail to look after themselves, the consequences can be serious. Chronic stress can cause illness, lead to compassion fatigue and may even result in burnout. This has implications not just for the workers, but for their colleagues, the people they are working with and their employers (Jackson, 2014). Helping a learner to understand the importance of establishing a good self-care strategy at the beginning of their career is another way that you, as a practice educator, can support the development of their resilience.

Remember, informal learning experiences are just as influential as more formal teaching. This means that the practices that you and your team model and promote will set the expectations for self-care for new workers and students. If you don't take a lunch break and never say no, regardless of how busy you are, the pressure for the learner to do the same will increase. Practise what you preach and encourage others to do the same. Being involved in supporting a student or any other learner may provide a timely opportunity for you and your colleagues to review and improve your own self-care practices.

Ideas for practice

Because no two people are the same, or have the same 'care' needs, it can be a good idea to encourage each learner to draw up a personalised care plan in the early days of their learning experience. Plans can be written in a variety of formats but in essence are 'contracts' that learners agree to with themselves. You can help to monitor and 'enforce' the plan over the course of the placement but, because the point of the exercise is for learners to develop sound self-care practices, the main responsibility for enforcement should rest with them. Ideas I have used with learners range from formal action plans, incorporating a series of self-care targets, to letters written by learners to themselves which include lists of self-care promises.

If you don't want to create additional work for the learner, the same outcomes could be achieved through a recorded supervision discussion or through a reflective diary entry. The format the learner uses can be tailored to meet their preferences – the most important thing is that they do something which has personal meaning and emphasises the responsibility they have for looking after themselves both in the placement and throughout their career. You could support the development of a plan within supervision by helping the learner to think about what they want the plan to include and how it will help them to:

- establish a good work/life balance – ensuring that they maintain the things that are most important to them in their life outside of work;

- manage their work time effectively – taking regular breaks and working reasonable hours;

- know when and how to seek support and advice;

- be appropriately assertive, know their own limits and stick to them;

- look after themselves physically by eating well and getting enough exercise;

- consider practising relaxation, meditation, mindfulness, etc.

Make sure your discussions include some consideration of how the plan will be monitored, updated and evaluated and what they will do if 'targets' are missed or 'promises' are not kept. As in other areas, making links to relevant domains within the PCF (BASW, 2018) may also be useful in reinforcing the importance of this aspect of their capability.

Chapter summary

- Stress and burnout are a serious problem in the social work profession, with 80 per cent of respondents in a recent *Community Care* survey indicating that they were considering leaving their jobs as a result of work-related stress.

- Some people are more able to withstand stress than others – these people are considered to have high levels of resilience.

- High levels of resilience have been found to be underpinned by the sorts of personal skills and coping strategies that enable people to manage their emotions and deal with the challenges of life without long-term negative effects. Relevant skills and strategies are thought to include: emotional intelligence, critical reflection, social competencies, e.g. assertiveness, communication and having an understanding that setbacks are part of life.

- Research indicates that it is possible to develop the attributes that underpin resilience through educational and work-based experiences.

- Practice educators can support learners to develop their resilience by helping learners to identify and understand more about the sources of their stress, helping learners to understand and manage their emotional responses to stress, promoting effective coping strategies and promoting strategies for self-care.

FURTHER READING

Davys, A and Beddoe, L (2010) *Best practice in professional supervision: a guide for the helping professions.* London: Jessica Kingsley.

See Chapter 9 – Promoting professional resilience.

Grant, L and Kinman, G (2014) *Developing resilience for social work practice.* London: Palgrave Macmillan.

Rajan-Rankin, S (2013) Self-identity, embodiment and the development of emotional resilience. *British Journal of Social Work*, 44 (8), pp2426–42.

Chapter 14

Applying learning from Domains A–C when working in marginal or failing placements

Introduction

My first experience of a failing placement was almost twenty years ago but the memories are still painfully fresh today. The day that I broached the possibility of failure is particularly clear in my mind and the emotional turmoil that followed as the placement spiralled towards the point of no return is something I have never forgotten. In some ways it was one of the most personally and professionally challenging experiences of my career. Not because the student made it particularly hard, but because of the huge sense of responsibility I felt for my role in bringing an end to her career. Was I right to do so? Did I expect too much? Should I have done something different? If I had been a better educator would she have been a better student? These and other questions kept me awake at night and although I knew that my first duty was to the vulnerable people who used our services, I did feel a responsibility for the student too.

When I reflect back on working with that student, I am fairly sure that I would have made the same decisions today. Although at some point in the future she may have been able to return to complete her education, right then she lacked the emotional maturity to succeed. However, I can see clearly see how my inexperience contributed to uncertainty and my lack of knowledge caused me to doubt the soundness of my judgement. Experience and increased knowledge have since developed my confidence, but have not (and I suspect never will) made working with a learner who is not meeting expectations a straightforward, certain or comfortable thing to do.

So, while I can't claim that this chapter will make it easy for you to be part of a failing or marginal learning experience, the material included has been designed to help increase your knowledge and build your confidence. We will consider a range of ideas and strategies for practice and provide opportunities to reflect on approaches that you could take from the point that a problem is first identified through to when a fail decision may have to be reached. Throughout the chapter we will hear from people who have been involved in failing placements, including students, a practice educator and a learning and development officer. I hope that the inclusion of their voices will help us to understand their different perspectives and provide an insight into what has helped and hindered them in the challenging situations they faced.

We start the chapter by looking at how to recognise, analyse and evaluate the kinds of problems that could arise when working with learners. Then, using an extended case study, we will explore strategies that have been designed to proactively maintain a partnership with the learner and focus on developing, working towards, monitoring and evaluating solutions to those problems. We consider what happens if the solutions don't work and the failing placement becomes a failed placement and end the chapter by considering the importance of providing access to an appropriate support network for all of those involved in work-based learning. This chapter dovetails with Chapter 10 on assessment, particularly to sections on judging or weighing evidence and reaching and documenting an assessment decision.

How will I know when there is a problem?

This is a difficult question to answer, largely because every learner and every placement is different and what would be a cause for concern in one context may be less worrying in others. On rare occasions, concerns about a learner's suitability for the profession can be so serious that there is little room left for doubt about the future of their placement. Under such circumstances the learner's university or employer will have clear policies and procedures to follow with regard to who should be involved and how to manage the suspension or termination of the placement. Make sure you are aware of these policies and procedures from the start and know who to contact when concerns, serious enough to warrant considering immediate placement termination, are identified.

More usually, concerns about placements grow over time. Failure to meet a standard once or even twice is not normally a cause for concern and most learners will improve their performance if they are given clear feedback and opportunities for further learning. However, practice which continues to be less than 'good enough' in one or more of the domains of the PCF (BASW, 2018) (or other appropriate benchmark standard) for a sustained period of time, despite feedback and developmental support, will become a cause for concern which, at the very least, requires further analysis and evaluation.

Why talk about a failing placement – surely it is the learner who is failing?

When a student is not performing at the level expected in a placement it is natural for the practice educator to be concerned that the student is not good enough and to think that he or she may be at risk of failing. But is it really that simple? Is it always true that a learner who is failing to provide evidence of capability is a learner who lacks capability?

Because so many aspects of the work context are outside of learners' direct control there can be significant differences between what learners actually do and what they are capable of doing. For instance, a learner who is sent to undertake an assessment without adequate training might produce a poor assessment report and, as a result, be judged to lack capability. But that student may have had the inherent ability to produce a good report and may have done so had appropriate training and support been provided. You could of course argue that the student not only lacked capability because they produced a poor report but also because they failed to recognise that they needed more training to undertake the task. However, it is important to remember that it is difficult for learners to anticipate what they don't know (see Chapter 5 for the 'conscious competence model') and challenging for them to question what they are instructed to do by someone in a position of power.

Even experienced social workers lack the complete freedom to choose between good and problematic practice as their performance will always be influenced by the nature of:

- the work they are doing;
- the people for whom they are providing services;
- the support and guidance available to them;
- the resources available to them;
- the organisation in which they are working.

If this is true of experienced workers, then it seems likely that the impact of these external factors will be even more significant for those, like students and newly-qualified workers, who have yet to develop a strong sense of confidence or professional identity. This means that assessments of the quality of a learner's practice will be the result not only of their inherent ability but will also be dependent on the tasks they are given, the support and training that is provided, their observations of others, the culture in the organisation in which they are placed and their perceptions of what is expected.

The following real-life account of two different placements undertaken by the same student very powerfully illustrates just how significant the context in which they are practising can be. (The name of the student has been changed.)

Cara's account

The first placement …

I think it was just the on-site supervisor's (PS) personality. The power was so much it was quite scary but I kept telling myself if I just keep doing what I need to do, it will soon be over. It felt like the PS wanted to break me. It did have an impact on my practice. I froze. Even to make a phone call I would wait until she wasn't there. I struggled to write a letter. I would continuously be worried. I knew I needed to have my work checked but I was afraid to do anything. It slowed everything down. There was a lack of constructive feedback. If she saw me talking to a team member, asking questions, she would call them immediately to ask them what it was about. I could not ask other team members for any help. I was afraid of my PS.

The second placement …

In my repeat placement I was worried that I would freeze again even though my practice educator (PE) had assured me that it would be a different experience and I did worry at the beginning. There was so much support from the whole team; people

---

would say how about doing it this way. In no time at all I felt free. I could go to managers and anyone and ask questions. I felt I could make a mistake and not be judged. Even with a very complex case, they checked that I was happy to carry on and I was. I was happy to do it because I knew I had their support. For most of the placement I was in a different office to my PE yet whenever we met, she would give me all the feedback she had been given from others. I just think it was the way the team did things. She would go through my work and I always felt she was trying to bring out the best in me even when she was correcting me; I felt motivated to remain focused. My PE and PS were very supportive of me using my own initiative and I kept them informed. I trusted them and I trusted the team. They wanted me to feel that I was in a safe learning environment as a student.

I was able to work to the best of my ability without being overstretched. I was able to bring research information to the team and felt the team valued my contribution. I quickly became independent; I could check everything in supervision. The team wanted to be involved in my learning such that in preparation for my assessed presentation, the whole team of social workers, including the practice managers, watched it and gave me feedback. It was good to feel valued as an individual.

Comment

We can see from these accounts that the way Cara felt about herself and the way she was able to learn from her experiences was affected very significantly by her environment. In the first placement her learning was limited by her fear and discomfort, and this had an impact on her ability to develop her practice and to generate appropriate evidence. In the second placement the support Cara received enabled her to take advantage of the learning opportunities offered, develop her practice and evidence her capability.

REFLECTION POINT

Arguably, social work students need to be prepared to work in challenging situations once they qualify and not all will go on to work in a supportive team with good supervision. How much adversity do you feel that it is reasonable for a student to have to cope with and still be expected to demonstrate capability?

The complex relationship between learning, practice and context will always mean that there is a potential source of error in judgements made about capability in work-based learning situations. So, when a learner is not performing at the level expected or is not making progress, questions will always need to be asked about why this is the case.

Field et al. (2014) suggest that the key to solving placement difficulties is early recognition, open discussion and the prompt implementation of an appropriate action plan. I would agree that this is of the utmost importance but would add that the ultimate success of such an approach will be dependent on the willingness of all involved to understand and address the involvement of the whole placement context and not just focus on the learner's performance. Later in the chapter we will explore how a systems-based strategy can be used to achieve these objectives. However, before doing so we will look in more detail at the kinds of problem that can arise in work-based learning situations.

What can go wrong when people are learning in a workplace?

Table 14.1 includes some, but by no means all, of the reasons why a work-based learner can run into difficulties. We include examples directly connected to the learner as well as others relating to the practice educator and the wider placement that could have an impact on the learner and their ability to practise effectively. Although, for convenience, we have presented these problems in neat boxes, it is worth remembering that real life is often much messier than the table suggests. Learners in difficulty often have more than one problem (some more obvious than others) and the existence of any individual problem can trigger a chain reaction that then leads to related issues in other areas of their practice or environment.

ACTIVITY 14.1

Select one of the 'problems' from Table 14.1 and spend a few minutes putting yourself into the position of the key people involved in the placement (the practice educator, the learner, your manager and the people who are using your services). How do you think they will be thinking/feeling about the problem? Once you have done this, come up with two different ways in which you could initially raise the issue with the learner. What are the advantages and drawbacks of each approach? Which are you most likely to try first and why?

Comment

Remember that the way that you raise and discuss issues with learners will influence their engagement in the process and the quality of the relationship you sustain through a potentially challenging time for you both (Lefevre, 2005). It is important to think carefully about the way you communicate and use your power within the relationship (Eno and Kerr, 2013; Finch and Taylor, 2013). As you plan your approach, take into account the things you know about this specific learner, their learning environment and about adult learning in a more general sense. Think about the impact of their anxiety on learning, the factors which can affect their motivation and the significance of the approach taken by the learner to their learning. Explaining that you will be seeking to work with the learner to understand the problems that have arisen with a view to developing solutions rather than attributing blame will increase your chances of maintaining an effective partnership. It is also worth bearing in mind that the learner will be much more likely to work positively with you if they believe that they can succeed, so it will be important to take a positive, problem-solving approach and to communicate your belief that all but the most serious issues can be resolved (Parker, 2010).

Table 14.1   Problems relating to placements

Problems related to	The learner	The practice educator	Wider placement
Failure to engage	e.g. not valuing the placement, more interested in 'student life' than learning, just wanting to pass (be 'just' good enough), not a team player.	e.g. practice educator lacking time and/or commitment, not prioritising learner or their needs. Unfriendly and unsupportive.	e.g. team members/manager/organisation not committed to the support of learner learning. Not sharing responsibility with the practice educator. Unwelcoming environment.
Personal or health issues	e.g. absent from placement and/or reduced capacity to engage or complete tasks.	e.g. absent from placement or reduced capacity to engage or complete tasks.	e.g. staff shortages and/or low morale.
Additional learning and/or other needs	e.g. dyslexia or other specific learning needs causing difficulties with written work and /or organisational skills. Specific cultural or religious needs or caring responsibilities that require non-standard work patterns.	e.g. own additional learning needs preventing provision of appropriate support. Lack of knowledge about how to meet specific additional needs. Lack of flexibility in approach.	e.g. lack of flexibility/understanding of specific additional needs. No support available for staff from Black, Asian and minority ethnic (BAME).
Lack of confidence	e.g. in own ability to practise and/or meet academic requirements. Poor levels of resilience in the face of challenge. Self-doubt regarding judgement and decision-making.	e.g. in own ability with some or all aspects of the role. Poor levels of resilience in the face of challenge. Self-doubt regarding judgement and decision-making.	e.g. other team members lacking confidence in their ability to contribute to the learning/ assessment process. Manager lacking confidence providing supervisory support to practice educator regarding the practice education role.
Critical reflection and analysis	e.g. limited or no ability/commitment to critical reflection. Lack of self-awareness.	e.g. little or no support for critical reflection and development of critical practice. Lack of self-awareness.	e.g. non-reflective culture.
Lack of professionalism	e.g. not following university and/or placement organisation's policies/ procedures, poor time/workload management, not using supervision effectively, issues with boundaries, not taking responsibility for own learning, etc.	e.g. not following policies/procedures, not fulfilling commitments as practice educator, not using their own supervision effectively, issues with boundaries within the practice education relationship, poor role modelling. Lack of CPD.	e.g. policies and procedures not readily available, essential training delayed or not available, essential equipment not provided, e.g. phone/computer access. Learning role not respected. Poor role modelling by team and other professionals. Lack of CPD.
Issues with values	e.g. not taking into account appropriate professional values in reaching decisions, demonstrating appropriate professional values in practice and/or recognising impact of own values on practice.	e.g. not applying professional practice educator values. Failing to take power differences into account and misusing power in the supervisory relationship.	e.g. team members/organisation providing poor role modelling of professional values. Power misused within organisation.
Issues with learning/assessment	e.g. not providing evidence of capability at the appropriate level and not making expected progress.	e.g. inappropriate learning opportunities/ objectives/assessment criteria for stage of development. Lack of timely feedback.	e.g. learning objectives and assessment criteria not understood by wider team and other professionals.

Providing adequate and effective support for Black, Asian and minority ethnic (BAME) students can be a particular challenge in practice placements (McCaughan et al., 2018) Research has shown that students from this group are among those with a disproportionately high chance of being considered marginal or failing. McCaughan et al. (2018) suggest this is at least in part due to the endemic racism within our society but say that by listening to each individual student's voice we can tune into their specific needs and gain a greater understanding of how their professional development can be nurtured. Thomas et al. (2011) found that the provision of specific support systems, such as a BAME student support group, can improve the likelihood of completion and improve confidence. Other groups with disproportionate failure rates are men (Schaub, 2015), students with disabilities and gay, lesbian, bisexual and transgender students (Finch, 2017). It seems likely that an approach which provides tailored support to meet the specific needs of people in these groups would go some way towards redressing this balance.

Managing a failing or marginal placement – taking a systems approach

Once concerns about performance or progress have been raised with a learner, careful consideration needs to be given to how you will manage a situation which, at least in your opinion, has become failing or marginal. The problems that have been identified will have placed a sharper focus on your responsibilities as a practice educator (SWTF, 2009a; Sowbel and Miller, 2015) and balancing the provision of support to the learner while gatekeeping for the profession may become an even more significant challenge. It is important to remember that while it will sometimes be necessary to recommend a fail, not all failing or marginal placements will inevitably end in this way. It is therefore important to take immediate steps to work with the learner to gain a deeper understanding of the issues that have arisen and put in place an action plan aimed at rectifying both the presenting problems and their underlying causes.

Munro (2011) suggest that a deeper and more meaningful understanding of problems that occur in complex situations can be gained by taking a systems approach which includes:

- gathering accounts about the 'problem' from key players and taking time to gain an understanding of their perspectives and to identify pivotal points;

- recognising and understanding the impact of the environment on practice;

- looking beyond the basic facts and uncovering what the individuals involved were thinking and feeling;

- establishing responsibility not blame; and

- working in collaboration with the people who were involved to analyse the information gained and develop action plans that are based on strengths as well as needs.

In a work-based learning situation these outcomes can be achieved through reflective discussions with the learner and, if necessary, with others involved in the placement such as work-based supervisors, mentors, line managers and colleagues. The practice educator will normally take the lead in this process and initially hold a relatively informal discussion with the learner in a supervision session. The first time a concern is raised in supervision it is important that it is fully explored and clearly recorded. It is of the utmost importance that a shared understanding is reached about the nature of the problems identified and any actions that are agreed. Clear timescales and explicit points of review must also be negotiated, agreed and recorded. Including an explicit discussion about the criteria that will be used to measure achievement of the agreed objectives should be part of this process.

Depending on the nature and seriousness of the problems it may be beneficial or even necessary to involve others such as university tutors, line managers or learning coordinators in this investigative and action-planning process. Each university and employer will have a slightly different approach to dealing with problems that occur within work-based learning situations and it is important that you make sure you understand the procedures that you need to follow when problems occur.

Although some universities and employers have policies that require the involvement of others in work-based learning problems at an early stage, it is often only when more serious issues have been identified or when an initial action plan has failed that a more formal process is instigated. This process will usually start with an additional meeting (sometimes called a concerns meeting) chaired by a tutor from a student's university or in the case of a newly-qualified worker a senior member of staff from your organisation. This meeting gives all present the opportunity to discuss concerns and agree a formal action plan. As with the informal action plan, it is important to agree timescales, points of review and criteria for measuring outcomes. All discussions should be recorded and copies given to all present. Following the local procedures that have been developed can help provide a structure in an emotional and difficult situation. The following has been written by Kay Renshaw, a learning and development officer at Dorset County Council, about her experiences of providing support and coordination for failing placements. It gives us an insight into the challenges faced by those involved in managing a failing placement and the support she can provide for the process through her role.

Kay's account

The emotions evoked from both the practice educator and the student can be very similar if a student is considered to be marginal or failing. These include feelings of anxiety, vulnerability, inadequacy, anger, fear and distress. The student, practice educator and the team can experience a significant loss of confidence and undertake a lot of reflection and questioning of themselves such as 'What did I do wrong? What have I missed? Why didn't I do that? How could I have done better?'

Once concerns about the student's practice are raised, there is significant activity which includes additional meetings and reviews, and action plans that clearly take up additional precious time for all concerned. Questions are asked and the practice educator and the student can feel that they are being scrutinised. It is therefore most important that these situations are dealt with as soon as possible, with honesty and

(Continued)

(Continued)

transparency and the greatest respect to all. 'Good practice', professionalism and emotional resilience are required from the practice educator.

As placement coordinator I can help the practice educator and the student unravel the complexities within a placement that is not going to plan and help reduce some of the stress. This could be through discussion of additional evidence from team members, documents, etc. or perhaps using the PCF as a tool to evidence or not evidence the student's performance.

Kay Renshaw

Senior Learning and Development Officer

Using a systems approach to manage a failing placement – a case study

We have established that a work-based learning situation is a complex system in which a learner's performance is affected by context. We have also discussed the importance of gaining an in-depth understanding of problems that arise as a basis for action planning. In this section, we will use a case study to help us explore how applying some of the principles of a systems approach to a failing or marginal placement can help us achieve these objectives.

CASE STUDY 14.1

Mike is undertaking his first social work placement in an inner-city voluntary sector organisation working with young people who have been involved in gangs. He is a 27-year-old white man who describes himself as working class. He has a degree in English and has worked in various administrative jobs since completing his first degree. He is using savings to fund his return to university but is also working part-time in a bar to cover everyday living expenses. At the start of the placement Mike was enthusiastic about the learning opportunities available, made a good impression on the team and on Akil, the 52-year-old male, North African practice educator who would be working with him for the duration of the placement. Mike had no previous professional experience of working with young adults or of facilitating groups but presented as very confident, motivated and self-assured.

Six weeks into the placement Akil is beginning to feel frustrated with Mike's lack of progress in direct work with service users. Since the beginning of the placement he and Mike have been co-facilitating a group for ten young North African men who had been arrested and cautioned for minor offences related to their gang involvement. The group has been set up to give the young men an opportunity to discuss the challenges they face living in an area dominated by a violent gang culture and provide access to an appropriate support network.

Mike has been very quiet in the group, only rarely participating in discussions. He is often late and when he does arrive, sits slightly turned away, looking sleepy and yawning with arms and legs folded. Akil has gently raised the issue of his lateness and of his apparent lack of engagement in three consecutive supervisions and has given Mike the opportunity to discuss any anxieties he may have about participating in the group. Each time Mike has avoided in-depth discussion by saying he is sorry, given acceptable reasons for lateness, joked about how it is tough to get a word in edgeways and by saying that he will try harder next time. Akil has got to the point where he feels that Mike's lack of ability/motivation to communicate with the service users in this group could be a cause for concern.

ACTIVITY **14.2**

Taking into account only the information you have so far, answer the following:

- *If you were Akil would you be concerned? What would you specifically be concerned about?*

*Now go to the BASW website (**www.basw.co.uk**) and have a look at the PCF (BASW, 2018) expectations for social work learners at the end of their first placement. Which domains, if any, do you think Mike should be meeting through this work? How do you think Akil should use the PCF to discuss his concerns with Mike?*

Comment

You will probably have identified several clear areas of concern regarding Mike's behaviour in the group that can be explicitly linked to the PCF (BASW, 2018) capabilities (Domains 1, 2, 3, 4, 7 and 8). For example, in Domain 1, Mike is not demonstrating professionalism when he arrives late and sits yawning through the session and, in Domain 7, Mike's lack of participation means he is not demonstrating core communication skills.

Linking concerns to specific capabilities in the PCF or other appropriate benchmarks should help a practice educator feel more confident about their expectations for learners and will enable them to be clear that concerns are both significant and evidence based. If Akil used the PCF as a basis for his next supervision discussion he would also be in a good position to suggest and negotiate some specific objectives to support Mike's development.

CASE STUDY **14.1** *continued*

In the next supervision session Akil has decided to explore his concerns with Mike more explicitly and plans to use the PCF (BASW, 2018) to discuss the capabilities that he would

(Continued)

CASE STUDY *14.1 continued*

be expecting Mike to be demonstrating through his work with the group. However, although he begins the discussion as intended, when he asks Mike how he thinks he is getting on in the group, Mike says he is really enjoying it and is learning a lot from listening and watching Akil interact with the young people. He talks enthusiastically about Akil's communication skills and says that it would be impossible for him, with the limited knowledge he has of local services, to be of as much help to the young men as Akil. He sounds surprised that Akil is concerned about his lack of engagement and is fairly dismissive of the concerns saying, as he has done in previous supervisions, that he will get more involved next time because, thanks to the opportunities he has had to observe Akil, he is now feeling more confident and knowledgeable. Akil feels flattered by Mike's comments and thinks that Mike has raised some good points. He now thinks that he wasn't clear enough previously about his expectations and had indeed expected too much too soon. He suggests that Mike looks at the PCF, before the next group session to plan how he can start generating evidence through his work with the group and says they will review progress in the next supervision.

ACTIVITY *14.3*

Do you think Mike was being honest and telling the whole story or do you think that he may be deflecting discussion by being optimistic and flattering Akil? Do you think that Akil was right to conclude from their discussion that he could have been unclear about expectations or had expected too much too soon?

Write a list of the possible factors that you think could be contributing to Mike's current behaviour. Remember to keep an open mind, consider the 'whole system' and not just what Mike has said so far and what you know about his practice in the group. Consider what Mike's mindset could be and what may have influenced the way he perceives the group situation and his role in it. Ask yourself how Akil and/or the group members may be (inadvertently or not) triggering, amplifying or maintaining Mike's behaviour? Also consider if there is anything that may be an issue for Mike outside of the placement that could be affecting his ability to practise more effectively.

Comment

You may have taken a less optimistic view than Akil and realised that there could be more to 'the problem' than has been uncovered so far. I expect that you have identified a wide range of factors that could be contributing to Mike's lack of engagement (adding some different dimensions to the rather positive and superficial story presented by Mike in his last supervision).

However, at the moment, the ideas you have come up with, although obviously informed by your knowledge and past experiences, are little more than guesswork. The 'facts' we are working with are that an apparently confident and initially motivated student is failing to engage in a group situation despite what the practice educator currently believes are clear prompts and frequent opportunities to do so. If you base your assessment of the student on these 'facts' you too may be tempted to say that the student is failing. However, as the last activity has hopefully made clear, there could be a range of other explanations or at the very least a range of factors that are contributing to Mike's lack of engagement in the group. A systems approach could help Akil drill down into the issues that have been identified to gain a deeper understanding of the reasons why Mike is failing to engage, and to inform an action plan aimed at improving Mike's performance in the placement. A good starting point for Akil would be to use reflective questioning with Mike to encourage and support him to be more open about what is really happening in the placement.

CASE STUDY **14.1** *continued*

Mike arrived on time for the next group session and Akil was pleased to see that he looked more engaged. However, despite this improvement Mike still only made one contribution to the discussion and that was when Akil specifically asked for his opinion. The session made Akil realise that the problem was not going to just go away and that he needed to make it clear that his concerns were potentially serious and could ultimately lead to Mike failing the placement. At the beginning of the supervision session he told Mike explicitly about his concerns by making links to PCF (BASW, 2018) capabilities and the expectations of the organisation. He then gave Mike space to talk about his perception about what had been happening in the group and in the placement more generally. When Mike simply repeated what he had said in previous sessions, Akil used critical questioning to help him explore the following aspects of his experience in greater depth:

- *his overall experience of being part of the group (providing an overview);*
- *occasions when he could have participated but chose not to (turning points);*
- *what he was thinking and feeling at these points (his mindset);*
- *his reasons for not participating (factors influencing his thoughts and actions at the time);*
- *what he felt he did well in the last session and could build on in the future (his strengths);*
- *what he specifically intends to do differently in the next session (his learning).*

Akil's aim was to provide opportunities to Mike to discuss his thoughts and feelings about himself and the group but also to broaden out the discussion and gain a deeper understanding of how the wider placement system and Mike's perceptions of the system were impacting on his practice in the group context. Through the discussion they uncovered a number of issues which helped them both to understand why Mike was not meeting his expectations for participation in the group:

(Continued)

1. *Mike believed he lacked skills in communicating with young people and did not feel his induction or subsequent practice experiences had provided him with sufficient support to develop these skills. His understanding was that observing Akil in the group was part of his ongoing learning and that he would only be expected to participate more fully at a later stage in the placement, as his confidence and knowledge grew.*

2. *Mike found it difficult to participate even at a basic 'social level' because he felt that the young people looked to Akil to answer questions and facilitate the discussion. Whenever there was an opportunity to participate in discussion, Mike felt that the young men wanted Akil to respond and not him. He didn't think there was a very clear role for him in the group and he felt he was intruding in what was a close-knit and successful group. He also did not feel culturally competent to participate in much of the discussion that took place.*

3. *Mike did not yet fully understand why the young people were attending the group as it was quite unstructured and Akil had not really explained what he was trying to achieve. This meant that when opportunities to contribute arose he was not quite sure what to say and was afraid of getting things wrong.*

4. *Mike did not realise he was being formally assessed on his participation at this point as Akil had not discussed learning objectives or assessment criteria explicitly with him. No links between the PCF (BASW, 2018) and the group had been included in supervision.*

5. *Mike is exhausted and very worried about being able to pay his bills. He was finding it hard to keep his concentration levels up in the group, particularly when he didn't understand what people were talking about. He had been working some additional shifts at the bar and was not finishing work until 2 a.m. on a regular basis.*

ACTIVITY **14.4**

Now you have the additional information, do you still think that Mike is at risk of failing the placement or have you begun to think that the situation is more complicated? How has the new information changed the way you are thinking about the placement as a whole? What do you think that Akil should do next?

Now write a bullet pointed action plan in two sections that will:

(a) *address the key issues raised by Mike about the placement; and*

(b) *provide clear targets, linked to the PCF (BASW, 2018), for Mike to achieve over the next four weeks.*

Don't forget to include an agreement on how and when targets will be reviewed and stipulate what will happen next if targets are not met.

Comment

The action plan you have just drawn up should have included some targets for Mike regarding additional learning about young people, the cultural background of the group members, group processes, etc. Depending on his preferences, this may include his undertaking reading, further shadowing, supervision discussion or role play to develop knowledge skills and confidence. Targets should also be agreed about improvements to his timekeeping, his professionalism and the contributions he needs to make to the group. It will be important to discuss and agree specific learning and performance objectives as well as the criteria that will be used to measure success.

Don't forget to use the rich information gained from the reflective supervision discussion as it may help to inform the way that targets are agreed and set. For example, it may be a good idea to focus on the pivotal points when Mike could have contributed but held back – consider what sort of target you think could be set to turn non-participation into participation at these points. It may also be helpful to set a target that gives Mike a specific role in the group, as a lack of clarity over purpose was one of the main issues that Mike raised. In some ways, the most difficult issue to address is the one that relates to Mike's personal life and the need for him to work outside of the placement. Since not working is probably not an option, Mike and Akil will need to consider what can be done to ensure that Mike's tiredness and stress do not impact to such a large extent on his performance in the placement.

As there was clearly a range of issues impacting on Mike's performance that were outside of his direct control, such as failure of communication between himself and Akil as well as shortfalls in the induction process, it seems unlikely that Mike will be able to engage more fully until these issues have been resolved. The action plan will therefore also need to include action points that ensure Akil is clearer with Mike about his expectations and that he provides the additional opportunities Mike needs to develop his skills, knowledge and understanding. Akil may also need to review his approach to supervision to make it easier for Mike to be more open about concerns in the future.

Although the discussions between Akil and Mike have highlighted some of the underlying causes of Mike's lack of participation, it is quite possible that there are further issues that have not yet been uncovered. It may therefore be helpful for Akil to reflect further on the way that he has fulfilled his role and how the wider organisation has supported Mike within the placement so far. Any further issues uncovered through Akil's reflections and discussions with others that follow on from these reflections will, of course, need to be discussed with Mike and, if appropriate, incorporated into the action plan. The following checklist may help Akil with this process of critical reflective and discussion:

- Was the placement well prepared and did everything that was planned take place as expected, e.g. induction, shadowing opportunities, specific training? Were the learner's identified needs actually met by the induction and initial training provided? Were plans put in place following induction to meet any outstanding training needs?

- Is everyone involved in the placement clear about their role and what is expected of them? Has everyone fulfilled their role as agreed? Has power been discussed and used appropriately?

- Was the learning agreement clear and was the learner actively involved in negotiating the agreement? Does the learner understand what he or she is expected to achieve? Have there been opportunities to revise the agreement?

- Is all assessment fair and transparent? Has the learner understood the assessment criteria being applied in each situation? Were criteria appropriate to the stage of development and clearly linked to the PCF (BASW, 2018) or other relevant standards? Has clear and constructive feedback been given with advice on how to meet required standards? Have varied assessment methods been used? Have other assessors been involved?

- Has the practice educator spent enough time getting to know the learner? Have they taken what they know about the learner into account and been learner-centred in their approach? Have the learner's specific/additional needs been met within the placement?

- Has the learner been encouraged to play an active role in managing and evaluating their own learning? Have any concerns or anxieties they have raised been addressed?

- Have sufficient learning opportunities been provided?

As writer and readers, we have invested a lot of time in Mike and Akil's story and I'm sure we all want to know how it ends. Since, as writer, I am in control of the story, I have decided that things went well! The action plan Mike and Akil agreed was effective. Mike engaged enthusiastically with the process and was able to increase his knowledge, skills and confidence. With more focused support from Akil, both in supervision and within the sessions themselves, Mike was able to meet the performance objectives they had agreed. Although there were some difficult times and the relationship between them become a little strained, Akil's positive attitude and willingness to listen and make changes paved the way for a more open and trusting relationship.

However, it is worth bearing in mind that if either Akil or Mike had reacted less constructively, the outcomes may not have been so positive and Mike could conceivably have continued to fail to meet expectations. It is also possible that, even with additional support and guidance, Mike may have been incapable of improving his performance at that time and in that context. Had the initial action plan failed, Akil would have needed to contact Mike's university and start a more formal concerns process. This process could have ultimately resulted in the termination or failure of the placement.

The impact of a failing placement on the learner

So far, we have mainly considered failing placements from the perspective of the practice educator. We will now take a little time to think more about how it feels to be a learner who is failing or at risk of failing. The following describes how James, a social work student, felt about his situation. (Not the student's real name.)

> *It's really hard when you know you are putting the work in and really pushing yourself but know on some level that you're not meeting the targets or the standards. It's crushing.*

At school you were taught that you should know the answer and should be able to answer immediately. As an adult it's even harder to ask the questions or ask for help because you are meant to be more independent or able. You are there to learn but you are also meant to be more independent and autonomous.

The experience of being part of a failing placement can be difficult for everyone involved. However, for social work learners their placements represent key components of their qualifying education and the cost of failure is very high (Parker, 2008). The learner will already have invested time and considerable amounts of money in reaching this point in their education and failure or even the possibility of failure can be devastating.

The stress of the situation they are facing may make it difficult for them to fully engage in learning tasks and you will need to take their emotional reaction to their situation and its impact on their learning into account – for instance, making sure that feedback is fully understood. They may become angry and resentful and seek to place blame with others. This can sometimes lead to a serious deterioration in the relationship with you, as the practice educator, and other team members.

Is there any such thing as a good fail?

Although we have established fairly conclusively that involvement in a failing place-ment will always be a challenging experience, according to Eno and Kerr (2013) a 'good fail' is possible when the following conditions are met:

- *There is consensus about the judgement by all concerned.*

- *The potential for future success is positively acknowledged and seen as achievable.*

- *A robust, fair and defensible assessment is given with issues and problems iden-tified in specific terms and fully understood by the learner both in terms of magnitude and direction of travel needed (linked to evidence).*

- *Discussion about how to progress is included in the process.*

- *The practice educator feels confident and supported.*

The following quote from a student who recently failed a placement very effectively illustrates some of the points made above.

I think it's important to accept that you are not meeting the requirements and that you have failed the placement and that it's up to you to reflect on that and develop from it. You need to take responsibility and own that. It would be easy to shy away from that and put the blame on someone else. People can support you but at the end of the day you have to make the decision as to whether you want this. Without acceptance I think nothing would really change and you wouldn't learn from it. That took at least a month. I had a lot of anger and denial. It's really only since my repeat placement that I can see the difference and look back and see where things went wrong.

Why do practice educators sometimes delay or even fail to raise problems?

The Social Work Task Force report that *specific concerns have been raised about the robustness and quality of assessment, with some learners passing the social work degree who are not competent or suitable to practise on the frontline* (2009a, p24).

As we have already seen, working with a learner who is failing or at risk of failing is very challenging for all involved. Research has shown that practice educators do not always find it easy to acknowledge that something is going wrong and, as a result, learners are sometimes passed who should be failed (Waterhouse et al., 2011; Basnett and Sheffield, 2010). The following has been taken from an account written by an experienced practice educator. It provides an insight into how she feels about working with failing learners and how she has come to terms with the need to fail.

Gail's account

Failing learners has caused me a maelstrom of emotions. It is difficult to tease out all the intertwined elements. It seems to me that issues for me fall into two main areas: professional and personal.

Professional issues

When involved in failing learners I have found myself questioning if I am actually right in my judgements. Am I setting the standard too high? Has the reason for the problems been due to me? Have I been unclear in my planning within the placement? Have the action plans that I have worked on with the learner to help them achieve the required standard been thorough enough? Have I provided too little support? Has it been my inability to ensure that the right learning environment has been provided, or my inability to accurately get over just what is required? Is there anything that I could have done differently that would have led to a more positive outcome for this learner? My confidence is undermined, and I have felt responsible for the learner's failure – if only I could do my job better, they may have been able to pass.

When a failing learner has requested a second opinion, challenging my decision, I have felt vulnerable and exposed – will this affect my professional standing? I know that my assessment will come under considerable scrutiny and I've worried that I in turn will be criticised. Although initially the idea of a second opinion has evoked anxiety for me, I have come to see it as reassuring. The whole weight of the decision no longer rests just with me. It has helped me to feel more confident in myself, and has enabled me to learn. So, ultimately, despite the stress, I have felt more confident in myself and my assessment.

Personal issues

I am so aware that learners' hopes and dreams lie in completing the course successfully. As a social worker, my values of supporting vulnerable people are challenged.

I know that if they fail, the learner loses so much – their self-esteem, their career, and the financial, emotional and time investment that they have put into their studies. I feel pressurised to help them achieve a pass on a personal level. I have usually developed good and trusting relationships with my learners, and the process of failing them puts a huge strain on this. I want to be liked. Some failing learners can become very angry and defensive, and the relationship can become very strained – particularly if they do not accept my decision. Others have become very distressed and tearful, and have been willing to do anything they can to get themselves to the required standard. I have found both responses very hard to deal with. I don't want to acknowledge to myself, or them, that sometimes some people will never have the ability to do the job. I have shared their distress and hurt. Alongside this I cannot but help myself feel sorry for them, and have a strong desire to go into 'rescue 'mode. I want to make it all right. I think that these emotions have led me at times to be too accommodating, and I have tried too hard to fix things. It has taken me time to come to realise that being clear with failing learners is really important. If I feel they are not right for the job, for whatever reason, it is important for them that they know earlier, rather than later. It is not fair to them to keep them hoping. It is better that they can start to consider what their alternatives might be. This has helped me be more positive and constructive at a time that is upsetting for all. It has also helped me to relook at my priorities – the practice educator's ultimate responsibility is to services users and carers. If the learner is not up to the job, it is the service users and carers who ultimately will suffer. They are often some of the most vulnerable people in our society, and it has reassured me to think that it is their needs that I am there to support.

Gail Stewart – Practice Educator

The thoughts and feelings described by Gail in her account will be familiar to many practice educators who have been part of a failing placement. The maelstrom of emotions she describes is similar to the experiences that I refer to in the opening sentences of the chapter. Although Gail talks about coming to terms with the need to fail, some practice educators find it more difficult to do so and this can have serious consequences on their ability to gatekeep effectively.

RESEARCH SUMMARY **14.1**

Finch and Taylor (2013) interviewed twenty practice educators with experience of failing placements and grouped their reactions to their experiences into these major themes:

- *guilt – about the impact of the failure on the learner;*
- *anger – towards the student, themselves and/or the university;*
- *role confusion – the struggle of combining nurture with judgement;*

(Continued)

- *the idealised learner – where actual learner was compared to an ideal and fell short;*

- *internalised failure – it was my failure as well as yours.*

They concluded that the strength of emotions evoked in practice educators involved in failing placements had the potential to obscure the assessment process – sometimes leading to students being passed inappropriately.

Because of the very real danger that assessment decisions can be skewed by emotion, it is important for practice educators to take a critically reflexive approach to their role and make good use of the support available from others to check out their judgements and proposed actions.

We have established that being reflective about the impact of emotion is important, but is there anything that practice educators can do to make it easier for them to manage a failing or marginal placement? If we return to Gail's account of her experiences she talks about coming to terms with the need to fail. She links this to her clear understanding of the importance of her gatekeeping role and the need to be fair to the student by being realistic about their chances at as early a stage as possible. One of the most interesting findings from Jo Finch's original research (2009) was that practice educators who find it easier than others to work with failing and marginal students:

- explicitly or inexplicitly acknowledge their gatekeeping role and the implications of this role on the relationship with the learner;

- acknowledge the potential for role confusion but are able to bring the 'split' together;

- have clear boundaries in place and a clear understanding of the role of the practice educator;

- have clear expectations of the student as an 'adult learner';

- make a clear differentiation between 'your work' and 'my work';

- take a reflective approach – avoid 'drama' – see experience as a learning opportunity.

Although all of the above could be considered 'best practice' for working with any adult learner, it is often only when confronted with a failing and marginal placement that you find out whether you are actually doing what you intended to do. Finch's research highlights the importance of both establishing and maintaining these sorts of 'best practice' approaches – taking the time to plan and prepare placements, getting to know learners, negotiating and agreeing effective contracts that clearly establish expectations and set appropriate boundaries, and making sure that you are self-aware and make time to reflect honestly on your own practice. We can also see how important it is that both practice educators and learners are aware of the possibility of a failing placement right from the start of any work-based learning experience. This may sound very negative (and clearly discussions about the possibility of 'failure' need to be handled with great sensitivity), but it is much more likely that problems will be addressed and resolved quickly when strategies for failing placements have been agreed as part of the overall management strategy at an early stage (Sharp and Danbury, 1999).

Where can those involved in a failing placement go to for support?

When things go wrong, the emotional and practical support needs of those involved in any learning situation are likely to increase. However, it is important that appropriate support networks are in place long before there is even a chance of a problem arising. Before you agree to take responsibility for a learner, you should consider and agree who you can turn to for support. Sources of support will differ according to local circumstances but are likely to include: your line manager, your mentor, colleagues, other experienced practice educators, a practice educators group and the training and development officer for your organisation. If you are working for a small organisation with no other practice educators or are self-employed, there may be few obvious places to turn to for support and advice. You need to think carefully about the implications of this both in terms of your own well-being and the possible impact of a lack of support on your ability to cope with challenging situations.

Of course, learners will also need to establish at an early stage where they can turn to for support. In the first instance, this will normally be a tutor or learning coordinator within the organisation. However, additional help to meet specific needs may also be available through universities or placement providers (e.g. learning support, groups for people from minority ethnic or cultural backgrounds, etc.). It is likely that they will also look to friends, colleagues and family to act as sounding boards and for help to meet the emotional challenges encountered within the placement. Although their preparation for the placement at university (or, for newly-qualified workers, their induction) should have encouraged them to consider where they could go to for help, the importance of making use of support is something that can still usefully be brought up in supervision sessions. This is because while learners may be aware, in principle, of what is available, they may see the need for support as a weakness or not fully appreciate how accessing additional help could enable them to cope more effectively. Grant and Kinman (2012) identified the ability to develop effective personal and professional support networks as a key aspect of building a social work student's resilience. Helping learners to understand the value of support and the importance of proactively building an effective network could therefore be considered a central part of the practice educator's role.

Chapter summary

- A small proportion of placements and other work-based learning experiences will end in failure and some groups such as BAME students make up a disproportionate amount of those who fail.

- Work-based learning situations are complex systems and the quality of a learner's performance will always be influenced by the tasks they are given to perform, the support available to them and the environment in which they operate.

- Taking a systems approach can help practice educators to work in partnership with learners to analyse and evaluate problems that arise in work-based learning situations. Information gathered can then be used as a basis for problem-solving and action planning.

- Practice educators often find it difficult to acknowledge problems and/or reach a fail decision. Research has shown that factors such as guilt about the impact on the learner, uncertainty about who or what is to blame and role confusion can be factors contributing to this difficulty.

- Involvement in failing or marginal placements is a challenging experience for all involved. Practice educators who explicitly acknowledge their gatekeeping role, have clear boundaries in place, have expectations of the student as an adult learner, make a clear differentiation between 'my work' and 'your work' and take a reflective approach are likely to find it easier to cope with a failing or marginal placement.

- Organising and accessing appropriate support networks is vital for all involved in work-based learning.

FURTHER READING

Basnett, F and Sheffield, D (2010) The impact of social work student failure upon practice educators. *British Journal of Social Work*, 40, pp2119–36.

Finch, J (2017) *Supporting struggling students on placement – a practical guide.* Bristol: Policy Press.

Furness, S (2011) Gender at work: characteristics of 'failing' social work students. *British Journal of Social Work* (online).

Sowbel, L and Miller, S (2015) Gatekeeping in graduate social work education: should personality traits be considered? *Social Work Education*, 34 (1), pp110–24.

Taplin, S (ed.) (2018) *Innovations in practice learning.* St Albans: Critical Publishing.

This book has useful chapters on listening to Black students and working with students with dyslexia.

Part Five
Domain D: Effective continuing performance as a practice educator

Introduction to Domain D

As seen throughout this book, before we can enable others we need to enable ourselves. As a practice educator you need to feel confident not only in your ability to facilitate the development of transferable skills in others but also in your ability to develop these skills within your own practice. You should be applying the methods and standards you are advocating to yourself first, in order to model the processes and develop your own understanding of them. Understanding your views of knowing and learning, your approach to learning, your learning style preferences, and developing a reflective competency all become the basis of lifelong learning for practice educators. Part Two explored a number of these views, approaches and preferences and showed how they can affect the way you enable and facilitate others and therefore impact on your potential achievement as a practice educator.

Part Five now develops these and other ideas further in our final chapter to enable you to create an individual approach for effective continuing practice and fulfil the requirements of Domain D. This part of the book may be shorter than the others and concentrated in just one chapter, but its ideas are the foundation upon which good practice is established and sustained.

Chapter 15
Continuing learning and development

Maintaining currency as a practice educator

In line with HCPC's re-registration requirements it is recommended that to maintain currency all PEs should take full responsibility for a social work student at least every two years. It is also recommended that PEs record their role as a practice educator and reflect their 'scope of practice' as defined by the HCPC, e.g. by the use of a portfolio. Therefore practice educators should ensure that CPD relevant to their role as a PE is included specifically in CPD documentation and can be presented as evidence for re-registration (if requested by the regulator). Considering oneself as an ongoing learner therefore seems essential for this process.

Critically understanding yourself as a learner

As Lefevre (2005) argues, creating supportive, safe and trusting environments in which learning is facilitated and risks can be taken requires enhanced self-reflection and self-awareness to ensure you are sufficiently conscious of the impact of your behaviour on the learner, and can realistically evaluate the nature of the environment you are co-creating.

ACTIVITY 15.1

Using the material from Chapter 5, write an insightful profile of yourself as a learner (e.g. on the practice educator programme). Using this profile, note the aspect that appears to influence your learning the most. How can being more aware of this help enable:

- *your own learning?*
- *the learning of others?*
- *anyone enabling you – for example, your mentor?*

Comment

Understanding yourself as a learner can unlock further potential. The key is to find ways to maximise the good aspects and minimise the bad ones, and these may differ in respect of whom you are interacting with and the nature of your role with them. For example, being an active learner may mean that you have high levels of motivation – you can make the most of this by allowing yourself the necessary time to put your ideas into action properly.

On the other hand, a mentor or supervisor may ask you to take time to stop and think as well, and you will need to remember to check to see whether your active enthusiasm is overwhelming less confident learners.

Professional learning and development

A holistic approach

A review (Webster-Wright, 2009) of professional development has advocated a 'continuing professional learning' (CPL) approach, focusing on professionals being engaged holistically in self-directed, ongoing learning. This approach avoids the potential limitations of the phrase 'professional development', which can view professional practitioners as deficient and in need of development through enforced training, which remains at a surface level. The CPL approach sees the learner, the context and the learning as interrelated, and therefore the learning is deeper and more personal.

Whatever terminology is applied, though, the development of your own practice can only become more meaningful when experiential (informal) as well as more formal learning activities are planned and engaged with in such a way that they enable significant, relevant insights and new understandings to emerge. As we highlighted in Chapter 1, recognising the need to make the most of informal as well as more formal learning should become a natural feature of practice. Informal learning covers areas like observation, feedback, dialogue and co-working, and usually results in new knowing or understanding that is either tacit or regarded as part of a person's general capability, rather than as something 'learned'. Nevertheless, it is a key area for professional development. For example, Becher (1999) reports that professionals learn six times as much through non-formal as through formal means.

Independent, self-directed learning

It is, therefore, practitioners who have the skills, abilities and attributes of self-directed and reflective learners who should be able to make the most of the potential for learning found within all work situations (Rutter and Brown, 2015). However, the ever-present danger, as with any skill set, is that it becomes routine and unexamined. Here, again, an embedded, holistic and critical stance can help to foster a more critical engagement, which will lead to deeper and more meaningful self-directed and ongoing learning.

We can look at this in more detail by listing the skills and abilities of self–directed, reflective learners and adding to each of them the extra element that a critical approach brings.

- Take the initiative in diagnosing your learning needs – a critical approach also asks:

    - What type of information informs this diagnosis – feedback, evaluation, meetings, learner reactions, gut feeling …?

    - Who provides the input and how – colleagues, supervisors, managers, learners …?

    - How honest and/or informed am I about my areas of strength and weakness?

    - What prompts me to take action, and what stops me?

- Recognise and capture the learning potential of everyday events – a critical approach also asks:

    – How and when do I note colleagues' ideas, tips, methods of working as useful or as areas of need within *my* working practices?

    – If a learner is not performing well, how do I analyse *my* part of the responsibility?

- Critically reflect on your practice and its outcomes – a critical approach also asks:

    – Who critically questions me?

    – Have I actively sought a direct observation of my practice?

    – Did/do I record my reflection and use it for the practice educator programme?

    – Do I ensure my reflection is strengths-based as well?

    – Am I aware of the 'shortcuts' I take in practice, and of the 'social norms' within the office – how may these be seen by learners?

- Create your own learning objectives – a critical approach also asks:

    – How do I use any input or diagnosis to form an objective for myself?

    – Do I discuss it with anyone?

- Identify, locate and evaluate the resources needed – a critical approach also asks:

    – What happens if the resources are not there?

    – Who else could help me?

- Choose and implement appropriate learning strategies – a critical approach also asks:

    – Do I review a full range of styles and approaches as well as my particular preferences?

    – How do I ensure that new knowledge, skills or ideas are put into practice and not left as a collection of notes or handouts?

    – How do I try to overcome the negativity associated with an organisation or team culture that is not conducive to learning?

- Evaluate learning outcomes – a critical approach also asks:

    – Do I revisit my learning objectives?

    – Do I test whether my practice has changed and how?

    – Do I actively seek and reflect on more critical feedback from learners or colleagues in order to gain a different perspective?

    – Do I reflect on feedback from assessed work undertaken within the practice educator programme or other programmes?

    – No one can be expected to practise perfectly – how do I judge whether my aims and expectations are set too high?

- Digest and generalise learning in order to facilitate its transfer – a critical approach also asks:

  - When I reflect on the learning gained from a specific situation, do I start to articulate it in more general ideas and concepts? For example, *I want to use the reflective question my supervisor used on me with other students – it was such an effective deep-learning prompt …*

  - Do I connect this to learning theories or research findings I have used or seen? How do I make connections between different areas of learning and different situations looking for common elements (e.g. across supervision, mentoring or coaching situations) or for different types of learners?

As we can see, it is not enough to have experiences and passively expect to learn from them. It is important that you take an active approach to learning and practice, and engage in all aspects of planning, undertaking, monitoring, reflecting on and evaluating your learning (Jarvis, 1992), bringing experiential and critically reflective processes together.

Stress and emotions

However, the more emotional and personal elements of learning must also be appreciated. We know that elements such as anxiety, fear and demotivation become barriers to learning, but so do more mundane but fundamental issues such as lack of time, support and resources for learning. Indeed, there seems to be much less time, opportunity or support for deep reflective thinking at work (Clutterbuck, 2001). On top of this, excessive work pressures and managerialist cultures create feelings of helplessness, anxiety and of being out of control, which all conspire against reflective practice. This is the reality of practice today for many people, and so a key part of being a professional is the need to find your own approach for dealing with it as best you can (i.e. to minimise the adverse effects on yourself, your colleagues and your service users). Thompson and Thompson (2008, p135) show that the busier we are, the more reflective we need to be in order to think more clearly and carefully before we act – *if the pressure to get things done means that we do not have time to think about what we are doing, then the potential for things to go wrong is high,* and that could waste a lot more precious time.

Of course, we are only human and there are times when the strategies we use to cope can be instinctive but not the most appropriate for long-term survival. Berne's (1996) work looking at 'the games people play' still appears very relevant in helping explain what happens to us. I'm sure we all know people who go into 'controlling parent' or 'disruptive child' mode when the pressure is on, and I'm sure we must all have gone down the 'ain't it awful' route, moaning about how bad things are but then actually wallowing in it as everyone joins in. It is always worthwhile revisiting this book and others like it to help become more aware of, and re-evaluate, our behaviour and coping mechanisms, and re-establish a more 'adult' approach where necessary.

On a personal note, when trying to write this book we have both felt deep levels of stress, frustration and anxiety, and resorted to avoidance, denial and a range of displacement activities as the pressure mounted. However, what we both found was that once we made a decision to not let the pressure get to us or 'go under', we were more able to reassert ourselves and find a few solutions (e.g. renegotiating certain deadlines) that helped us to manage the situation more effectively. The initial feeling of being overwhelmed seemed not only to demotivate us but also disempower us, and this was the pivotal issue we needed to address first. As noted in Chapter 5, key 'resilience markers' are the need to feel in control and to influence outcomes, to see new things as opportunities to learn, and to become involved in our environment and the learning taking place there (Maddi and Khoshara, 2005). The first priority should be to ourselves and our health, remembering to exercise self-care with the aid of others where necessary.

ACTIVITY 15.2

What can you do to avoid the spiral of helplessness and demoralisation that results from excessive pressure of work and time constraints?

Comment

Noting that this is actually happening is the first step and making a concerted effort to manage it as best you can is the next – maintaining self-awareness as well as retaining some measure of control are key starting points. Forcing yourself to stop and think, even if it is only for a few minutes, brings that element of control back into the process. Thompson and Thompson (2008) also stress the importance of not losing sight of what you are doing and why, and being aware of your own role in the process too. They provide useful discussion around minimising the impact of other barriers such as lack of organisational commitment or value placed on reflective practice, which may be helpful to you.

Critically informed practice

Keeping up to date

Critically informed practice involves keeping up to date with the world of practice education, i.e. finding out about new knowledge, processes, ideas and policies, etc., from a wide range of individuals, groups and organisations. It also means keeping in touch with learning and training developers within your organisation and the learning providers within your area, finding out what is on offer and supporting their work.

ACTIVITY 15.3

Research a range of local and national groups associated with social work practice education. Note the types of information, advice and help available from each.

Comment

Most universities offer some form of support to practice educators working with their qualifying students. You should be given information about what is available when you are approached about organising a placement. There may also be local support groups to be aware of, as well as some key national organisations, such as:

- Social Care Institute for Excellence (SCIE – **www.scie.org.uk**);

- National Organisation for Practice Teaching (England) (NOPT – **www.nopt.org**);

- Health and Care Professions Council (HCPC – **www.hcpc-uk.org/registrants/cpd**);

- Skills for Care (SfC – **www.skillsforcare.org.uk**);

- Scottish Organisation for Practice Teaching (ScOPT – **www.scopt.co.uk**).

After you have finished your practice education programme, many university resources may no longer be available to you. In this respect, several of the national sources outlined above, as well as your local and agency resources, may be useful to locate relevant theory, research, legislation, policy and quality-assurance guidance.

Linking knowledge, knowing and action

In order to link knowledge, knowing and action, a slightly different emphasis needs to be applied to the more traditional notions of theory–practice integration and to evidence-based practice (while still adhering to the essence of accountable and informed practice). We need to open up these notions and allow a more critical and holistic approach to the use of knowledge within your practice as an educator.

We have seen that students and novice practitioners may want more direction and 'rules' to follow and will look to more formal, external knowledge to provide it, as their range of experiential knowledge and more tacit knowing will be limited. Similarly, in your early days as a practice educator you will be looking for 'external' answers that can help you (e.g. from books or journals). You will not want to let your learner down any more than you would a service user. However, you will also be drawing on your existing knowledge and tacit understanding (e.g. about interacting and working with people), asking advice from others and building up a bank of experience and expertise in the process.

To demonstrate this we can work through an example using you and Liz, a second-year student. Liz does not seem motivated in her placement with you, she is not engaged with the service users and appears uninterested in learning. You want to find out more in order to help you decide what to do and your questions will reflect this. (The following section is adapted from work by Ashford and Lecroy (1991).)

If you start with the practice situation then your tactical questions will be situational and specific:

- *How can I motivate Liz?*

  You may struggle to answer this question on your own if this is your first experience with a student. You may know that this is not Liz's first choice of placement and obviously suspect this is a major part of the problem.

More strategic questions would prompt you to seek other people's ideas to help:

- *What do other practice educators do to motivate students on placement?*

- *What does Liz's university tutor know about this?*

Using these types of questions you can gain more information from different perspectives about the situation, and also a range of ideas that helped in different situations and which may be applicable here. Liz's tutor may tell you more about her specific learning needs. A practice teacher who works near you may say that, in her experience, demotivated learners are always hiding something and it is always worth 'digging' further. A report on the SCIE website may note how students get very blinkered about meeting particular professional requirements on placement.

Knowledge-seeking questions allow a wider perspective on the problem and more general understandings which help you to construct your answer:

- *What is learner motivation?*

- *Which factors are likely to increase learner motivation?*

The 'answers' found using more formal sources (e.g. books and journals) will be general and perhaps vague but they may provide additional insight into the problem. You might read up more on theories about motivation – extrinsic/intrinsic – or revisit Maslow's (1943) theory of human motivation and 'hierarchy of needs' model.

All these ideas can be evaluated in their own right and then related to the situation and appraised against what you know about Liz and the learning context to see how relevant they are and how they might help. For example, you may then decide that you respect the practice teacher and trust her advice, that the tutor has highlighted an issue about the PCF that Liz didn't mention, and you can see that motivation theory highlights the link between anxiety and motivation and this resonates with other behaviour you've noticed in Liz. You may decide to revisit the learning contract with Liz and critically question her understanding of her own needs. You may see that Liz is really worried that the type of work she is doing is not relating to the professional standards she needs to address this year – it is her fear that is the demotivating factor. By more fully addressing the links between the work and the PCF successfully, Liz becomes much more motivated.

There are three key points to reiterate here. First, the type of 'evidence' you use in practice can include informal as well as formal types and sources (Humphries, 2003; Trevithick, 2007), i.e. knowing as well as knowledge. Other people's ideas, reflective output, experiential learning, feedback and values should have a key place alongside more formal types of knowledge such as theory, research, policy and quality guidelines. Second, knowledge and knowing can be used in a number of ways. They can help at all stages of problem forming and solving rather than just being applied mechanistically to provide an 'answer'. This helps ensure that the best understanding of a situation is created at the outset, which, in turn, informs aims, choices, decisions and outcomes, as illustrated in the process below.

- *What is going on* – name and frame the situation. Knowledge and knowing provide awareness, description, explanation and understanding of wider, specific and underlying (assumptions, givens) or hidden issues (ethical, moral), etc.

- *What is needed* – establish purpose/develop feasible aims and objectives. Knowledge and knowing provide ideas, directions, possibilities, alternatives, etc.

- *What to do about it* – consider alternatives. Knowledge and knowing provide general approaches and strategies as well as specific techniques and methods for consideration, etc.

- *Make a decision* – knowledge and knowing provide further direction and detail on chosen approaches, strategies and methods, etc.

- *Noting what might happen* – take account of impact and outcomes with monitoring and review stages. Knowledge and knowing provide awareness of possible effects, implications, dangers, results, etc.

The third and final point concerns evaluation. All types of knowledge and knowing need to be evaluated in respect of authority, reliability, credibility and accessibility and, of course, relevance and ability to understand the situation and answer your questions. The criteria used need to be appropriate to the source. Obviously, you cannot judge the applicability of a piece of research in the same way as a theoretical model or reflective learning outcomes. A range of criteria for critical appraisal of arguments, research and theory can be found in Rutter and Brown (2015).

ACTIVITY 15.4

Which criteria do you use to evaluate someone else's ideas gained from their experience and learning?

Comment

The range of criteria which may be useful probably relates to the idea of 'authority' or 'expertise' – does this person know their 'stuff' (e.g. judging the type and range of experience this person has had which may affect their reliability and credibility)? Other aspects may relate more to the type of person they are and the approach they take to others (e.g. their values, self-awareness, the way they talk and listen to others, especially those less experienced or less 'powerful'). How we view the opinions of others can also take a less critical path by unconsciously valuing only those who look, talk or act like us or who we like. We sometimes need to consciously reappraise these opinions and our view of them.

By using a range of knowledge and knowing and allowing it to inform practice through a set of critical review and thinking processes the 'best' outcome is more likely to be achieved. The overall point to be made is that good practice is an ongoing process of information-gathering and evaluation – knowledge and knowing need to be kept up to date and evaluated, as well as made meaningful to the situations in which you are working.

Critically reflective practice – knowing, acting and being

Reflection – a review

We know that critically reflective practitioners are self-aware, critically analysing, evaluating, reviewing and updating their values, skills and knowledge, practising flexibly and reflexively, exploring alternative approaches and being open to change in all contexts – not just those concerned with learning. They are, in effect, demonstrating professional capability and criticality in all aspects of Barnett and Coate's (2005) model (knowing, acting and being). This means that ongoing learning and development are not just about updating knowledge and skills, they are also about reconsidering your ability to make sound judgements and decisions. They involve engagement with and reflection on experience, which facilitates the promotion of professional values and principles which guide action (Tyreman, 2000, p122).

As we have seen, reflection should be:

- active – lead to active output or change;

- holistic and meaningful – integrate knowing, acting and being;

- developmental – explicit to implicit areas of practice, recognise and develop own methods;

- critical – evaluating competence and capability, looking at strengths and weaknesses;

- deep – any frameworks being used need to encompass critical levels of description, analysis and evaluation;

- enhanced by dialogue and critical questioning with others.

A humble stance

The type of criteria that may prove useful here could relate to the idea of 'authority' or 'expertise', i.e. asking whether this person knows their 'stuff'. You will be judging this person's experience which affects the reliability and credibility of their ideas. However, although many competency-type skills may be easily reflected on and self-appraised, your disposition at work and the approaches you take to work situations will be so closely tied in with your personality and previous history that a truly honest reflective examination can be very difficult to achieve. As we know, reflection can become very negative unless it is also strengths-based, but it can also become self-justifying and self-serving – 'I reflect, therefore I am OK!'

The need for humility as well as honesty within a reflective stance is perhaps a key point here. It especially holds true when you are working in a partnership of trust with a learner. You have to model reflective behaviour in order to be credible but the extra awareness that humility can bring to the process may help address some of the power issues between educators and learners; it may enhance sensitivity towards the learner's perspective.

CASE STUDY **15.1**

Carol had critically thought through how she could help Vik to manage his learning more productively. She thought Vik was a great student but quite disorganised in his approach. Carol thought that Vik needed a system and, as she didn't want to impose her own, she spoke to him about the need for a more systematic approach and provided him with a

(Continued)

CASE STUDY 15.1 *continued*

range of ideas he could adopt. From Carol's point of view she thought she had helped him. However, Vik thought about it very differently – in his mind Carol was now criticising him and it made him doubt himself. He knew he was a little disorganised but it hadn't affected his work in any significant way. In fact, Carol had praised his work in the past but now he doubted whether she had meant it. He became hypercritical about everything he was doing and the anxiety this provoked made him start to resent Carol. In their meetings Vik became unresponsive. Carol sought his opinion but Vik didn't feel confident or safe enough to give it. The relationship began to deteriorate. Carol noticed this and reflected with a trusted colleague about it. Gradually it dawned on her that whatever she had thought of Vik's disorganised way, this was only her view of the situation. She had judged it as 'wrong' and something that needed to be changed, but in the bigger picture, even though he was a bit disorganised, it didn't really matter – Vik was still a great student. By imposing her own interpretation on the matter, no matter how well thought through it had been, she had effectively 'oppressed' Vik, and this had undermined his confidence and motivation. In their next meeting Carol made an unconditional apology and discussed how her need to be in control of the placement had blinded her to the fact that it was two-person responsibility. She admitted she was worried about Vik's disorganised methods but she should have talked about this first with him to establish together, in partnership, whether they were an issue or not, rather than judging the situation alone and trying to take control.

Just as it does for your learners, developing practice in this way can prove threatening and provoke anxiety for you. It is hard work, involving self-doubt and mental blocks, and therefore needs to be supported and enabled in empowering work-based relationships and partnerships, i.e. genuine learning cultures. Some of you may be fortunate enough to work in a positive learning culture that encourages sharing of knowledge, plus feedback and evaluation of services; others of you may need to seek such a relationship more actively: for example, on a one-to-one mentoring basis with a colleague you trust.

REFLECTION POINT

Where are your risk-free, safe opportunities for:

- *emotional support?*
- *discussing different perspectives?*
- *critical questioning and challenge?*
- *exploring alternative approaches, ideas, outcomes?*
- *fully exploring how you deal with complexity, risk, uncertainty?*
- *making new theory–practice connections?*
- *feedback?*

As we noted at the start of this chapter, an ongoing approach to professional development sees the learner, the context and the learning as interrelated, and therefore the whole experience is deeper and more personal for you. This approach not only requires your commitment and dedication, it also requires recognition, value, encouragement and support from others around you.

Summary of Part Five
Domain D

> - *You need to feel confident not only in your ability to facilitate the development of transferable skills but also in your ability to model their use within your own practice.*
>
> - *Critical engagement will lead to deeper and more meaningful self-directed and ongoing learning.*
>
> - *Part of being a professional is the need to find your own approach for dealing with stress – maintaining self-awareness while retaining some measure of control are key starting points.*
>
> - *Good practice is an ongoing process of information-gathering and evaluation – knowledge and knowing need to be kept up to date and evaluated, as well as made meaningful to the situations in which you are working.*
>
> - *There is a need for humility as well as honesty within a reflective stance to ensure the best type of partnership can be established with your learners.*

FURTHER READING

Fook, J and Gardner, F (2007) *Practising critical reflection: a handbook.* Maidenhead: Open University Press.

This very accessible book takes a theoretical and a practical approach, offering skills, strategies and tools.

Maddi, S R and Khoshara, D M (2005) *Resilience at work.* New York: Amacom.

This text provides knowledge, tools and encouragement that you can actually learn and develop to enhance your resilience.

Rolfe, G, Freshwater, D and Jasper, M (2001) *Critical reflection for the nursing and helping professions: a user's guide.* London: Palgrave.

This practical user's guide offers a range of clear frameworks and structures for reflective practice, including individual and group supervision, reflective writing and reflective research.

Rutter, L and Brown, K (2015) *Critical thinking and professional judgement for social work,* 4th edn. London: Sage.

A pragmatic look at some ideas associated with critical thinking, especially those linked to learning and development.

Thompson, S and Thompson, N (2008) *The critically reflective practitioner.* Basingstoke: Palgrave Macmillan.

This is essential reading for making sense of reflective practice, looking at what it is not and what it can be at its best.

Conclusion

So, what effects will work-based learning and critical reflection have on qualifying practitioners and established staff? What should the enabling and facilitation of learning be achieving? How will practitioners be developing? If you refer back to the Barnett and Coate (2005) theory of professional capability, by following a creative approach to the enabling of learning and professional development you should be facilitating practitioners to work and learn independently and to deal with complexity and embrace change, i.e. develop and enhance critical practice, become more emotionally intelligent and build their resilience.

As we have seen, critical practice is constructive, creative and optimistic, and takes calculated risks as part of a positive strategy of addressing issues and problems rather than avoiding them (Adams et al., 2002, p94). It is worth repeating, though, that critical practice is not about 'being certain', but about being able to deal with uncertainty using sound, valid and accountable processes and, where appropriate, maintain a position of 'respectful uncertainty', or at least hold onto doubt for longer and seek out other possible versions (Taylor and White, 2006). Critical practice therefore deals creatively with uncertainty and complexity rather than following prescriptions, and is capable of change. As Fook et al. (2000) also show, developing professional expertise is a process of learning to work with uncertainty using a wide range of knowledge, skills and understanding. When developing expertise, professionals start to create their own 'theories' of practice – their constructed knowledge about the best way to do things.

By developing your learners to approach their learning in active and critically reflective ways, and by using student-centred, active and critically reflective methods yourself, the learning situations you create will better enable such techniques and attributes of critical practice and expertise to develop or become enhanced. In addition, the best type of work-based learning can help all participants to see their processes of reasoning and judgement more realistically and to become more reflexive, analytical and systematic in their 'sense-making' activities (Taylor and White, 2006, p950). So, we may all learn from this involvement in learning as the relative importance of learning from experience becomes greater the more expert we become. Many of our students are amazed at how much they learned about themselves and their own practice while undertaking an enabling role. Indeed, one of the points to emphasise here is that the development of professional capability and expertise is a complex form of growth, which is never complete. The journey begins at the pre-qualification stage of a professional's career but will be a lifelong learning task, and so your part in another's development will be just that – a part – and in your own life it will form just another strand within the growth of your expertise.

Perhaps this is a way to build true communities of practice which reject the separation of training and learning from practice (Lave and Wenger, 1991) and enable the organisation to learn as well through more pervasive and distributed routes (Gould, 2000). This is what makes the role of the practice educator so crucial to the enabling of learning organisations and is why the Practice Educator Professional Standards were introduced.

Overall, enabling learning requires innovation, courage and the willingness to try new methods and experiment. Enthusiasm and adaptability are key factors. However, it can also create its own set of anxieties, especially when new skills are being developed. As with any type of activity, much is learned through trial and error to see what will best fit your particular situation. 'Mistakes' help create a bank of expertise, so don't worry too much when things don't go to plan. It is important to review the learning schemes you design, involve the learner in a true partnership, evaluate how well you are doing, be flexible, and adapt and change where necessary. Being enthusiastic about your work and caring about the learners you are working with are the main attributes they require from you.

We hope this book has helped you to understand yourself as an enabler and to form your ideas about what good practice should entail. Finally, we wish you the very best in all your future 'enabling' endeavours.

References

Adams, R, Dominelli, L and Payne, M (eds) (2002) *Critical practice in social work.* London: Palgrave.

Anderson, L W and Krathwohl, D R (eds) (2001) *A taxonomy for learning, teaching, and assessing: a revision of Bloom's taxonomy of educational objectives.* New York: Longman.

Argyris, C and Schön, D A (1974) *Theory in practice: increasing professional effectiveness.* San Francisco: Jossey-Bass.

Argyris, C and Schön, D A (1978) *Organisational learning: a theory of action perspective.* Reading, MA: Addison Wesley.

Ashford, J B and Lecroy, C W (1991) Problem solving in social work practice: implications for knowledge utilisation. *Research in Social Work Practice, 1,* pp306–18.

Askheim, O, Berresford, P and Heule, C (2017) Mend the gap – strategies for user involvement in social work education. *Social Work Education, 36* (2), pp128–40.

Atherton, J S (2009a) *Learning and teaching: advance organisers.* Available at: **www.doceo.co.uk/l&t/teaching/advance_organisers.htm**

Atherton, J S (2009b) *Learning and teaching: learning curves.* Available at: **www.learningandteaching.info/learning/learning_curve.htm**

Bandura, A (1977) *Social learning theory.* New York: General Learning Press.

Barnett, R (1997) *Higher education: a critical business.* Buckingham: Society for Research in Higher Education and Open University Press.

Barnett, R and Coate, K (2005) *Engaging the curriculum in higher education.* Maidenhead: Open University Press.

Basnett, F and Sheffield, D (2010) The impact of social work student failure upon practice educators. *British Journal of Social Work, 40,* pp2119–36.

BASW (2018) *The professional capabilities framework.* Available at: **https://www.basw.co.uk/professional-development/professional-capabilities-framework-pcf** (accessed 31 July 2018).

Baume, D (2004) *Reflective competence.* Available at: **www.businessballs.com/consciouscompetencelearningmodel.htm**

Baxter Magolda, M (1996) Epistemological development in graduate and professional education. *Review of Higher Education, 19* (3), pp283–304.

Becher, T (1999) Quality in the professions. *Studies in Higher Education, 19* (2), pp225–35.

Beddoe, L (2009) Creating continuous conversation: social workers and learning organizations. *Social Work Education – The International Journal, 28* (7), pp722–36.

Beddoe, L (2017a) *Harmful Supervision: ScOPT.* Available at: **https://www.scopt.co.uk/archives/3936#comments** (accessed 21 July 2018).

Beddoe, L (2017b) Harmful supervision: a commentary. *Clinical Supervisor, 36* (1), pp88–101.

Berne, E (1996) *Games people play.* New York: Ballantine Books.

Beverley, A and Worsley, A (2007) *Learning and teaching in social work practice.* London: Palgrave Macmillan.

Biggs, **J** (1999) What the student does: teaching for enhanced learning. *Higher Education Research and Development,* *18* (1), pp57–75.

Biggs, **J** (2003) *Teaching for quality learning at university,* 2nd edn. Buckingham: SRHE and Open University Press.

Bloom, **B S** (ed.) (1956) *Taxonomy of educational objectives, the classification of educational goals – Handbook 1: Cognitive domain.* New York: McKay.

Boud, **D** (1999) Avoiding the traps: seeking good practice in the use of self-assessment and reflection on professional course. *Social Work Education, 18,* pp121–31.

Boud, **D, Cressey, P and Docherty, P** (eds) (2006) *Productive reflection at work.* Abingdon: Routledge.

Boud, **D, Keogh, R and Walker, D** (1985) *Reflection: turning experience into learning.* London: Croom Helm.

Bowlby, **D** (1969) Attachment and loss: Vol. *1 Attachment.* New York: Basic Books.

Brockbank, **A and McGill, I** (2002) *Facilitating reflective learning through mentoring and coaching.* London: Kogan Page.

Brookfield, **S** (1987) *Developing critical thinkers.* Milton Keynes: Open University Press.

Brown, **G** (2001) *Assessment: a guide for lecturers,* Assessment Series No 3. London: Higher Education Academy. Available at: **www.heacademy.ac.uk**

Brown, **K and Rutter, L** (2015) *Critical thinking and professional judgement in social work,* 2nd edn. London: Learning Matters.

Brown, **K, Fenge, L and Young, N** (2005) Researching reflective practice: an example from post-qualifying social work education. *Research in Post Compulsory Education, 10* (3), pp389–402.

Brown, **K, Keen, S, Rutter, L and Warren, A** (2010) *Partnerships, CPD & APL: supporting workforce development across the social care sector.* Birmingham: Learn to Care.

Bruner, **J** (1960) *The process of education.* Cambridge, MA: Harvard University Press.

Cabiati, **E and Raineri, M** (2016) Learning from service users involvement: a research about changing stigamitizing attitudes in social work students. *Social Work Education, 35* (8), pp982–96.

Cartney, **P** (2000) Adult learning styles: implications for practice teaching in social work. *Social Work Education, 19* (6), pp609–26.

Chapman, **A** (c.2009) *Conscious competence learning mode.* Available at: **www.businessballs.com/conscious competencelearningmodel.htm**

Clarke, **N** (2006) Developing emotional intelligence through work-based learning. *Human Resource Development International, 9* (4), pp447–65.

Clutterbuck, **D** (2001) *Everyone needs a mentor: fostering talent at work,* 3rd edn. London: Chartered Institute of Personnel and Development.

Coffield, **F, Moseley, D, Hall, E and Ecclestone, K** (2004) *Learning styles and pedagogy in post-16 learning: a systematic and critical review.* London: Learning Skills Research Centre (now LSN).

College of Social Work (CSW) (2012a) *The Practice Educator Professional Standards.* Available at: **www.tcsw.org.uk**

College of Social Work (CSW) (2012b) *Integrated critical analysis and reflective practice.* Available at: **www.tcsw.org.uk**

College of Social Work (CSW) (2012c) *Understanding the PCF.* Available at: **www.tcsw.org.uk**

Collingwood, **P** (2005) The three stage theory framework: building an Identikit picture. *Journal of Practice Teaching, 6* (1), 6–23.

Collingwood, **P, Emond, R and Woodward, R** (2008) The theory circle: a tool for learning and for practice. *Social Work Education, 27* (1), pp70–83.

Collins, S (2008) Social workers, resilience, positive emotions and optimism. *Practice: Social Work in Action, 19* (4), 255–69.

Community Care (2015) Social workers too stressed to do their jobs. Available at: **www.communitycare.co.uk**

Cowburn, M, Nelson, P and Williams, J (2000) Assessment of social work students: standpoint and strong objectivity. *Social Work Education, 19* (6), pp627–37.

Cree, V (2000) The challenge of assessment. In V Cree and C Macauley (eds), *Transfer of learning in professional and vocational education.* London: Routledge, pp27–52.

Crisp, B, Green Lister, P and Dutton, K (2006) Not just social work academics: the involvement of others in the assessment of social work students. *Social Work Education, 25* (7), pp723–34.

Croisdale-Appleby, D (2014) *Re-visioning social work education: an independent review.* DfE. Available at: **www.gov.uk**

Curtis, L, Moriarty, J and Netten, A (2009) The expected working life of a social worker. *British Journal of Social Work, 40* (5), pp1628–43.

Davies, H and Kinloch, H (2000) Critical incident analysis: facilitating reflection and transfer of learning. In **V Cree** and **C Macauley** (eds), *Transfer of learning in professional and vocational education.* London: Routledge, pp137–47.

Davys, A M and Beddoe, L (2009) The reflective learning model: supervision of social work students. *Social Work Education, 28* (8), pp919–33.

Davys, A M and Beddoe, L (2010) *Best practice in professional supervision: a guide for the helping professions.* London: Jessica Kingsley.

Davys, A M and Beddoe, L (2015) Going live: a negotiated collaborative model for live observation of practice. *Practice, 27* (3), pp177–96.

Department for Education (2018) *Post-qualifying standard: knowledge and skills statement for children and family practitioners.* Available at **https://www.gov.uk/government/publications/knowledge-and-skills-statement** (accessed 5 December 2018).

Department of Education (DoE) (2015) *Post-qualifying standard: knowledge and skills statement for children and family practitioners.* Available at: **https://www.gov.uk/government/publications/knowledge-and-skills-statement** (accessed 31 October 2018).

Department of Health (DoH) (2002) *Requirements for social work training.* London: Department of Health.

Department of Health (DoH) (2014) *Knowledge and skills statement for child and family social work.* Available at: **www.gov.uk**

Department of Health (DoH) (2015) Available at **https://assets.publishing.service.gov.uk/government/uploads/system/uploads/attachment_data/file/411957/KSS.pdf** (accessed 5 December 2018).

Disability Discrimination Act (1995) Available at: **www.opsi.gov.uk**

Doel, M (2010) *Social work placement: a traveller's guide.* Abingdon: Routledge.

Doel, M and Shardlow, S (1998) *The new social work practice: exercises and activities for training and developing social workers.* Aldershot: Arena.

Doel, M, Sawdon, C and Morrison, D (2002) *Learning, practice and assessment.* London: Jessica Kingsley.

Doel, M, Shardlow, S, Sawdon, C and Sawdon, D (1996) *Teaching social work practice.* Aldershot: Arena.

Edmondson, D (2014) *Social work practice learning – a student guide.* London: Sage.

Eno, S and Kerr, J (2013) That was awful, I'm not ready yet, am I? – Is there such a thing as a good fail? *Journal of Practice Teaching and Learning, 11* (3), pp135–48.

Entwistle, N and Ramsden, P (1983) *Understanding student learning.* London: Croom Helm.

Eraut, M (1994) *Developing professional knowledge and competence.* London: Falmer.

Eraut, M, Alderton, J and Cole, G (1998) *Development of knowledge and skills in employment.* Brighton: University of Sussex.

Fairtlough, A, Bernard, C, Fletcher, J and Ahmet, A (2013) Black social work students' experiences of practice learning: understanding differential progression rates. *Journal of Social Work, 14* (6), pp605–24.

Field, P, Jasper, C and Littler, L (2014) *Practice education in social work – achieving professional standards.* Northwich: Critical Publishing.

Finch, J (2009) *Covering bad practice – story telling or collusion.* Student doctoral conference, University of Sussex. Available at: **www.sussex.ac.uk**

Finch, J (2017) *Supporting struggling students on placement – a practical guide.* Bristol: Policy Press.

Finch, J and Taylor, I (2013) Failing to fail? Practice educator's emotional experiences of assessing failing students. *Social Work Education, 32* (2), pp244–58.

Fook, J and Gardner, F (2007) *Practising critical reflection. a resource handbook.* Maidenhead: Open University Press and McGraw-Hill Education.

Fook, J, Ryan, M and Hawkins, L (2000) *Professional expertise: practice, theory and education for working in uncertainty.* London: Whiting & Birch.

Ford, K and Jones, A (1987) *Student supervision,* BASW Practical Social Work series. London: Macmillan.

Ford, P, Johnston, B, Mitchell, R, Brumfit, C and Myles, F (2005) Practice learning and the development of students as critical practitioners – some findings from research. *Social Work Education, 24* (4), pp391–407.

Fraser, S and Matthews, S (2008) *The critical practitioner in social work and health care.* London: Sage.

Furness, S (2011) Gender at work: characteristics of 'failing' social work students. *British Journal of Social Work* (online).

Gardner, H (1993) *Frames of mind: the theory of multiple intelligences,* 2nd edn. New York: Basic Books.

Gates Foundation (2013) *Measures of Effective Teaching* (accessed 24 July 2018). Available at **https://www. gatesfoundation.org**

Gould, N (2000) Becoming a learning organisation: a social work example. *Social Work Education, 19* (6), pp585–96.

Gould, N and Baldwin, M (eds) (2004) *Social work, critical reflection and the learning organisation.* Aldershot: Ashgate.

Grant, L and Kinman, G (2012) Enhancing wellbeing in social work students: building resilience in the next generation. *Social Work Education, 32* (5), pp605–21.

Grant, L and Kinman, G (2014) *Developing resilience for social work practice.* London. Palgrave Macmillan.

Grey, D (2002) *A briefing on work-based learning,* Generic Centre Assessment Series No.11. London: Higher Education Academy.

GSCC (2002) *Guidance on the assessment of practice in the workplace.* London: General Social Care Council. Available at: **www.gscc.org.uk**

GSCC (2005) *The revised post qualification framework for social work education and training.* London: General Social Care Council. Available at: **www.gscc.org.uk**

GSCC (2006) *Specialist standards and requirements for post-qualifying social work education and training: practice education.* London: General Social Care Council. Available at: **www.gscc.org.uk**

Hafford Letchfield, T, Leonard, K, Begum, N and Chick, N F (2008) *Leadership and management in social care.* London: Sage.

Hastings, M (2000) User involvement in education and training. In **R Pierce** and **J Weinstein** (eds), *Innovative education and training for care professionals*. London: Jessica Kingsley, pp97–110.

Hawkins, P and Shohet, R (2000) *Supervision in the helping professions*, 2nd edn. Buckingham: Open University Press.

HCPC (2012) *Standards for proficiency for social work*. Available at: **www.hpc-uk.org**

Hobbs, V (2007) Faking it or hating it: can reflective practice be forced? *Reflective Practice: International and Multi-disciplinary Perspectives, 8* (3), pp405–17.

Hofer, B K (2002) Personal epistemology as a psychological and educational construct: an introduction. In **B K Hofer** and **P R Pintrich** (eds), *Personal epistemology: the psychology of beliefs about knowledge and knowing*. Mahwah, NJ: Lawrence Erlbaum Associates, pp3–14.

Honey, P and Mumford, A (1982) *Manual of learning styles*. Maidenhead: Peter Honey.

Horwath, J (1999) It's not that I'm not good, it's just that I'm scared: managing anxiety associated with practice learning. *Issues in Social Work Education, 19* (1), pp17–34.

Hughes, M (2017) What difference does it make? Findings of an impact study of service user and carer involvement on social work students' subsequent practice. *Social Work Education, 36* (2), pp203–16.

Humphrey, C (2007) Observing students' practice (through the looking glass and beyond). *Social Work Education, 26* (7), pp723–36.

Humphries, B (2003) What else counts as evidence in evidence-based social work? *Social Work Education, 22* (1), pp81–91.

Ixer, G (1999) There is no such thing as reflection. *British Journal of Social Work, 29*, pp513–27.

Jackson, K (2014) Social worker self care – the overlooked core competency. *Social Work Today, 14* (3), p14.

Jarvis, P (1992) Quality in practice: the role of education. *Nurse Education Today, 21* (1), pp3–10.

Johns, C (2017) *Becoming a reflective practitioner*, 5th edn. Chichester: Wiley Blackwell.

Juwah, C, Macfarlane-Dick, D, Matthew, B, Nicol, D, Ross, D and Smith, B (2004) *Enhancing student learning through effective formative feedback*. Higher Education Academy. Available at: **www.heacademy.ac.uk**

Kadushin, A and Harkness, D (2014) *Supervision in social work*, 5th edn. New York: Columbia University Press.

Karpenko, V. and Gidycz, C. (2012) The supervisory relationship and the process of evaluation: recommendations for supervisors. *Clinical Supervisor, 31*, pp138–15.

Keinemans, S (2015) Be sensible: emotions in social work ethics and education. *British Journal of Social Work, 45*, pp2176–91.

Kemp, E (2000) Partnership in the provision of education and training. In **R Pierce** and **J Weinstein** (eds), *Innovative education and training for care professionals*. London: Jessica Kingsley, pp81–96.

Kinman, G and Grant, L (2011) Exploring stress resilience in trainee social workers: the role of social and emotional competencies. *British Journal of Social Work, 41* (2), pp261–75.

Knott, C and Scragg, T (eds) (2010) *Reflective practice in social work*, 2nd edn. Exeter: Learning Matters.

Knott, C and Scragg, T (eds) (2016) *Reflective practice in social work*, 4th edn. Exeter: Learning Matters.

Knowles, M (1980) *The modern practice of adult education: from pedagogy to andragogy*, 2nd edn. Englewood Cliffs, NJ: Prentice Hall.

Knowles, M (1990) *The adult learner – a neglected species*, 4th edn. London: Gulf Publishers.

Kolb, D A (1984) *Experiential learning: experience as the source of learning and development*. Englewood Cliffs, NJ: Prentice Hall.

Kondrat, M E (1992) Reclaiming the practical: formal and substantive rationality in social work practice. *Social Service Review, 66* (2), pp237–55.

Lafrance, J, Gray, E and Herbert, M (2004) Gate-keeping for professional social work practice. *Social Work Education, 23* (3), pp325–40.

Laming, Lord (2009) *The protection of children in England: a progress report.* London: Stationery Office.

Lave, J and Wenger, E (1991) *Situated learning: legitimate peripheral participation.* Cambridge: Cambridge University Press.

Lefevre, M (2005) Facilitating practice learning and assessment: the influence of social work education. *Social Work Education, 24* (5), pp565–83.

Levin, E (2004) *Resource guide 2: Involving service users and carers in social work education.* London: SCIE. Available at: **www.scie.org.uk/publications**

Lusk, M, Terrazas, S and Salcido, R (2017) Critical cultural competence in social work. *Human Service Organisations: Management, Leadership and Governance, 41* (5), pp464–76.

McCaughan, S, Hesk, G and Stanley, A (2018) in S Taplin (2018) *Innovations in Practice Learning.* St Albans: Critical Publishing.

McGill, I and Beaty, L (1995) *Action learning: a guide for professional, management and educational development,* 2nd edn. London: Kogan Page.

Maclean, S and Lloyd, I (2008) *Developing quality practice learning in social work.* Rugeley: Kirwin Maclean Associates.

Maclean, S and Lloyd, I (2013) *Developing quality practice learning in social work,* 2nd edn. Lichfield: Kirwin Maclean Associates.

Maddi, S R and Khoshara, D M (2005) *Resilience at work.* New York: Amacom.

Martin, G, Carlson, N and Buskitt, W (2010) *Psychology,* 4th edn. Harlow: Pearson.

Marton, F and Säljö, R (1976) On qualitative differences in learning: 1. Outcome and process. *British Journal of Educational Psychology, 46,* pp4–11.

Marton, F, Hounsell, D and Entwistle, N J (1984) *The experience of learning.* Edinburgh: Scottish Academic Press.

Maslow, A (1943) Theory of human motivation. *Psychological Review, 50* (4), pp370–96.

Masocha, S. (2015) Reframing black social work students' experiences of teaching and learning. *Social Work Education, 34* (6), pp636–49.

Merriam, S. B and Bierema, L L (2014) *Adult learning: linking theory and practice.* London: Wiley.

Miettinen, R (2000) The concept of experiential learning and John Dewey's theory of reflective thought and action. *International Journal of Lifelong Education, 19* (1), pp54–72.

Moon, J (1999) *Reflection in learning and professional development.* London: Kogan Page.

Moon, J (2002) *Learning journals: a handbook for academics, students and professional development.* London: Kogan Page.

Moriarty, J, MacIntyre, G, Manthorpe, J, Crisp, B R, Orme, J, Lister P G, Cavanagh, K, Stevens, M, Hussein, S and Sharpe, E (2010) My expectations remain the same. The student has to be competent to practise. Practice assessor perspectives on the new social work degree qualification in England. *British Journal of Social Work, 40,* pp583–601.

Morrison, T (2007) Emotional intelligence, emotion and social work: context, characteristics, complications and contribution. *British Journal of Social Work, 37,* pp245–63.

Morrison, T. (2005) *Staff supervision in social care*, 3rd edn. Brighton: Pavilion Publishing.

Mullins, L (2005) *Management and organisational behaviour*, 7th edn. Harlow: Prentice Hall.

Munro, E (2011) *The Munro review of child protection: final report – a child centred system*. DfE. Available at: **www.gov.uk**

Murphy, R (2013) *Testing Teachers*. Sutton Trust (accessed 24 July 2018). Available at **https://www.suttontrust.com/wp-content**

Narey, M (2014) *Narey's report on initial training for children's social workers*. DfE. Available at: **www.gov.uk**

Neary, M (2000) *Teaching, assessing and evaluation for clinical competence*. Cheltenham: Nelson Thornes.

Newell, R (1992) Anxiety, accuracy and reflection: the limits of professional development. *Journal of Advanced Nursing, 17* (11), pp1326–33.

Nixon, S and Murr, A (2006) Practice learning and the development of professional practice. *Social Work Education, 25* (8), pp798–811.

O'Donoghue, K, Wong Yu Ju, P and Tsui, M (2018) Constructing an evidence-informed social work supervision model. *European Journal of Social Work, 21* (3), pp348–58.

Parker, J (2004) *Effective practice learning in social work*. Exeter: Learning Matters.

Parker, J (2006) Developing perceptions of competence during practice learning. *British Journal of Social Work, 36* (6), pp1017–36.

Parker, J (2008) When things go wrong! Placement disruption and termination: power and student perspectives. *British Journal of Social Work Advance Access, November*, pp1–17.

Parker, J (2010) *Effective practice learning in social work*. Exeter: Learning Matters.

Pink, D (2010) *Drive: the surprising truth about what motivates us*. New York: Canongate Books.

Pearl, R, Williams, H, Williams, L, Brown, K, Hollington, L, Gruffydd, M, Jones, R, Yorke, S and Statham, G (2018) Simply pass/fail or a learning tool. *Social Work Education, 37* (5), pp553–64.

Postle, K, Edwards, C, Moon, R, Rumsey, H and Thomas, T (2002) Continuing professional development after qualification – partnership, pitfalls and potential. *Social Work Education, 21* (2), pp157–69.

Prosser, M and Trigwell, K (1999) *Understanding learning and teaching: the experience in higher education*. Buckingham: SRHE and Open University Press.

Race, P (2010) *Making learning happen*, 2nd edn. London: Sage.

Rajan-Rankin, S (2013) Self-identity, embodiment and the development of emotional resilience. *British Journal of Social Work, 44* (8), pp2426–442.

Ramsden, P (1992) *Learning to teach in higher education*. London: Routledge.

Rogers, A (2002) *Teaching adults*, 3rd edn. Buckingham: Open University Press.

Rogers, C R (1980) *Freedom to learn for the 80s*. New York: Free Press.

Rolfe, G, Freshwater, D and Jasper, M (2001) *Critical reflection for the nursing and helping professions: a user's guide*. London: Palgrave.

Ruch, G (2000) Self and social work: towards an integrated model of learning. *Journal of Social Work Practice, 14* (2), pp99–112.

Rutter, L and Brown, K (2015) *Critical thinking and professional judgement for social work*, 4th edn. London: Sage.

Säljö, R (1979) *Learning in the learner's perspective: 1: Some commonplace misconceptions.* Reports from the Institute of Education, University of Gothenburg, p76.

Schön, D (1983) *The reflective practitioner: how professionals think in action.* London: Temple Smith.

Schuab, J (2015) Issues for men's progression on English social work honours and postgraduate degree courses. *Social Work Education, 34* (3), pp315–27.

SCIE (2004) *Learning organisations: a self-assessment resource pack.* Available at: **www.scie.org.uk/publications**

Senge, P (1990) *The fifth discipline: the art and practice of the learning organisation.* New York: Doubleday.

Shardlow, S I and Doel, M (1996) *Practice learning and teaching.* Basingstoke: Macmillan.

Sharp, M and Danbury, H (1999) *The management of failing DipSW students.* Aldershot: Ashgate.

Shaw, I (2004) Evaluating for a learning organisation? In N Gould and M Baldwin (eds), *Social work: critical reflection and the learning organisation.* Aldershot: Ashgate, pp117–28.

Sherman, J. (2017) *Practical tips for successful supervision.* Jane Sherman Consultancy. Available at **https://janesherman. co.uk/publications**

Singh, G (2001) *Assessment in social work.* London: SCIE. Available at: **www.scie.org.uk**

Smedley, A and Morey, P (2010) Improving learning in the clinical nursing environment: perceptions of senior Australian bachelor of nursing students. *Journal of Research in Nursing, 15* (1), pp75–88.

Smith, M K (1996, 2005) The functions of supervision. *Encyclopedia of Informal Education.* Available at: **www.infed. org/biblio/functions_of_supervision.htm**

Smith, M K (2001) David A Kolb on experiential learning. *Encyclopedia of Informal Education.* Available at: **www.infed. org/ b-explrn.htm**

Social Work Reform Board (2010) *Building a safe and confident future: detailed proposals from the Social Work Reform Board.* DfE.

Social Work Reform Board (2012) *Building a safe and confident future: maintaining momentum.* DfE.

Social Work Task Force (2009a) *Building a safe confident future.* London: Department of Health/Department for Children, Schools and Families.

Social Work Task Force (2009b) *Facing up to the task – the interim report of the Social Work Task Force.* London: Department of Health/Department for Children, Schools and Families.

Sowbel, L and Miller, S (2015) Gatekeeping in graduate social work education: should personality traits be considered? *Social Work Education, 34* (1), pp110–24.

SWRB (2010) *Building a safe and confident future: one year on.* Available at: **www.education.gov.uk**

Taplin, S (ed.) (2018) *Innovations in practice learning.* St Albans: Critical Publishing.

Taylor, C and White, S (2006) Knowledge and reasoning in social work: educating for humane judgement. *British Journal of Social Work, 36,* pp937–54.

Tedam, P (2013) The Mandela model of practice learning. *Journal of Practice Teaching and Learning, 11* (2), pp60–76.

Thomas, G, Howe, K and Keen, S (2011) Supporting Black and ethnic minority students in practice learning. *Journal of Practice Teaching and Learning, 10* (3), pp37–54.

Thompson, N (2000) *Theory and practice in human services.* Buckingham: Open University Press.

Thompson, N (2005) *Understanding social work: preparing for practice,* 2nd edn. London: Palgrave.

Thompson, N (2006) *Promoting workplace learning*. Bristol: Policy Press.

Thompson, S and Thompson, N (2008) *The critically reflective practitioner*. Basingstoke: Palgrave Macmillan.

Tisdell, E (1995) *Creating inclusive adult learning environments: insights from multicultural education and feminist pedagogy*, Eric Information Series 361. Ohio State University.

TOPSS (2002) *National occupational standards for social work*. TOPSS. Available at: **www.skillsforcare.org.uk**

Trevithick, P (2007) Revisiting the knowledge base of social work: a framework for practice. *British Journal of Social Work, 37* (3), pp1–26.

Turner, J C (1991) *Social influence*. Milton Keynes: Open University Press.

Tyreman, S (2000) Promoting critical thinking in health care: phronesis and criticality. *Medicine, Health Care and Philosophy, 3*, pp117–24.

University of York (2000) *Facts, feelings and feedback: a collaborative model for direct observation*. York: University of York.

Walker, J, Crawford, K and Parker, J (2008) *Practice education in social work: A handbook for practice teachers, assessors and educators*. Exeter: Learning Matters.

Wareing, M (2017) Me, my, more, must: a values-based model of reflection. *Reflective Practice, 18* (2), pp268–79.

Waterhouse, T, McLagan, S and Murr, A (2011) From practitioner to practice educator: what supports and what hinders the development of confidence in teaching and assessing student social workers. *Practice: Social Work in Action, 23* (2), pp95–109.

Webster-Wright, A (2009) Reframing professional development through understanding authentic professional learning. *Review of Educational Research, 79* (2), pp702–39.

Wenger, E (2000) Communities of practice and social learning systems. *Organization, 2*, pp225–46.

Williams, S and Rutter, L (2010) *The practice educator's handbook*, 1st edn. Exeter: Learning Matters.

Williams, S and Rutter, L (2012) *The practice educator's handbook*, 2nd edn. Exeter: Learning Matters.

Wonnacott, J. (2012). *Mastering social work supervision*. London: Jessica Kingsley.

Index